Cities Destroyed For Cash

Cities Destroyed For Cash

The FHA Scandal at HUD

BRIAN D. BOYER

Follett Publishing Company
Chicago

Library of Congress Catalog Card Number: 73-82197

ISBN: 0-695-80421-9

First printing

Dedication

This book is dedicated to all of the people who showed me
the way through the Federal Housing Authority, especially
Dick Still, Jerry Buckley and Francis Turk of the House
Subcommittee on Legal and Monetary Affairs; Jack Blum
of the Senate Subcommittee on Antitrust and Monopoly;
Milton Semer, former general counsel of the FHA; Bob
Lambrecht of the Michigan Mortgage Bankers Associa-
tion; Agnes Moore of the HUD-FHA Detroit area office;
Don Ball of the *Detroit News;* Don Bartlett and Jim Steel
of the *Philadelphia Inquirer;* and the National People's
Housing Coalition.

Special thanks go to the people whose voices are contained in these pages: Gail Cincotta of Chicago; Joyce
Renford of Detroit; Bill Whitbeck, director of the Detroit
district office of HUD-FHA; and John Waner, Whitbeck's
counterpart in Chicago. George Romney, former secretary
of the U.S. Department of Housing and Urban Development, extended his time and assistance in the face of an
effort he knew must necessarily criticize his administration of the department. I wish, with him, that Romney City
could be the name of a victory instead of a defeat.

It is further dedicated to Bob Lindsay and the late Nora Mabarak who figured together in a tragedy which seems to me to be a metaphor of the larger tragedy they acted in.

It could not have been written without the support of and hundreds of hours of work by Barbara Ann Leticia Belle-ttini Baier Boyer, who not only put up with my obsession and curious working hours over the past year, but who so often guided me by her extraordinary good sense.

But most of all, this book is for the victims. I have tried to explain what happened to them. I wish I could do more.

Author's Note

The Way It's Supposed To Be

There is no way to make the FHA scandal as simple to understand as, say, a street mugging. We are talking about the murder of cities, after all, and the ways in which men despoil the urban landscape to enrich themselves are both bizarre and Byzantine.

But the technical description of the game played, as laid out most formally in chapter one, "The $70 Billion Slum," and in chapter seven, "The Mortgage Bankers," isn't all there is to it by any means. There's also the human factor that must be considered—human beings who die violently (The Murder of Nora Mabarak), who have been economically ruined (Joyce Renforth, chapter eight) or, like George Romney (chapter fifteen) who claim they have been gulled and otherwise misled.

To explain how the FHA Scandal worked on a day-to-day basis in the big cities of the United States, I have constructed a book within a book, the Romney City chapters. They are "Romney City," "The Streets Are Paved With Gold," "We Buy Houses For Cash" and "The Sacred Trust." All of the characters in this section, and all of their various crimes and schemes, have factual parallels both in the real world and in the rest of the book. The Romney City quartet is the *In Cold Blood* of how cities are killed.

The entire book is based on my research and interviews, sworn Congressional testimony or other written material. What is extraordinary about all of it is that it's all true.

B.D.B.

Contents

Author's Note   vii

1 The $70 Billion Slum   3

2 The House Buyer Laments   24

3 Romney City   37

4 The Streets Are Paved with Gold   50

5 We Buy Houses for Cash   64

6 The Sacred Trust   79

7 Mortgage Bankers: the Mystery Unmasked   94

8 We Got Troubles   113

9 Country Ridge Baltimore—Life in the Swamp   133

10 Detroit—the Ruined, the Abandoned, and the Dispossessed   141

11 William Whitbeck   163

12 Chicago—the People Speak   176

Gail Cincotta Speaks   179

John Waner Speaks   187

13 The Philadelphia Story—Politics and Profit   197

14 Jack Blum   205

15 George Romney   221

16 Romney City Redû—One More Time   238

Cities Destroyed For Cash

1

The $70 Billion Slum

There is a part of Detroit called the Lower East Side which visitors, in awed voices, compare with the bombed-out cities of Europe after World War II and, later, of Vietnam. Half and more of the houses on any given block are boarded up with plywood squares. The gutters hang, rain washes in through the holes in the roofs. Ruined by the elements and gutted by thieves, the houses seem to be disintegrating like the stumps of rotted trees. Fires at night cremate the remains. The next day the family moves out of the house next door and another house is abandoned and eventually destroyed.

One equivalent of this area in New York City is known as the South Bronx; another is Brooklyn; a third, Harlem. The weary miles of abandoned houses in Chicago are in Woodlawn on the South Side, and in Austin on the West Side, next to Oak Park. Then, like a projected series of dismal color slides of what could be the same blighted blocks and wrecked hovels over and over again, the ruin is repeated in North Philadelphia, St. Louis, Seattle, Los Angeles and Lubbock, Texas.

What makes these vistas of urban ruin so compelling are neat little signs nailed on the doors. The signs tell you that the property is protected by the FBI and that it belongs to the secretary of the U.S. Department of Housing and Urban Development. The slums, in other words, belong to us.

To make the point, one of these signs reads:

"A theft from your government is a theft from YOU."

Another warns intruders:

"U.S. government property. Persons defacing this property will be prosecuted to the full extent of the law."

There is a kind of macabre humor to the idea that the majesty of the federal government sits behind these ruins, and the little children who play in the grassless yards of the broken houses seem to appreciate it.

"Is *you* the FBI?" they jeer at strangers. "You gonna arrest this house?"

The adults smile, with the bittersweet cool of people who have nothing left to lose. "That man ain't no FBI," they say. "He's a speculator, gonna buy up this house and trick some poor mother again."

As they say in almost every big city in the United States, "The neighborhoods have been FHA'd."

To be FHA'd is to be ruined.

Most people have had no idea of what has been going on in the government's housing programs. Especially people who are supposed to be experts. The director of the Ford Foundation's urban and metropolitan program, for example, told me the disaster was caused by ignorant buyers. Universities teach that urban blight is caused by social factors that nobody understands and only statisticians can chart, like distant scientists marking the destruction of a star by the radio waves being ejected. Most investigators see problems in terms of individual cases, but never as an overall problem. Liberals always blame the conservatives —the conservatives blame the programs.

Let me say at the onset that the disaster known as the FHA scandal was not caused by ignorance or unsophistication. Instead, it was a deliberate program of urban ruin for profit, under the cover of government housing law and with an endless flow of federal money. The destruction of the cities can be understood if put in old-fashioned cops-and-robbers terms—there were a bunch of bad guys who stuck up the cities and rode away with the gold. To trace their activities, all you need are land tract index books and FHA case files, if you can pry them from the hands of the secretive and careless government agency and its often corrupt personnel. The overall pattern and evidence in almost every major city points to widespread conspiracy between mortgage and real estate interests, with the help (sometimes for a price) of government officials.

The conservatives and Republicans cannot be blamed for the scandal, although the Republicans have administrated HUD-FHA during these recent years and made a thorough botch of it all, because so many of the large speculators, contractors, urban redevelopers and others who profited from the blight are staunch Democrats. And Democrats wrote the law. But the present housing law itself isn't as bad as the conservatives and Republicans maintain —it has just been criminally mismanaged by the Nixon Administration.

George Romney, who was so unprepared to be HUD secretary that he may be considered a burnt offering to the housing industry, never was close enough to the FHA problems to learn their full extent. That he found out about it at all is a kind of tribute to his decency. Some of his assistants would have preferred that he never knew. Romney almost never did find out.

The House Committee on Banking and Currency, on January 6, 1971, issued the first formal report on the FHA scandal. Up to then, nearly everybody in and out of government assumed that the expensive, sweeping, low-income housing programs enacted by the 1968 National Housing Act were going along very well, because new records in housing production were being reached and the blacks weren't rioting. Romney certainly thought so, and when the committee's criticism was made public the secretary, as usual, said it wasn't so. The same day, in fact, he called a news conference and assailed the committee's negative conclusions as "inaccurate, misleading and very incomplete."

I like to quote those words, because I rather suspect that the American housing industry and its protectors will use similar words to assail me for this book, with less reason than Romney had to assail the committee.

I presume the mortgage bankers and real estate speculators already knew the truth about their activities and the mess at the FHA, but Romney had to find it out the hard way. Simply put, he was lied to by top FHA executives—he says especially by the Philadelphia office—and was generally misled by his staff, few of whom he had control over in any case. It took Romney eight days to start to get his facts straight about that first report, but when he did he acted in character: He admitted he had been wrong, in public, to the press.

He said, "It is apparent the abuses are more prevalent than had previously been evident."

To rectify the situation, Romney ordered an internal HUD investigation and punished the urban poor by taking away from them the subsidized mortgage interest program, even though they weren't the ones who had abused it.

Well, by then the entire FHA low-income program was rotted through, and no frantic catch-up efforts by Romney or anybody else were going to save the tower from falling down. Despite himself, by the spring of 1972, after almost daily newspaper exposés of the scandal in Detroit and Philadelphia, and months of hearings by the U.S. Senate and House, and federal investigations, even Romney knew his department sat on one of the worst government scandals in the nation's history.

He told the forty-first annual convention of the National Housing Conference in Washington, D.C.:

"The . . . federal subsidy program that would permit the poor to rent, or purchase homes of their own . . . was so poorly conceived and so uncautiously developed that we estimate the federal government will, in the next few years, have more than 240,000 units in default—and with little resale value except at catastrophic levels of loss."

Romney would later maintain that he didn't mean that all 240,000 units would be foreclosed, although he clearly drew that conclusion himself.

Later in 1972, Cong. Wright Patman also spoke of a loss of 250,000 units, not necessarily the same units Romney mentioned, by any means. For while Romney spoke of the subsidized units—those houses and apartment dwellings on which the Treasury paid most of the interest costs— Patman was addressing himself to a larger problem: the defaults and foreclosures in the unsubsidized FHA programs under which the government does not help support interest payments.

How many of the unsubsidized units will end up in government hands is unknown, but about 25,000 of them are in Detroit alone. Subsidized FHA housing never got very far in Chicago, so the 5,000 or so foreclosures there come almost entirely under the bread-and-butter Section 203 program (see page 20). Likewise, the loss in New York City—5,000 or more houses—is due mostly to unsubsidized units. The unsubsidized loss in Los Angeles, I predict, will be second only to Detroit.

So government ownership of 100,000 houses in the unsubsidized programs—and maybe a good many more—is virtually assured. The way HUD keeps its figures it's very hard to tell. For example, when HUD-FHA tears down a house, it comes off its books and is said to have been "disposed of." But the land on which the house stood is owned by HUD. Indeed. When a district office clears 2,000 or 3,000 foreclosed houses from its inventory, only the naive would assume they had all been repaired and resold. The cynic would ask how many of them had been "disposed of" by other means. HUD probably won't tell him, but he can find out by counting empty lots in poor neighborhoods.

If we just use Romney's figure of 240,000, we are talking about a ruined city that would house more than one million people. Its price is at least $3.6 billion, at a bargain basement cost of only about $15,000 per house.

If we say that Patman's estimate of 250,000 houses in government ownership and Romney's figure of 240,000 houses overlap a great deal, and we throw in the 100,000 unsubsidized houses that nobody ever wants to discuss, mix it up and extrapolate a bit, it appears that the eventual HUD ownership of about 390,000 living units is in store for us, at a price of about $5 billion. Right now, tens of thousands of bankrupt apartment units are kept out of the foreclosure figures by such tricky techniques as forbearance, and government management, and signed-over deeds.

One of the sobering things about this numbers game is that the simple multiplication of houses foreclosed times $15,000 per each one doesn't actually reflect the cost. What Congress has never been told is that it costs an awesome pile of money to keep the foreclosed mortgages in HUD's steel files and the houses on the streets where the vandals can get to them.

In Detroit, for instance, HUD district director William Whitbeck told me that the holding cost is four dollars a day per house. Houses in the Motor City have remained in the HUD inventory for an average stay of forty-three months. That's about $5,000 more per house that the government spends, until HUD resells it or bulldozes it down.

The FHA inventory in Detroit, the most FHA devastated city in America, will reach at least 25,000 houses. The mortgage payoff by the FHA and the additional holding costs will run between $375 and $500 million, all of which has been paid to real estate speculators, con men, criminals and mortgage companies. In return, the government was presented with a deserted slum and the concomitant problems of rampant heroin addiction and the highest big city murder rate in the U.S.A.

But if you think that $3.5 or $5 billion for the foreclosed houses is a lot of money, you should see how much the interest subsidies will cost the taxpayer for houses and apartment units which don't foreclose. That cost will be about $66 billion, paid out in interest subsidies to the largest insurance companies, mortgage companies, banks and other investors. The total doesn't include the billions of dollars in tax breaks that will have been handed over to the rich for "investing" in what is called the Section 236 multifamily subsidized program.

There are two basic rent supplement programs. Because both are reflected as mortgage interest subsidies, the programs should be called moneylender interest subsidies. The Section 235 single-family program pays up to all but 1 percent of the interest due on mortgages for low-income homeowners—or lower middle-income buyers, since the poor, whom the program was designed to help, are not qualified. They are *too* poor, according to HUD's interpretation of the law.

When we talk about the results of the Nixon Administration's administration of the 1968 Housing Act—the foreclosures, the defaults, the interest subsidies and the tax breaks—we are really talking about a $70 billion slum.

I want to caution you that my figures about the scope of FHA foreclosures under the 1968 Housing Act are considerably higher than those presented by the government itself. I also want to say that my figures are closer to being accurate than those released by the FHA, because that agency manipulates its figures to hide losses and to focus the best possible light on the situation.

For example, the FHA always talks about the size of its inventory—that is, the number of houses that have been paid off by the FHA insuring fund and not otherwise disposed of. The person unenlightened in the ways of FHA statistics might see an inventory of 100,000 on the Twelfth of Never, 1974, and an inventory of 100,000 a full year later and assume that the problem of foreclosures has been stopped. But if he assumed that, he would be very, very wrong. For during those twelve months, the FHA may have had an additional 100,000 foreclosures, while fixing and reselling or tearing down the first 100,000 houses. The impression of a steady inventory is true and false at the same time, doublethink in the classical manner of modern American government.

So how bad is the problem, really? You can start to get at the truth of it by analyzing HUD's figures, with one eye on what they are and the other eye fixed on what they *mean*.

For example, as of December 31, 1971, HUD's Office of Property Disposition said the FHA had 110,281 defaults. On December 1, 1972, Romney told me the FHA had 250,000 defaults, which he defined as mortgages two or more months in arrears. In addition, as of March 31, 1972, HUD had an inventory of 44,396 foreclosed and abandoned houses; of them, 29,528 were in the inner cities.

What the hell does all of it mean? Well, it doesn't mean, as FHA spokesmen say, that defaults aren't foreclosures, because a goodly number of them are. For purposes of glossing over its troubles the FHA can keep a house in its default list for months, a year, and longer, postponing the fatal foreclosure label almost indefinitely. An active bull-dozer program in a city like Detroit, which destroyed more than 3,000 houses in the closing months of 1972, opens the foreclosure listing to 3,000 more government-owned houses that nobody knows have been added.

You may doubt that the government would play in such manner with figures. But I will tell you a delightful little true story about phony Detroit statistics and let you make up your own mind. It's the fairest thing I could possibly do.

In 1972, HUD officially announced that it had a Detroit inventory (owned outright) of 7,574 houses, with 5,888 more in default.

The fact of the situation was that HUD had more than 8,000 houses in its inventory. It had 3,000 more houses in a limbo called redemption, the technical name for the final part of the foreclosure proceeding. It simply means that there were 3,000 more houses in the Detroit inventory that FHA was calling something else and so didn't count. There were 23,000 more houses in serious default.

How many of these would end up being foreclosed? Bill

Whitbeck, director of Detroit's HUD-FHA office, said that about 50 percent of these houses would come into government hands. Thus, 8,000 houses plus 3,000 houses plus 11,500 houses to come totals 22,500 houses that are or will be owned by the FHA in Detroit, and this is a conservative estimate.

But Baltas Birkle, an assistant director of the Government Accounting Office (GAO), in 1972 told Congress that 75 percent of the houses in serious default will be foreclosed, or 5,750 more houses than Whitbeck estimated. Using Birkle's figures, we find the Detroit inventory at some 28,000 houses either foreclosed or certain of foreclosure.

You don't have to understand much about figures to know that there's one hell of a difference between 7,574 and 28,000.

If you are charitably disposed toward the government you would decide that HUD doesn't lie about figures, that it just doesn't know what's going on. I am not very affectionately disposed to the machinations of the HUD bureaucrats I've had to deal with, so, on the basis of good evidence, I think the very worst—that the agency lies and is incompetent. The incompetence of its personnel is legendary. Even George Romney has admitted that it takes a HUD bureaucrat a year to learn what a clerk in a private business could master in a couple of weeks.

Although some of the FHA's figures are plainly issued to confuse the uninitiated and put a rosy glow on a wormy apple, others just don't seem to make sense from any standpoint. One of my favorite examples of this was presented to me on April 24, 1972, by the Washington and Los Angeles HUD offices. All I was trying to do was determine how many low down payment Section 221-d-2 mortgages had been underwritten in the city of the angels from 1968 through 1971. The figures I got were:

	FROM LOS ANGELES	FROM WASHINGTON
1968	2,589	1,363
1969	7,177	5,355
1970	12,893	9,627
1971	19,123	13,334
Totals	41,782	29,679

The difference between the two totals represents about 12,000 houses and $180 million—not a small piece of change to lose between the main office and a district head-quarters. I called each office twice to get confirmation of the figures, and I also explained the discrepancy. Each office said its figures were correct. The $180 million differ-ence "would show up someplace," the statisticians sup-posed. I was the only one who cared.

In addition to all of its other problems, HUD—or the Republican administration—appeared to be determined to compound bad administration with foolish decisions that can only cost more money. That is, to end FHA mort-gages for the center cities. By September of 1972, HUD's offices in New York, Chicago, Detroit and Los Angeles had once again red-lined the core cities as effectively as the old policies of economic viability that existed up until 1968. In fact, no HUD office was insuring FHA mortgages in central city areas except in unusual cases, usually those involving the FHA's efforts to clear out its inventory by reselling foreclosed houses. This new reticence came about as a result of directives by Romney aimed at stop-ping the avalanche of foreclosures.

Then, to complicate matters still more, to guarantee inner city ruin, the Nixon Administration ordered on Jan-uary 4, 1973, the end of subsidized housing—an order that effectively ended the FHA's resale of its repossessed houses, since the only way the government can sell fore-closed houses in central cities is to give away a subsidy with them.

There is a further catch: Black-listing FHA mortgages in the inner cities means that homeowners, who live there and faithfully make their mortgage payments, will not be able to resell their houses, at least not if they bought their property FHA. Here's why.
- As a result of price fixing, central city housing prices increased 200 to 300 percent from 1968 through 1972.
- The central city markets became dominated by the FHA.
- FHA foreclosures have ruined neighborhoods, making the value of central city houses less than the 1968 level.
- To sell a house FHA costs the individual owner a great amount of money, because he must pay to bring the home up to FHA standards for a homeowner sale.
- FHA has stopped mortgages in these areas, anyway.

- The owners have no equity in their FHA houses.
- To resell, they must either price their property at no more than 50 percent of what they paid for it, or pay high costs for FHA mortgages to new buyers (who are no longer available, in any case).

So, conscientious homebuyers must abandon their property if they ever want to move, letting it foreclose, further ruining the neighborhood and adding to the FHA inventory, and keeping in motion the economic wheels that make the man next door also abandon his property.

John Mogk, a professor at Wayne State University in Detroit and an expert in inner city problems, estimates that up to 100 percent of all Section 221-d-2 and Section 235 program mortgages in the core cities must end in abandonment and foreclosures because of these factors. His prediction has not been disputed by anybody close to the situation.

So it's possible to anticipate that the nation's largest inventory of foreclosed properties could be in Los Angeles which, of all major cities, started core city FHA business last, and where the scandal has just begun to surface. (Of the Section 221-d-2 mortgages, 41,782 were made in Los Angeles.)

Supporting this argument is the foreclosure pattern in Detroit, where most of the symptoms of the disease have been seen, although not treated. In four years, the foreclosure rate under the Section 223-e program (high risk) had risen to 34.6 percent of all the houses sold in 1968. Of the 221-d-2 houses sold in 1968, 19.1 percent had foreclosed. Of the subsidized houses sold in 1969, 15.4 percent had already entered HUD ownership. And the figures continued to rise rapidly. In fact, it appears that 40 to 45 percent of the 61,000 single-family mortgages made in Detroit from 1968 through September of 1971 will belong to the secretary of HUD.

The foreclosures in Detroit, New York, Philadelphia and other major cities have caused a serious drain on FHA insuring funds. The Committee on Government Operations said that for the fiscal year 1971, FHA's total insurance reserves of $1.7 billion were $1 billion below estimated reserve requirements, based on HUD's actuarial figures. It noted:

"If similar losses [to those in Detroit] are incurred in other cities, the solvency of these funds will be threatened."

One of the FHA accounts called the "special risk fund" had suffered an actual deficit of $2.1 million by the end of fiscal year 1971, with an estimated reserve deficiency up by $146 million from 1970. The special risk fund was created to absorb losses from foreclosed mortgages in core cities under the high risk section of the 1968 National Housing Act called 223-e. To keep it going, HUD had to borrow $80 million from the U.S. Treasury. George Romney said that someday the special risk fund will be solvent. I have not met anyone who agrees.

In HUD's budget for fiscal 1973, the department requested an additional $195 million to cover estimated special risk losses through the year. The House Appropriations Committee chewed on the request and spit it out, saying:

"While this request for $195 million is in essence a bookkeeping proposition to reimburse the Treasury, it makes no material addition in support of housing or urban development programs. It is a prime example of how Treasury borrowing constitutes 'back door' financing and provides additional subsidy and cost for housing programs."

Whether the FHA insuring fund and the Treasury will pay out $1 billion or $5 billion for abandoned houses in the central cities becomes almost insignificant when the cost of present rent supplement (subsidized) programs is added up.

From its inception in 1968, through 1971, a total of 143,500 mortgages were insured under Section 235. About 100,000 of these units were for new construction and were sold almost entirely to whites. About 43,300 subsidized mortgages were for existing buildings, and many of these were sold to black residents of the big cities. For a time, subsidized Section 235 mortgages were only given for standing housing when the FHA wanted to sell off a foreclosed house —it was frequently the only way that it could. As a result of the January 4, 1973, decision, even this policy was stopped. So most black Americans have been cut out of the FHA.

The second subsidized program, Section 236, pays up to all but 1 percent of the interest due on apartment building mortgages. The FHA's overall payment to the lender is figured out for the individual renter in terms of (theoretically) lower monthly payments. But as we will eventually find out, most of this break for renters has not been passed on.

How expensive are rent supplements? Romney told the House Subcommittee on HUD-Space-Science-Veterans that the long-term total federal exposure for Sections 235 and 236 "is approaching $100 billion."

The actual out-of-pocket cost, he said, is nearing $66 billion, for programs which by 1978 will have assisted only one out of four families who are eligible under present laws.

The payments for 1973 alone will total an estimated $1.88 billion, to pay for most of the interest on 2,250,000 housing units. Understood correctly, this supplemental money acts as a prop under the high interest rates, benefiting lenders but never really helping individuals. The almost $2 billion represented 40 percent of HUD's budget for 1973, which was up by 20 percent from 1972.

Romney's grand total of $100 billion—$34 billion for principal and 1 percent of the interest, and $66 billion in interest subsidies—purchased housing worth about $30 billion.

The government's $66 billion in interest supplements hasn't bought anything. It just went to private money-lenders for the benefit of private contractors. Additional billions of dollars were spent (actually, never entered the Treasury) for the extraordinary tax shelter provisions for investors in the Section 236 program.

Tax law is a complicated field. Tax law as it applies to HUD and FHA programs has created a group of specialists who interpret it for the wealthy. Basically, these specialists tell investors that they can invest as little as $20,000 in a $1 million project and claim the entire million in depreciation against ordinary income, in less than the life of the forty-year mortgage.

Although accelerated depreciation is not unique to Section 236 investments, certain provisions of the program give investors a nine-to-one depreciation for every dollar put into one of the projects, compared with a three-to-one depreciation tax advantage for other kinds of buildings.

As an example, consider Randy Arms, a hypothetical Section 236 apartment building that cost $1 million. The Internal Revenue Service will allow M.Y. Cash, the investor, to depreciate the property over about thirty years, the useful life of the building. After subtracting land value of, say, $200,000 and a salvage value of $50,000 for the property, $750,000 remains. Dividing the thirty years into $750,000, the investor gets a depreciation of $25,000 a year.

This procedure doesn't apply only to Section 236 projects. But what makes them extraordinarily attractive is the fact that the 236 investor has put only 10 percent or less of his own money into the project, compared with 25 percent or more required for the investor in conventional projects. His actual cash investment may be as little as 2 percent, or $20,000, of the whole $1 million. The tax advantages become enormous. M.Y. Cash, who's in the 50 percent tax bracket, will make $12,500 a year for thirty years in the form of taxes not paid—for an investment of $20,000. That is a return of $375,000 for $20,000. This doesn't include profits from the rentals.

There are other tax advantages for Section 236 investors. One has to do with what the government calls recapture. Recapture is what the government gets back in unpaid taxes if you sell the property before a certain number of years have passed. The owner of a conventionally financed project who sells it before 16⅔ years have passed must pay straight income taxes on any excess depreciation he has claimed. But the federal government has no income tax recapture from 236 investors after only ten years, except at the capital gain rate.

A third advantage is called rollover. It means that if a 236 project is sold to its tenants or to a tenant-oriented non-profit group, the investor pays no capital gain tax at all if he invests the proceeds into another 236 project. So you can keep building your money without having to stop for taxes along the way.

For the socially conscious rich man, there also are advantages of rehabilitation projects under the 236 program. Here M.Y. Cash can write off the entire cost of repairs up to $15,000 per living unit over five years. Talk about making money—the smart investor with $20,000 cash in a $1 million rehabilitation project can write off $200,000 a year against regular income. For the taxpayer in the 50 percent bracket, it means a return of up to $500,000 for $20,000— a cash return of five times his investment each year for five years.

It is supposed to be a way to help the poor!

To make these advantages even more attractive, to gild the lily as they used to say, Section 236 investments can be syndicated. The owner can and usually does sell part of his interest in the project to other investors, at a profit, of course.

The depreciation advantages are available proportionally to each of the individual partners. It is like stockholders in a company being able to take personal credit for corporate tax losses. So a whole industry has grown up of syndics who are in the business of bringing wealthy investors and projects together, especially for projects in Detroit, St. Louis, Chicago and New York. These offerings are not made available to the public as a whole, but only to a few sophisticated investors. This procedure makes it unnecessary to register with the Securities and Exchange Commission, which so far has let the syndics operate without regulation.

Investors can transfer their interest, up to a point. What they fear is foreclosure, because it means that they have to pay heavy capital gains. Some do go under, but the government, unlike its attitude toward individual homeowners, takes extraordinary precautions to prevent Section 236 foreclosure. (Despite official solicitude, as of August, 1972, 186 multi-family projects had been formally foreclosed.) In the summer of 1972, 36 of these apartment buildings, worth $44,480,818, had been assigned to HUD in a procedure that puts the burden of management on the federal government but still allows the investors to keep their tax breaks. This is despite the fact that the argument for the tax advantages, in addition to getting the largely unnecessary buildings constructed, is to give the management job to private interests, not to the government. The government is allegedly incapable of building management.

In addition, to save more properties from foreclosures, a bright young HUD loan assistant named Philip Harris made a mark for himself in the big HUD building by devising a scheme called deferred principal payments. The essence of this plan, which HUD officials claim has been looked at and pronounced legal by the Justice Department in the event it might seem shady to outsiders, is to have the government pick up the remaining 1 percent interest payment not already paid by the interest subsidy for projects in trouble.

The principal due on the interest (thus neatly reversing interest and principal) is deferred. As Harris explained it in August of 1972, during the deferment period, HUD would be paying $800 of a hypothetical $1,000 monthly mortgage payment instead of the forty-year average of $500 for principal and interest. That's like the average homeowner being required to pay only one dollar in five owed on his mortgage payment. The mortgage is "recast" after a time in deferment, thus keeping the tax write-offs for investors, and the badly managed, badly built, badly budgeted apartment building is kept out of the FHA's foreclosure files.

The number of crimes committed against homebuyers and the federal government in the criminal gutting of the central cities with FHA mortgages will probably never be known. But as Nixon threw sand into the FHA gears and early in 1973 prepared for his inauguration, federal grand juries were hearing evidence against speculators, mortgage companies, HUD employees, property managers and others in New York City, Philadelphia, Chicago and Detroit. Other grand jury investigations had been called for in Kansas City, St. Louis, Seattle and Los Angeles. Additional investigations were being conducted by the FBI, the Justice Department, the Internal Revenue Service, HUD, the Government Accounting Office, county prosecutors, and half a dozen congressional committees.

As of May 31, 1973, the federal government had won 116 indictments naming 250 people and a total of 324 charges, counting multiple charges. By city, the figures were:

CITIES	DEFENDANTS	INDICTMENTS	CONVICTIONS
Brooklyn	53	21	4
Chicago	36	31	13
Cleveland	4	1	0
Detroit	50	19	6
Los Angeles	4	4	0
Philadelphia	91	31	24
Portland	1	1	0
Seattle	10	7	5
Tampa	1	1	0

Early in June, an additional eight persons were indicted in Chicago. A Justice Department spokesman said that "a great many more" persons were expected to be indicted in late summer and early fall of 1973.

Toward the end of August, 1972, Jack Blum, then majority counsel for Sen. Philip Hart's Anti-Trust and Monopoly Subcommittee, told me that the New York grand jury was holding back 300 indictments until after the November presidential elections, for fear of embarrassing the Republican administration. Blum, who is perhaps the most knowledgeable man in Washington about the operations and scope of the FHA scandal—at least the most knowledgeable *honest* man—said Secretary Romney resigned his post the same day he learned of the pending indictments, because they pointed to corruption throughout the entire HUD agency. It was one of those Washington stories that explained Romney's sudden decision to leave HUD and the administration's butchering of the agency at the same time—one of those stories that should be true, whether or not it actually was based on fact.

For the most part, the activities of the Justice Department in investigating the FHA scandal, at least during 1972, had been rather commendable. At least part of the reason is that many of the large real estate speculators involved in the corrupt transactions were Democrats, part of the traditional butter-and-housing liberals who fought for social legislation that funneled federal dollars into their private pockets. Not that the administration has anything against freebooting capitalism—by Republicans. But the Justice Department did come into the investigation slowly, considering the evidence, allegations and testimony of FHA crimes that were easily available from the start of 1971.

The scandal was officially touched off January 6, 1971, when the House Committee on Banking and Currency issued a report that detailed 102 specific cases of FHA crimes. Doubting that it was so, HUD sent out its Office of Investigation to double check on the allegations. The investigators interviewed 511 individuals in thirty days. They found forty-one prima-facie cases of federal fraud against the FHA and forty-five additional cases of false statements and certifications concerning required repairs, mortgagor investments, and ownership of properties, forged certifications and fraudulent appraisal reports.

What made investigations move slowly in the opening months of 1971 were the attitudes of local and federal prosecutors. Most of them tended to think of FHA crimes as low priority "white-collar crimes." They were also ignorant about the FHA's incredibly complicated procedures. The real estate and mortgage industries take years to know and understand. In this shell game, not only uneducated homebuyers, but lawyers, accountants and federal agents could not see what was going on without a thorough learning process.

To compound the confusion, HUD itself didn't know what was going on, or its top brass weren't admitting it to anyone, for fear of losing their jobs.

In the fall of 1972, the Justice Department's entire investigative efforts were being conducted by fewer than 100 men. Two assistant U.S. attorneys were sent to each of four cities: Philadelphia, Newark, Brooklyn and Detroit. Three were assigned to Chicago. No city had more than twenty FBI agents working on the cases, and Detroit, where the problems were the worst, got only six. The other agents working on cases came from the IRS and HUD.

Many of the agents found it hard to get too excited about FHA crimes, because they are too complicated and not very sexy. After all, what can you get a man for? Fraud is about it. There is no criminal charge called "city homicide." If there was, it would have to be treated as an economic war crime. In any case, agents and many Americans tend to look at the abandoned houses, which are hovels, and at the bad neighborhoods and believe that the people brought it on themselves. Investigators do not tend to find anything suspicious in the fact that land speculators made an average profit in excess of 100 percent in their transactions, or anything criminal about the fact that at least 50 percent of the $5 billion loss in the unsubsidized programs will end up in private pockets, or that $66 billion for badly built new housing worth half of that is more dangerous to society than a man with a gun.

It has been very easy to steal from the federal government, but it is also a crime.

The greatest cost of the FHA scandal simply cannot be added up from a row of figures representing foreclosures, rent supplements and the like. It can only be guessed at by looking at crime statistics and heroin addiction, ruined dreams, human despair and our blighted city cores.

The real tragedy has been not monetary but human waste. Our cities have been ruined by deliberate and mismanaged government housing programs, money-hungry and indifferent investors, criminal speculators and crooked bankers. Romney argued that crime, blight and the desertion of the inner city began before HUD and the FHA entered it in 1968. He felt there are natural, or "structural," social problems in housing to which the government has fallen victim along with everybody else. I am convinced he has been wrong.

While the federal government didn't invent crime, the FHA and the large investment interests have destroyed deliberately the core cities where the nation's poor are congregated. Crime, violence, disease and addiction are nurtured by a ruined physical environment, and there is no poverty so degrading as the one where shelter rots in the day and burns at night.

The national solution to the black riots of 1966, 1967 and 1968 was the FHA low-income housing programs, but what they have done is destroy the homes and neighborhoods of the poor, giving millions of people a glimpse of hope yet quickly snatching it away.

In addition, the policies of the real estate and mortgage industries, compounded by the FHA programs, have created the flight of ethnic and working whites out of our cities into the suburban noose around the ghetto. They created class bitterness and hatred where none needed to exist. Where, at least, no new bitterness and hatred were called for. These industries and the FHA worked the economic levers that kept this society physically segregated. Some of it was the product of ignorance, but none of it was accidental.

Nor have urban blight and abandonment been the result of processes no man understood or could prevent, as the official line pretends. Instead, the destruction of our cities has come about solely for profit, part of the same equation that threw up the sprawling, jerry-built suburbs that cannot withstand the wind and the rain.

After we have explored the FHA scandal, you may not agree with my conclusions, but you will understand the background and the facts. The place to begin is with the programs themselves.

The Programs

Section 203. Enacted in 1934, Section 203 is considered the basic FHA mortgage insurance program. It provides FHA mortgage insurance to finance the construction, purchase or improvement of one- to four-family homes. The mortgage value on a single-family home can go up to $33,000. Although there is no minimum income to qualify for Section 203 mortgages, the buyer is expected not to pay more than 35 percent of his income for housing costs. Mortgages are thirty years long. The formula for down payments is: 3 percent of the first $15,000, 10 percent of the next $10,000 and 20 percent of the remainder, to the $33,000 ceiling. When banks get directly involved in FHA lending, they generally use only this program.

The Section 203 program embodies the basic FHA philosophy—to insure the mortgage lender against loss. No FHA program insures the buyer. The idea behind FHA insurance was to restore the confidence of lenders in making loans to the average homebuyer. It was created at a time when the United States was in the midst of the Depression, and mortgage capital had its confidence shaken. To stimulate residential construction in the depressed economy, it authorized the insurance of mortgages with relatively low down payments, and set up extended loan maturities.

In addition, to keep monthly principal and interest payments low, the interest rate was not to exceed a regulatory ceiling. Administrative expenses and insurance claims in the case of foreclosure were to be paid from annual mortgage insurance premiums collected from the homebuyers. The premium has traditionally been one-half of 1 percent of the outstanding loan balance, except for a short period in the early years of the program.

The program was intended to be self-sufficient, and it was, mainly because the FHA authority was operated much like a conservative bank. No identifiable risks were taken, and large areas of big cities were "red-lined" or black-listed because of racial and economic reasons. The rule was: "No mortgage shall be accepted for insurance under this section unless the Secretary finds that the project with respect to which the mortgage is executed is economically sound."

In thirty-five years the program insured about 8.4 million home mortgages, and built up an insurance fund reserve of $1.3 billion.

Section 221-d-2. The Omnibus Housing Act of 1954 established an urban renewal program, and 221-d-2 was designed "to assist private industry in providing housing for low- and moderate-income families and families displaced from urban renewal areas or as a result of governmental actions." It was created because of the limited income of many of the families displaced from housing which was to be rehabilitated or demolished for redevelopment at urban renewal sites.

The legislation permitted home purchases with a $200 minimum down payment, with provisions for a forty-year mortgage instead of one for thirty years. There is no "economic soundness" rule for the 221 section. However, "the property shall comply with such standards and conditions as the Secretary may prescribe to establish the acceptability of such property for mortgage insurance." In practice, it meant that less rigorous criteria for housing conditions were accepted, as long as "the requirements of all State laws, or local ordinances or regulations, relating to the public health or safety, zoning or otherwise, which may be applicable thereto" were met.

The program was used most extensively after the 1968 Housing Act.

Section 235. Section 235 was part of the National Housing Act of 1968. It established a mortgage interest subsidy program to support home ownership by low- and moderate-income families, generally those with incomes below 135 percent of local public housing limits. The government, depending on a homeowner's income, pays up to all but 1 percent of the interest due on the mortgage. The homeowner must pay at least 20 percent of his adjusted monthly income on the mortgage. Family income and mortgage limits are established for each section of the country. The program can go either for new or used housing. Mortgages are thirty years long.

There is no "economic soundness" requirement for Section 235 mortgage insurance, but a buyer and home can be accepted as "a reasonably satisfactory" risk.

Income limitations varied from state to state and county to county, as well as with family size. In Chicago, for instance, the income limit for a family of two was $6,480; and $8,100 for a family of four; and $9,720 for a family of six.

Section 236. This section deals with the subsidized, multi-family interest program.

Section 223-e. This section of the 1968 National Housing Act opened FHA mortgage insurance to older, declining urban areas in which somebody determined: 1, that the area is reasonably viable; and 2, that the property is an acceptable risk. The Special Risk Insurance Fund was intended to pay losses under this program.

Other programs. There is a "number soup" of other programs—such as Section 237 and Section 203-1, plus innumerable other subsections—and what mischief has been created by their use is known only to the profiteers and victims. But the real woes have come about under Sections 203, 221-d-2, and 235 and 236 subsidized mortgages, and that's what we'll be dealing with.

Keep in mind that the only thing the FHA does for the homebuyer is to enable him to get a house for a low down payment and to pay off the mortgage over thirty years at a controlled interest rate, except in the case of interest subsidies. The controlled interest rate became one of the most destructive mechanisms of the FHA scandal.

What the FHA does for the mortgage lender is to insure him against any possible loss in the event of foreclosure. In other words, it makes FHA loans a sure thing for investors.

2

The House Buyer Laments

"My name is Robert Lindsay. I been a buyer since 1944. I've been licensed in Michigan since 1953. I bought hundreds of properties. I bought 150 houses a year since 1968, for speculators and other people. I bought for all the investors. I bought for Detroit teachers who financed the property through the teacher's union. I bought for FHA [Federal Housing Authority] appraisers who then appraised it for resale after they put it in other people's names. I bought for welfare caseworkers who sold the house to their own clients. And there were some top-notch citizens loaning out money to the top speculators. I got $150 for every house I bought.

"Buying was my business. I never sold a house FHA or VA [Veterans Administration] in my life. But I dealt in cash, and most of the time bought houses for cash or land contract.

"The FHA came into the inner city in 1968, after the riot [of 1967].* The FHA was just a sitting duck, if you know

---

*Congress then passed the 1968 Housing and Urban Development Act, which created the Section 235 program.

what I mean. They were throwed right in the middle after the riot. They loosened the requirement for FHA and would insure houses by expressways, airports, in front of a factory entrance or in an area considered commercial.

"Before then, from 1963 to 1968, we wouldn't get [FHA] insurance on the East Side. It was all red-lined [black-listed]. No investor would buy in that area. You couldn't even give away that property.

"But what happened, sir, was this. When the riot happened, the FHA thought to give low-income people a home, to give them respectability, to give them a place in the community. So they loosened the requirements.

"I started buying these properties, cash. Some of the homes that I [and the speculator] bought, we flipped: we'd buy 'em for cash and sell to other investors or mortgage companies. Some of these things I bought for $2,500, $3,000 in 1968 and 1969. My commission was $150 no matter what I bought a house for, even if it was $6,500. When we flipped a house, I got a $300 commission—$150 for me and $150 for the speculator. If a person was short of money and the weekend came up, we would flip three or four houses just to get $450 or $600, so he could have a good time.

"Now you've got to understand, a lot of these houses were bought 'subject to.' That is, subject to a FHA appraisal. Because without the appraisal, these houses were no good no matter what you bought them for.

"That was some crew the FHA had—regular and fee appraisers. They were ignorant. The FHA appraisers and the fee appraisers was the most ignorant people that ever was. The speculator didn't put the price on the house. The FHA did. Naturally, I don't say that some of the appraisers wasn't friendly [on the take]. But in all my years, I never wined or dined no investors, no FHA appraisers and no buyers.

"Let me show you some of the houses I bought and what happened to them.

"Now lookie here. This house on East Forest, I bought for Paan Investment Company, owned by Paul M. Maba-rak. The house had building code violations on it at the time. I purchased it for $2,500 from a widow. The house was flipped to a mortgage company, sold under FHA and defaulted. It had so many violations on it I didn't want to buy it. I just picked it up for the company to make a rental out of it. [When investigated, the house had a concrete back yard littered with refuse and broken glass. The walls were falling inward. The roof was open.]

"Now here's a house on Canfield that I wouldn't buy because of all the violations. It's deserted now. It's got no windows, only screens across where the windows was. The house was sold FHA, and the buyer lived in it for one month.

"This house on Ludden I bought for $1,500. It was sold for $10,500 or $10,800, FHA. It is being lived in now. The reason I'm showing you this is to show you how the FHA didn't know the value of the property. It's got no basement. This S.O.B. shouldn't of never been in FHA, you understand.

"Here on Preson, well . . . it's deserted now. The walls are covered with tar paper. The lady who lived here was sick. Her son in New York came and got her. It sold for $3,500, Nora Mabarak sold it for $12,800, and she never did any work on it.

"This double on McClellan is deserted now. A man walked into the office one day and he wanted to sell it. It had so many violations on it and two tenants not paying rent. I told the man, 'I don't want it.' He said, 'You are here and can take care of it.' I bought the house for $2,000, for Paan. Paan flipped that S.O.B. to William Hahn for $3,250. William Hahn got a $14,700 FHA mortgage on it and flipped it to Brookfield Investment for $7,500. They sold it FHA for $14,700 after a cosmetic job.

"It was lived in for one month.

"This house on McClellan was condemned at one time and was stripped. It belonged to the estate of a slumlord. It was fixed up and sold FHA, when it needed to be torn down.

"Finally, lookie here at this one on Chene. I bought it for $1,800. It's got tar paper walls and the walls are not straight. The speculator tried to get FHA on it and it was rejected as unlivable. They ran it through another mortgage company and sold it for $10,800 with a cosmetic job.

"When I bought a house for $1,800, I was buying right. Now these houses, without a FHA appraisal on them, wasn't worth anything but what I paid for them. It was the appraisal that made it all work.

"Say that we would buy a place for $4,000 and flip it to another speculator for $4,500. They'd get a commitment on it for $10,000. Then they'd sell the house and commitment for $5,000 or $6,000. They sold the commitments on the street, just like you'd sell stock.

"Now the speculators didn't use their own money for this. They had interim financing on it. All of it. But to get the interim financing on the property they had to pay 2 percent a month, between 18 and 24 percent interest a year.

"Because of all the money, the mortgage companies were running PR men up and down Mack Avenue, like pool hustlers. The big ones and the small ones. When the easy money came you found all the suburban guys come into the city. You had all the out-of-state mortgage companies come in. They came out of New York, Ohio, Wisconsin. They came into this city like a swarm of bees.

"Some of the mortgage companies owned the speculators. Then they made money on both ends of the deal. The people who were selling, well, they didn't know what was happening. I enjoyed buying after people had listed with two or three brokers. I bought out from under them. What the speculators did was get the FHA appraisal first, before I bought the house. You'd get a $10,000 appraisal. Then I'd buy it for $2,500. The owners, they couldn't get the appraisals. They couldn't sell FHA themselves. Only the speculators could. You figure it out for yourself.

"Before they started the easy FHA money, we really had to fix a house up to sell it. We'd paint it inside and out, sand the floors, put rat wall around it, repair steps and replace broken glass. Afterwards, all we did was cosmetic repairs. Sometimes we didn't do anything at all—just sold them FHA. The buyers, those welfare mothers and poor people, didn't know nothing about houses.

"There wasn't any city certification then. But the city inspectors would come around, and ask for donations —for 'church' or something. They wanted cash. They wouldn't take a check to the church, you understand.

"Now, even if you fixed a house up it didn't do any good. A lotta times we got appraisals on property and then it was vandalized. Theft was so prominent that you could fix up a house today and tonight it'd be stripped. What caused that was these repairmen. They'd steal stuff from one property and put it into another property.

"There was people, that was workers, who was vandalizing one place, and naturally the stuff would end up in somebody else's property. We'd have to have armed guards sit in a place all night long before we could ever close a deal the next day. They steal bathroom fixtures, doors, radiators, paneling, furnaces, everything. And, of course, contractors would buy the stuff through the grapevine. Oh, they robbed us blind. Everybody was getting something out of the FHA.

"Finally, I quit because there was so much of this stuff going on. I called the Government Accounting Office. I talked to the main man. I told him the FHA oughta get out of the business. They don't know the first principle about investments. They don't know value and they don't have the personnel. I sent telegrams to the FHA in Washington. They said they'd look into it. But they haven't.

"The FHA is just throwing good money out after bad money.

"But what are you going to do? Without the speculators, they're not going to sell any property in the inner city. It takes a special breed of people to operate in the inner city. You see, I go armed. That's because it's dangerous out there. You have to go out at eleven o'clock at night, or early in the morning, to look at a house, so that the robbers are asleep and won't get you.

"Now what's happened to the people who lived in these houses? Where did they all go? Well, 90 percent of the people I bought from, they left the city. The people that bought the houses FHA and got foreclosed on, they are doubling up with one another.

"I'd buy from white and colored, and as fast as I would buy, they'd leave town. They're leaving this town at ninety miles an hour. They don't let their shirttails hit their back. Now the city is dead. The neighborhood is ruined. I hate the FHA. I hate the word FHA. I hate the FHA worse than I hate a rattlesnake."

Robert Lindsay
Detroit, Michigan
Spring, 1972

The Murder of Nora Mabarak

For me, it didn't begin with Bob Lindsay—it started with a sweaty dream of many houses, ruined houses, and a question: "Who got the money?"

But Bob Lindsay taught me what it was all about. Bob Lindsay took me out in the streets where the underbelly of American real estate and property is inhabitated by thugs, con men and the suede-shoe boys who have eaten away our cities with the grim tenacity of human termites. Bob Lindsay lifted my eyes from the land tract index and governmental file to show me the greed that feasts on misery and the dead neighborhoods nobody will ever resurrect.

His family name was Screws. Just about six feet tall with a fanatical look under the vaguely Amish, flat-brimmed black hat, Robert carried himself swiftly and nervously on his black-laced shoes. He talked that way, too, with a Southern accent. There was the urgent exhortation of the old evangelistic preacher in his voice: "Hell—the FHA has been our ruin."

Early in 1972, alarmed by what I then believed to be the loss of 10,000 houses and $100 million in the Federal Housing Administration's insured mortgage program in Detroit, I had begun to investigate and write about the spreading disaster. (The loss in Detroit alone may reach $500 million.) On March 3, David Hess of the Knight Newspapers' Washington bureau transmitted a bulletin to the *Detroit Free Press* where I worked.

"A man named Robert Lindsay, 50, in Detroit called me Friday morning in response to the housing abuse story that ran in the *Free Press* Thursday. Mr. Lindsay says he has been engaged in buying and selling real estate in the city for a number of years. He says he can document abuses by the mortgage lenders and realtors and 'knows for a fact' that certain parts of the city are red-lined. I told him that I would pass the word on to you with the suggestion that a good investigative reporter look into Mr. Lindsay's charges. . . . If Mr. Lindsay knows what he's talking about, it could be a helluva story."

So I gave Lindsay a call and he said, "Yes, Mis-Ter BaYer [Boyer], ah know all about what's goin' on."

He would not elaborate over the telephone, but only hinted darkly that "them guys that got the big money" was—were—involved.

I made a note which I promptly filed and forgot. But a few days later Lindsay called me, to say that he knew names and could describe the inner workings of the scandal that turned old houses into new money. He would talk to me. I asked him to come into the newspaper office at night because I worked the city desk until 11 P.M., and the office is quiet then. The following day Bob Lindsay, in his black shoes and black hat, with a nickel-plated .38 tucked into his pants under a green cardigan sweater, appeared in the city room with a huge briefcase of notes and records tucked under an arm.

"Mis-Ter BaYer?" he asked, smiling through the gaps in his teeth. "I don't want you to say nothin'. I just want you to listen. Do you hear me now?"

I decided two things. I would be very careful with a man who walked around wearing a gun. And I wanted to hear what he had to say.

That night, and on subsequent nights and days, I sat writing feverishly while Lindsay preached about how real estate speculators used the FHA program to defraud the government and the poor. I went with him into the streets ("I carry me a gun 'cause it's dangerous out here. All the fella's in this business do.") to look at houses he had purchased for as little as $2,000 that were resold for as much as $18,000. I checked land tracts and titles to find out if his figures were correct, and they were.

Lindsay, who had once been a preacher, seemed to grow more and more excited about FHA crimes as he explained them to me. His own feelings of guilt appeared to grow, until, spitting with excitement, he'd curse the real estate business and defend his own role in it. "I was only a buyer. Remember that. I didn't sell the houses or nothin.' Do you hear me now? Can you hear what I'm telling you?" He was, I decided, trying to clear his soul of complicity in what he considered to be momentous crimes against the poor of Detroit.

Bob had been a housebuyer for one of the city's largest real estate investors, the Mabarak family, and its various members and companies. The jobs he had done for them and for others who he said included FHA officials, social service employees, politicians, policemen and thugs, made his conscience boil.

Eventually, I wrote an article about the things that Lindsay told me, using his words but keeping his name out of it. Immediately afterward, Lindsay called me to say that his life had been threatened.

"Mis-Ter BaYer?" he said. "I think I should tell you this. There has been a contract [to kill] put out on my life. I've heard it four places now. Once from a colored man and from three whites. The threats has come through a mortgage company, but I can't tell you its name. Also, I been gettin' six crank telephone calls."

I asked him what he intended to do.

"Well, I'm not going to worry about it," he responded. "They can't frighten me off. But listen here, now. I want to tell you this. If I do wind up dead, I want you to take my papers."

I told him to be careful. He said he would be, but he intended to keep on with his life as usual and try to find who was behind the threats. If a "hit man" confronted him——

"It doesn't make a difference to me. Face to face like that, I'd like to see him. I'd like to know who it was that got me."

True enough to his prediction, Lindsay's story ended in murder. But not his own. On April 10, 1972, the state of Michigan charged that Robert Lindsay murdered Nora M. Mabarak, age 44, in her real estate office on Detroit's Near East Side.

The events leading to the murder were, for Lindsay, extraordinary and fraught with consequence. They also all connected in a way that linked Bob Lindsay, Nora Mabarak and·me with the FHA in a series of events that seemed to make death as logical a consequence as the climax of a Greek play.

First, there was the article and the threats against Lindsay's life. Then early in April came a call to me from Robert Simms, a CBS television producer for the Walter Cronkite news show. Simms is a large, handsome black man with a pleasant voice and a sweet disposition, who must regret ever placing the call to me from the office of Richard Still, staff director for the House Legal and Monetary Affairs Subcommittee in Washington, D.C.

Simms had a problem. He had been assigned to produce

a special news segment for CBS about the FHA scandal and its impact on American cities. Plenty of information was available. But outside of showing ruined houses and blighted blocks, the subject didn't lend itself to television. Too many statistics and too much complicated explanation of them made bad viewing. Did I know of anyone in Detroit who knew about the scandal and would talk about it for national broadcast?

I told him about Bob Lindsay and explained that while I thought Lindsay was emotionally unstable, I believed him to be the most knowledgeable and colorful FHA participant I had met. I would call Lindsay and test his interest. I did. The housebuyer and the television producer spoke to each other for the first time on April 5.

On April 9, a Sunday, Simms and a CBS television crew flew into Detroit. On Monday, Simms, with a crew of three persons and David Cohan, the correspondent for CBS, went to Detroit's Lower East Side area where they shot film to demonstrate how the FHA scandal had ruined the neighborhood.

Simms had an appointment to meet with Lindsay on Tuesday, April 11. But Monday, after the film crew had finished, Simms returned to his room at the St. Regis Hotel where he received a telephone call from Lindsay at 5:30 P.M.

"Lindsay requested that I accompany him on something of a mercy mission," Simms recalled. "That he had received a call from a very distraught woman who said she was going to kill herself. The reasons were because of the situation involving her home. Her house had been repossessed. I take it this all had to do with the [FHA] story that we were investigating here.

"Eventually, the woman had reached the end of the rope and had called Mr. Lindsay and said that she was going to kill herself, and Mr. Lindsay called me and asked me to get a tape recorder and join him in trying to dissuade the woman from blowing herself in."

Simms, because he was unsure about Lindsay, declined to go with him on the "mercy mission."

According to Lindsay's wife, Lindsay had spent the day preoccupied, as usual, with the FHA. At noon she said, Lindsay announced his decision to "help" George Romney, former secretary of the U.S. Department of Housing and Urban Development, of which the FHA is a most difficult part. She said that Lindsay had decided that "the mortgage companies and not Romney" were to blame for the troubles in Detroit.

At 1:30 P.M. he got a telephone call from an elderly black woman who used the name Aileen Price. Mrs. Lindsay recalled that Bob said Mrs. Price lived on Iroquois in the 4000 block. After he talked to the caller, he placed a telephone number and address in his pocket. Lindsay told his wife that the woman said she had purchased the house from Nora Mabarak and that she couldn't make her mortgage payments on it any longer. It was a house that Lindsay believed he had purchased for the Mabaraks.

"The woman was either going to walk out of it [the house] or kill herself," Mrs. Lindsay said. "This is what Bob called Simms about, to arrange an interview. At 5 P.M. he called the woman back and didn't get any answer. He told me he thought it was a 'setup.'"

Lindsay decided that he would find out what was going on. With the pistol in his belt, he drove to the house, a once-pleasant brick home now in shambles, and found it deserted. His fear that somebody was trying to set him up appeared to be confirmed. Why would somebody call him to a deserted house unless they intended to harm him in some way?

He apparently decided that his former employers, the Mabarak family, and specifically Nora Mabarak, were responsible for the call. Nobody knows why. The only recent contact he had had with Nora Mabarak had been shortly after the *Free Press* article appeared. Mrs. Lindsay said that Nora had called Bob and said, "What bothered her [Nora] the worst was the fact that he [Bob Lindsay] told the *Free Press* that the Mabaraks never entertained appraisers."

It meant that Lindsay had denied a kind of wrongdoing that actually went on—kind of a "we're much worse than you let on." It was a jocular, not a threatening, statement.

Whatever his reasons were, Lindsay left the deserted house and drove to the Mabarak real estate office on Mount Elliott. He arrived at 6:40 P.M.

When he got there, he found the entrance locked. He knocked on the door and a neighborhood friend of Miss Mabarak, Wilbert Pace, let him in.

"Hi, Willie," Lindsay said.

"Hi, Lindsay," Willie responded.

"Is Nora in?" Lindsay asked, and Willie told him that she was in her office. Also in the office, but in another room, was a bookkeeper. Nora Mabarak was in her office with an unknown woman customer, taking rent or writing out an insurance policy. She was also talking on the telephone to her brother, 27, also named Robert, who was another member of the family in the real estate business.

Robert heard Nora say, "Hi, Lindsay," and then heard Lindsay say, "Listen to me, do you know anything about a home on Iroquois?"

Pace and Robert Mabarak both heard Lindsay and Nora argue. Pace had heard the two of them argue before, about business, never anything personal, and didn't think anything of it. He considered both of them friends.

But suddenly, the middle-aged woman who had been in the office when the quarrel began ran outside, leaving her pocketbook behind in her haste.

Listening on the other end of the telephone, Robert Mabarak "heard my sister say 'No.' He [Lindsay] asked if she knew anything about this house, and I heard my sister say 'No' and I believe she said 'No' a couple of times. And then she said, 'Is it a big home?' and he said, 'No.' And then I heard more of the conversation. Mr. Lindsay was saying something about being set up. Then all I heard was my sister say 'NO, LINDSAY, NO.' Then two seconds later, gunshots and that was it."

The deputy chief medical examiner of Wayne County said that Nora Mabarak died of a single bullet in the left side of the head, slightly behind the left ear and about four inches from the top of the head. Gunpowder stippling indicated that when the gun was fired at her from about a foot away, her hands were raised as if to protect her face.

When the gun went off, Willie was sitting with the bookkeeper. He jumped up and ran toward Nora's office. He saw Lindsay coming out of the office holding the gun, a .38 caliber nickel-plated revolver.

Gun in hand, Lindsay walked past Willie and out the front door where he calmly unlocked his car, got in and drove away.

On the street, Thurman Lilly, a 40-year-old barber, Herman Thomas and Arthur P. Anderson, Sr., were on their way to a grocery store when they saw a woman run out of the office and cross the street, shouting, "There's a man with a gun in there. Someone's going to get shot."

Fifteen or twenty seconds later, Thomas said, they heard a shot and saw "this white man come out of the office carrying a nickel-plated gun.

"He looked like he was loading it or unloading it," Thomas remembered. "He walked to his car, a bronze, late-model Chevy. He wasn't in any hurry, but was looking to see if anyone was watching him. He seemed very deliberate. He stood by the side of the car, took the keys out of his pocket and unlocked the car. He got in, but didn't start off in any hurry."

Lilly shouted, "Get the license number," which Anderson took down. They stopped a passing Detroit police station wagon, told the policemen what happened, and gave them the license plate number of Lindsay's car.

Inside, Pace found Nora lying dead on the floor of her office, blood coming from the wound in her head.

The woman who had been with Nora rushed back into the office and retrieved her purse from the desk beside the murdered woman. As the police arrived, Lindsay calmly drove home.

Mrs. Lindsay said that Bob entered the house and told her, "I just shot Nora."

"I didn't believe it at first," she said.

Lindsay put the gun containing one spent shell and five unused bullets on a book shelf in the dining room, picked up the telephone and called Simms at his hotel room.

Simms got the call at 7:05 P.M.

"This is Bob Lindsay. I can't make the 8 A.M. shooting [filming] schedule. I killed her."

Simms didn't believe Lindsay, either.

"I thought he meant that figuratively," he said later.

Lindsay told Simms that he had gone to the house on Iroquois, found it abandoned and vandalized, and came to the conclusion that it was a place for an attempt on his life.

"He then said that he recognized the voice of a woman, whom he had talked to earlier," Simms stated. "He [Lindsay] said he then went to an office, confronted the woman, and then he said, 'I killed her.'

"After a repetition of the words, 'I killed her,' I said, 'Well, what are you talking about?'

"He said, 'I pulled out my .38 and I shot her, once between the eyes.'"

The conversation ended when Simms heard someone with Lindsay—his wife—say, "the police."

A very puzzled Simms called me at 7:10 in the evening at the *Free Press*.

"What is with this guy?" Simms asked. "Is he a practical joker?"

He told me about the telephone conversation he had just had with Lindsay and wanted to know if it could be true. I asked him if the woman Lindsay said he had killed was Nora Mabarak. Simms said he "didn't catch the name."

I called my police reporter and asked him to find out if Miss Mabarak had been slain. A few minutes later he confirmed that Nora had been murdered, and that Bob Lindsay was already in custody for the crime.

An examination was held in Detroit's Recorder's Court on April 20, 1972, at which time Lindsay was bound over for trial on a charge of murder in the first degree. Lindsay did not take the stand at the examination. He appeared to be in a stupor, perhaps because of the heavy dosages of tranquilizers he was being given to dampen his emotions. The only time during the examination that he appeared to be conscious of what was going on was when the FHA scandals were mentioned. At that point he looked at me, nodded his head slightly and winked.

Bob Lindsay eventually was ruled not guilty by reason of insanity. He was sent to Ypsilanti State Hospital in Michigan where he was held and treated for mental illness for several months before being released as no longer dangerous.

It may not be correct to say that the FHA drove Bob Lindsay to kill Nora Mabarak, but it would not be wrong to say that that's what he thought was responsible for his troubles. Bob Lindsay believed himself to be a victim of the blight brought about by the FHA scandals, and held himself personally responsible for the ruined houses and displaced citizens whose dreams of home ownership were dashed by individual fraud and governmental bungling.

Poor Bob Lindsay, mad and a murderer, too, kept his promise and left me all of his records, the scribbled notes about hundreds of houses bought cheap, sold dear, foreclosed, vandalized and destroyed. Nora Mabarak is dead. The neighborhoods are in ruins. "Romney City" is the name of the slum.

3

Romney City

Romney City is the sixth largest city in the United States, with 350,000 houses and a population of about 1,400,000, and ranks between Detroit and Houston proper. Unlike most cities, of course, Romney City doesn't exist in a single place; rather, its parts are scattered about in twenty and more other cities in the United States, from New York, Boston, Philadelphia and Washington, D.C., in the East; to Detroit, Chicago and St. Louis in the Midwest; to Dallas in the South; and to Seattle and Los Angeles in the West. It was created by criminal manipulation of the 1968 National Housing Act, under the administration of George Romney, then secretary of the U.S. Department of Housing and Urban Development.

Another way in which it is unique is that the suburbs of Romney City are eight or ten times larger than the city itself, with nearly three million houses and apartment units and a population of ten million or so. The suburbs are fascinating because they consist almost entirely of what folk singer Pete Seeger called "little boxes made of ticky-tacky, and they all look just the same." The mile after mile of apartment units have the same cracker-box appearance to them that the houses have, as if an immense cookie press had deposited row after row of the same building in what had been cornfields and cleared pastures and woodland.

As a third difference from other cities, Romney City's population is almost entirely black or Puerto Rican with, perhaps, a smattering of Mexicans. Nearly half of the people who live here live with another family, a curious thing because about half of the houses in Romney City are empty and boarded up. Pretty soon, all of the houses will be abandoned and boarded up, and where the people will live then is something that worries them very much. The thought of more than a million homeless black people spilling over the city's boundaries into the suburbs would terrify the white people, especially the million whites who lived inside Romney City until four years ago when the blacks came. But the whites feel secure in knowing that whatever else happens, the blacks can't move into their neighborhoods. Actually, they don't know why they believe that, but since the facts support their prayers it doesn't make any difference.

Anyway, they have much more important things to worry about, such as the lack of schools for their children and the dawning realization that their houses, which are still new and won't be paid for until three or four decades have passed, seem to be falling apart. Even those whose house payments and rents are being aided by the government are dismayed, for they cannot understand why the government backs such terrible buildings. Everybody in the suburbs continues to wonder about that, and some of the housewives have begun passing petitions asking the government to force the builders to repair what's gone wrong.

One thing that outsiders notice about the Romney City metropolitan area is there is only one nice section. It's on the very outskirts, where fine old houses and tree-lined streets tell you immediately that the people who live here are quite a bit different from all of the rest. These people are very rich. Some of them have made their money from real estate, construction or mortgage banking. Every house in Romney City has been sold by them at least once, and the owners of the occupied houses owe from $15,000 to $20,000 each.

The mortgage lenders and speculators built and financed

the suburbs, too, with money backed by the United States government, which they stand behind with fervor. They should, because the government that backs their endeavors also has arranged a nice deal in which is forgiven most of the otherwise staggering taxes they would have to pay on their profits for building the houses and apartment buildings, which make the money for them.

The richest people here are the bankers and the mortgage bankers and the people who own the insurance companies. Next come the builders, some of whom are wealthy enough to own their own mortgage banking firms and some of whom are owned by them. A few of the contractors and mortgage bankers have side businesses, in illegal gambling, narcotics and prostitution. Federal investigators believe that the "Mafia" has infiltrated the businesses in Michigan and Florida, both to "wash" dollars raised in criminal activities and to make more money.

At an almost equal level with the contractors, but generally much younger, are a group of high-livers who call themselves real estate investors but who are called speculators by others. They are sometimes the sons and daughters of the kindly old slum landlords, who called themselves real estate investors, too. But the new breed is smarter, and much better educated, and has made a lot more money than their parents and mentors did. These bright youngcomers even taught the bankers a trick or two, and are acceptable at anyone's cocktail party where their parents were generally closed out. The realtors, a name which real estate brokers are called if they belong to the right trade association, have also done well in Romney City. They are assiduously courted by the money people. They are marketing specialists, who live by picking up a piece of the action here and another piece there, and by easing the way with a kickback to one side and a payoff to the other. Payoff is a word that is never used in these refined circles, so the side money is called gratuity and has a traditional standing.

One of the most interesting groups of people who live on Nice Heights works for the federal government, and if you saw their paychecks you would have to wonder how they could afford the amenities of gracious living. But these government workers are all employed by the U.S. Department of Housing and Urban Development and work for the Federal Housing Administration. In addition to their salaries, these workers are supported by gratuities from the speculators and real estate people and mortgage bankers, and are said to be "friendly." Everybody likes the friendly FHA employees. Not only this, some of the HUD executives are "on loan" from the mortgage companies and real estate firms to the government and are just there to do a stint for the public good. Others have come up through the ranks, but plan to go to work for the private business interests as soon as their dedication falters.

The biggest building in Romney City was the federal HUD headquarters building, with an American flag proudly out in front and large photographs of President Richard M. Nixon and the HUD secretary inside the entrance. Near the HUD building, and even inside of the same structure, were the well-appointed offices of the mortgage bankers. Mortgage bankers decorate their offices with large American eagles, because when they have authority to do FHA business they can, as they say, "fly the eagle." American eagles are nice to display, because they look so official.

The real estate people keep their offices scattered about through the area, except in the abandoned neighborhoods where all the business that could be conducted is now finished. The contractors work entirely in the suburbs and never go downtown unless it's to talk to the HUD director or the banker. All of these people do business together during the day and socialize at night and know how to get along.

It was only a short time ago that Romney City, as we know it now, didn't exist. The suburbs weren't there—they hadn't been built—and the farmers cultivated their crops on the land that has since been covered with concrete. Romney City itself was a very different place, and actually quite a pleasant one. Most of its neighborhoods, although built in the earlier years of this century, were sturdy places where a polyglot population pursued its different and similar interests. If there is a word that described its flavor, it would be one that is very popular, now that what it describes has virtually ceased to exist—ethnic. The neighborhoods were ethnic enclaves of very different kinds of people—urban villagers who followed their own religious expressions, customs and cuisines. The neighborhoods were linked together only by a common experience of remembered immigration, a love of America and a passion for houses.

You might remember what these neighborhoods were like, for millions of Americans grew up in them—Irish, German, Bohemian, Serbian, Italian, Croatian, Greek, black, of course, and more recently, Puerto Rican. It would be fair to say that early Romney City was mostly white and perhaps no more than 25 percent of its residents were black.

All of these neighborhoods were not the equal of each other, but as the lot of their people improved, traditionally their housing did, too. An important part of the upgrading came as the upper classes sought new locations and left behind sound buildings for large families. Even more important was how the people in the neighborhoods improved them, for a little more money meant another wing or a dormer, new plastering and a new roof, a fresh coat of paint and, if fate smiled on a man, a down payment for another house or an apartment building to be rented out. House-proud people lived in Romney City. The home was more than a place to live in. It was a symbol of strength, a native art object, and the major investment of a person's life.

There were several traditional ways to buy a house, some of them better than others. The best way, if you could afford it, was to buy with money borrowed from a bank. That usually required a good wage and 25 or 35 percent down payment, and you were expected to give the bank its money back in ten to twenty years. The banks thoroughly approved of a lot of money down and fast repayments, because the risk was lessened and the return seemed to be higher. A person who had put $3,000 or $4,000 into a $10,000 house wasn't about to miss one of his payments, or let the property be foreclosed and lose his investment. Bankers thought of him as a good manager of the property that acted as collateral for the loan, and they were absolutely correct.

If you didn't have much money, but had proved your good character by paying bills on time and working steadily in the mills, the bountiful government of the United States stood ready to help you buy a house. That was through the FHA program, which insured the mortgage money lent to you. The benefit of the insurance, if you were so unfortunate as to lose the property, went to the lender, but the procedure was a reasonable one. Bankers, accustomed to all of the protections of high equities, weren't about to lend $9,000 to a person who hadn't proved himself. The government was acting like a rich uncle who said, "This boy's OK by me. Lend him the money, and if he gets in trouble, I'll pay it back." The other nice things about the FHA program were the low down payments, long-term loans and interest rates that were frequently lower than the market rate.

The system wasn't perfect, and when hard times came more people lost their houses, but overall, the FHA program's loss was less than one-half of 1 percent of all FHA mortgages. Crimes committed against the program generally were by eager buyers who fudged about their income in order to qualify for a mortgage, or who tried to get FHA home improvement loans to spend the money on other things. The government kept a careful eye on that kind of activity.

The government kept an extremely careful watch on the kinds of houses it would insure, too. They had to be in good shape, generally better than houses sold in other ways, because FHA had no intention of being stuck with a house that couldn't be resold quickly. Congress, which had written the laws for FHA in the first place, didn't want the voters to live in bad houses. Good living quarters for everyone was an honored American dream. Places that weren't good—near factories, high crime areas, on commercial blocks and on floodplains—weren't insured. It was as simple as that.

But there were houses in these places, and buyers for them who couldn't afford conventional mortgages or qualify for FHA insurance. They bought on contract. In theory, there was nothing wrong with contract, but the goodness or badness of it was—and still is—contingent on who did business with whom. The contract rules are simple. The buyer makes his own deal with the seller—how much down will be paid, and how much interest will be charged, and for how long. Unlike a regular sale in which a warranty deed giving ownership goes along with the mortgage, no deed passes hands in a contract deal. The original owner still owns it, until the very last dollar is paid. If the seller isn't the very best kind of person, the buyer can be taken for an expensive ride. One trick the unscrupulous had was to peg the monthly payments at a level higher than the buyer could reasonably be expected to pay while charging him a down payment equal to all of his cash reserves. One missed payment and the seller had his property back, and the buyer was out on the street with his pockets emptied. Another trick was to arrange the payments so that at the end of the contract period, frequently twelve years, the buyer would have one large cash payment due. That amount could be anything up to the entire principal if monthly payments were set up so that only the interest was being paid. Many contract buyers found themselves at the end of twelve years looking at eviction instead of a home. People who had no other choice kept buying on contract, hoping that things eventually would work out and they could convert the contract to a conventional mortgage. Some of the folks in the high rent districts of Romney City got there by Yo-Yoing contracts from buyer to buyer.

A general rule was, if you were not white, you couldn't get conventional mortgages or FHA mortgages, and usually not contract mortgages unless you were dealing with a shark. Black people were renters, though certainly not by choice. Like everybody else, they thought home ownership was the front yard of the American Dream. So they lined up for contract sales when they had a job and the chance, and they also lined up for the old second- and third-mortgage trick called the "Black Tax."

It worked this way. A real estate speculator would buy up a property for $6,000 and put perhaps $1,000 worth of repairs into paint and a door knocker. His goal was to at least double his investment, but in the deal twice $7,000 isn't $14,000, it's actually $30,000 that the buyer owes, in three mortgages. In the first mortgage for $10,000, the speculator will sell it to an investor for nine dollars on ten, 90 percent. For the second mortgage of $10,000, the speculator will sell for fifty cents on the dollar. For the third mortgage of $10,000, he'll get $1,000—a total to the seller of $14,000, but debt owed by the poor buyer of $30,000. When one mortgage is paid off, the next one becomes due. The speculator has his money and the buyer has a hell of a payment to worry about. Whenever one mortgage is paid, the deal is recast, and the buyer is on an endless voyage of debt service and mortgage payments, for an inferior house.

A variation on the same theme is the home improvement loan, which ended up as a second or a third mortgage on the property. It was operated by the suede-shoe boys, the fast-buck roofing-and-siding salesmen who came from the same school that trained the furnace repair boys and other basic kinds of flimflammers.

A bad house needs repairs, and poor buyers want them.

The home repair operators do shoddy work for inflated prices and get in return second or third mortgages on the property for a five year period. To compound all their other troubles, the owners frequently signed blank contract slips, onto which the shady operators noted whatever prices they felt like charging, plus certification of completion.

Many ethnics in Romney City didn't know any of this was going on, and if they knew about it, they didn't care. Blacks were generally not held in high regard. Shoddy real estate practices captured their attention only when it snared one of them. Educated and rich people were rarely victims.

But, despite the nostalgic pleasures of the ethnic Romney City in which we have let ourselves drift, into the odors of kielbasa and bagels and pasta, and the solid comforts of well-trimmed lawns and painted siding, there were problems here that seemed to grow over the years after World War II. First of all, the houses were old and getting older. Although they were frequently well-built they didn't always have the amenities Americans were being taught they needed to live a civilized life, and their yards weren't big enough, and the economy was booming, and the FHA was beginning to tempt people to move away into the opening suburbs with the same good loans that enabled the working class to buy in the first place. There weren't enough houses, either, for all of the new families being formed after the war. Suburbia was, along with a new car, seen in a kind of Town-and-Country affluent haze. The good life began to appear over the horizon, in the next suburb and the newest subdivision. If Mama and Pop didn't want to leave their neighborhood, their kids did, and they could. They didn't like the old ways and the old cities. Besides, every day there seemed to be more black faces around the edges of the neighborhoods, only those people with dark faces weren't black people or even Negroes yet: they were niggers and coons.

What was right about that perception was that there were more black people around. Industry had started importing them from the South where they had been tucked away for a couple hundred years, because it needed labor during the war years and it needed labor afterwards to punch out consumer goods. In addition, the big cities continued to work their magic for the rural population, and after he has seen it, you can't keep a man down on the farm chopping cotton for fifty cents a day, at least not when he can pull down two dollars an hour working for Ford.

Only nobody thought about where they would put this new population. One thing for sure, you couldn't put them in with the working whites, because they were intolerant to simple ethnic differences, much less a color change. So the blacks were packed together in black districts, and they were packed in their slum apartments and urban shacks tighter and tighter. Here and there the population would spill over, but the lid was kept on as tightly as possible by the banks and mortgage companies and real estate firms that control, for every American regardless of how much money he has, where a person is going to live.

Housing was just one of the tribulations suffered by the blacks, but it was a problem that seemed to them to be much more critical than it appeared to the whites. Times were changing, tempers were heating up and blacks were increasingly reluctant to be kept in their place. Pop went the first riot. Bang went the second. Whoosh went the third, and American cities burned with a fierce, riotous light from 1966 through 1968.

A long way from Romney City, in Washington, D.C., where men politicize in marble monuments and sometimes pay attention to their constituencies back home, the word came that something had to be done about the blacks. You couldn't keep the people at gunpoint forever, and it looked bad overseas to send the tanks rumbling down streets more accustomed to old Chevrolets decorated with an occasional swan and white mud flaps. Martin Luther King, Jr., was a Negro, and the South was prejudiced, and the North was aflame. As the editorial writers liked to put it, the nation's conscience was pricked, and as always happens in America when a real crisis arrives, her elected representatives put their shoulders to the wheel to find a solution, by creating new legislative programs to solve the problems.

President John F. Kennedy—actually his brain trust and advisers—got to work to find solutions. Housing was a problem, unlike prejudice, that could be solved. With houses. The question was how to deliver the houses to the eager consumer—low-income blacks. Input came from the universities and authorities and housing officials and from the real estate lobbies and the banking lobbies and the home builders. A mechanism was available to take care of what was wrong, and it was called the FHA. The FHA had always worked well in delivering houses to the deserving worker. Couldn't it be broadened to cover every American, regardless of color or income? Of course it could, by stripping the FHA of all of the conservative financial approaches to housing and mortgages. There wouldn't be any problem because the FHA would act like a watchdog over the transactions, as Congress assumed it would. This problem was more important than future problems, anyway. Home ownership would tranquilize the people. It would make them steady and understandable, darker carbon copies of the white Europeans who scrubbed their kitchen floors seven days a week and used nail clippers to edge their lawns.

But the housing industry and mortgage industry reminded Congress that the nation was facing a general housing shortage. If people who didn't have houses were going to get them, new ones would have to come from someplace. But new houses would have to be financed, and private capital wouldn't be enough. John F. Kennedy died when the problem was still unsolved. President Lyndon Johnson took over and kept the housing trust at work. He was being assailed by Republicans for breaking the budget. It was evident that the government would have to put some money into the housing program, but several billions of dollars a year would further skew the budget. What to do?

The nation's mortgage bankers and financial interests came up with a solution. They would put up the necessary capital after all. Since there weren't enough well-heeled people to use it properly, the government would back their investment and help the people keep up their mortgage payments. "But we need a little incentive to make it all work," they told Johnson's housing boys. "We'd like a tax break or two. After all, it's our money."

What the government housing boys were stewing about when the money boys walked in with their solution were problems like this:

- We need $40 billion worth of housing.
- If the Treasury puts up the money for it in loans over the next eight years, that's $5 billion a year. If we give it away, that's $5 billion a year, too. We can't add $5 billion more to the budget. The GOP will crucify us for it.

What the money guys told Johnson's boys was that they could have their cake and eat it, too. How? By interest subsidies. You'll like the way they work. If the Treasury pays 6 percent of the 7 percent interest we (the money boys) want on our mortgage money, we'll throw $5 billion right now into new construction. Anybody can see that 6 percent of $5 billion is only $300 million. Think of it—$300 million buys $5 billion in new housing.

It was a deal that aides to Johnson, who were writing the law, and Congress and everybody else in government couldn't refuse. It was also a poisoned pawn. For what nobody stopped to figure out, except the capital sources who had it all figured out from the beginning, was that 6 percent interest on $5 billion over forty years turns into $10 billion. If the government agrees to finance a private investment of $40 billion in housing, it will eventually cost the taxpayer $80 billion, and it will cost property owners $40 billion more to pay back the loan. Interest doubles the cost over the life of the loan.

The best idea would have been to finance the construction in direct loans which would have been paid back, with interest, to the Treasury. But it certainly didn't seem very good at the time.

All of the President's plans and Congress's good intentions culminated in the 1968 Housing and Urban Development Act, a piece of legislation that was broadcast as the solution to riots, short housing and unrest, a sluggish mortgage market and tired blood.

The FHA commissioner and his staff, under the energetic prodding of President Johnson and the more cautious exhortations of HUD's secretary, Robert Weaver, laid down the word to the cautious bureaucracy of the FHA: deliver housing. Deliver it as fast as you can, and as much of it as possible, to anybody who wants it. They also said that the rules were to be followed, that used houses sold to the poor in Romney City were to be as good as building codes could make them, and that people shouldn't be put in a position where their payments were so out of line with their incomes that they couldn't possibly keep them up. Those cautionary messages were lost in the memos urging mortgage production. The FHA had a national mission—to house the poor.

What the government hadn't bothered to think through was that the FHA staff knew about as much about the inner city housing market and ghetto business practices as Pope Paul knows about the Mob. Not so much. FHA appraisers, who are the fellows who set the prices on the houses by deciding how much the government will insure it for, were almost entirely white, lower level bureaucrats who worked by the book and with very little initiative. They didn't know the territory. They were afraid of the turf, too, because some tough customers lived in it.

Higher level officials were even more ignorant because they spend their working lives entirely in grim governmental offices amid forms and applications and numbers where reality is the piece of paper on the desk, not a building on a street where people live. When things started going askew, they had no experience to tell how things were going wrong. Their work consisted of moving papers from one file to the next, and as long as the documents were correct on their face, the reality they described was true.

As a final apologia for the FHA, it was about to be forcibly mated with HUD, under a new secretary named George Romney, who has white hair, strong ideals and fervent loyalties to Richard M. Nixon, who wanted the FHA to continue its mission with dispatch, a smaller staff, and a new decentralized organization that didn't come running back to Mother Washington with every little thing that went wrong.

There was also a snake in the bushes, and its name was greed. It was an old pet of the real estate speculator, contract dealer and suede-shoe operator, and it was at least a speaking acquaintance of the mortgage banker and investment manager who act altruistically only when they are unfortunately in ruin. With their training in real estate, money and law, they carefully read over the provisions of the new housing act and attended the meetings with FHA officials who passed on the magic word "production" like a sacred trust, and they realized that some temptation is just too strong for a man to resist. All of them didn't realize it right away, and the strong had to lead the weak into the leaky basement where the government keeps its gold, but they got the idea, all right. The FHA and the poor, like an eager and inexperienced virgin, were going to get screwed.

Those who were going to do it included:

The Italian—Don Giovanni, and the staff of the Friendly Real Estate Company, whose slogan was "We Buy Cash" and "Welfare Mothers, Low Down Payments FHA."

The Comer—Fred Angelo, a juvenile delinquent *cum* lawyer who learned the tricks of the trade working part time for the FHA as an appraiser.

Windshield Willy—William Nefretti, a 45-year-old Civil Service GS-14 making $13,500 a year, with four kids, big debts and customary prejudices.

Uncle Max—An Armenian slumlord who taught his four sons and only daughter the business, set up his own mortgage company and put all of his former salesmen into business as speculators.

The Grandson—His father, grandfather and uncles are all listed as Mafioso personages. But Jack Black, at 26, builds new houses for the federal government. Nobody knows where he gets the money.

The American Eagle Mortgage Company—Sammy Goldstein and his whole family run the business like a personal checking account, while the business runs the FHA.

Forever Life Insurance Company—WASPs all, who intend to do the city good.

I. Clip—Wealthy investor.

Twice Built—Disrepair contractors.

Also Ran—Repair contractor owned by a black.

Fast Pencil—The fastest closer in Romney City.

Outstate National—Their mortgage portfolio was tattletale gray until the FHA took all the risk away.

FNMA—No lady is "Fannie Mae," the Federal National Mortgage Association.

The Victims—The residents of Romney City. Unscrupulous and greedy people paved the streets of the city with gold from the pockets and the dreams of their victims. Others will be introduced as they come along.

The following story is all based on real people and real incidents, some of whom have criminal charges pending against them. Names have been changed to prevent libel and to protect the rights of people facing trial.

4

The Streets Are Paved
with Gold

Don Giovanni was 27 years old in the spring of 1969, and
he didn't know what he wanted to do. He had a wife, Gloria,
and a couple of kids, and a long succession of jobs since he
dropped out of college after his freshman year and did his
time in the National Guard. He had worked briefly in the
office of a plumbing contractor, sold encyclopedias, and
graduated to hustling siding for a manufacturer of vinyl
covers that could be snapped over old wooden exteriors.
That led to real estate, which he had been in and out of
lately without too much success. He didn't have a state real
estate license so he usually had to divide his commission
with someone else who was licensed. It didn't seem as
though he was ever going to get rich.

But in April, when the rains came down and washed
some of the coal soot off the roofs and trees, an unexpected opportunity presented itself in the form of trouble
for somebody else. Uncle Max, Max Haberol, the canny old
Armenian slumlord who rented out shacks on Blessings
Street to the blacks, had gotten the short end of it from the
Romney City building department because some newspaper guys had decided to shake things up. After critical
articles in the *Romney News* about Max's operations, the

city started putting the heat on and Max was slapped with about 200 building-code violations that even his well-established connections with the building inspectors couldn't prevent. Some of the houses were even con-demned. It made no sense for Max to fix them up to meet city codes, because that would eat up capital without re-turning anything. You could only get so much rent out of one of those dumps, and $75 or $100 a month was the tops even if you turned the house into a palace. Max was doing what he always did when things got tight: He was liquidat-ing some of his property.

Don had been working the streets long enough to know that although a violation or condemnation follows a house, a new owner generally gets a reprieve. Usually a perma-nent one, because he can pay off the inspector the second time around. Max was unloading this batch of houses fast, which meant that they were available wholesale for as little as $3,000 or $4,000 each to the right people.

Don had worked for Uncle Max and had worked a couple of good third mortgages for him, so he went over to the old man's Blessings Real Estate office to discuss a deal. Max was, as usual, very courteous and very polite. But he was amused to discover that Don had only $500 in the bank and intended to repair the house he bought before resale.

"Sure, I can give you a contract," he said. "I can even give you a deed if you can find enough short-term money. I can give you that money myself. But then, where is the money to put into the house? Anyway, anything you put in will be stolen before you can sell. And you can't sell con-tract, or rent, and cover the 2 percent a month short-term. But come back to work for me. After you do, we'll see what we can work out."

Don, who had come in with visions of buying a house with his $500 and turning it over fast for a quick $1,000 or $2,000, left the Blessings office in a dark mood. It was too late in the afternoon to get anything else done, so he turned into the Telephone Bar, where some of the home improve-ment boys and fire-chasing repair contractors drank, and fell into conversation with two acquaintances who were arguing over the "new FHA."

The sense of their argument, as he understood it, was the FHA didn't know what in the hell was going on, and was going to give mortgages to the spades. One man was against it on principle: Those people couldn't even take care of their cars. The other one didn't give a damn what a man's color was. If he could buy a house, it was good for business. Don had had enough real estate experience to know what the FHA was but he didn't know how it worked because Max and the other guys he had worked for never sold that way. Their buyers couldn't qualify.

"Well, that's not the way it works anymore," said the beefy repair contractor, Glen something-or-other, who hated blacks. "The government's gonna give the houses away because it's scared to death. I mean, $200 down, and you got a welfare mother in a house."

"They got a right," his drinking companion said.

"Who can they buy houses from?" Don asked.

"Anybody," Glen said. "All you need to sell is an appraisal."

Don wondered how you got that.

Glen explained. "You call down to FHA and you say 'I got this house at such-and-such, and I want to get an appraisal on it for FHA.' So they send a guy out, and he takes a look at it and puts down how much he thinks it's worth. And he's supposed to put down what needs to be fixed up in the place. But the government just wants those people to get a house, so it isn't like it used to be when you had to fix everything up. You don't even have to own it to get it appraised."

"How do you know about it?" Don asked suspiciously.

"The word's out," Glen said. "Besides, I know this kid who works for FHA. He's an appraiser."

"What kind of a guy is he?" Don asked.

"A regular guy. He used to work the street a little bit on fires. Why?"

"I want to meet him," Don said. "What's his name?"

"He's a friend of mine," Glen said. "I'd have to give you an introduction."

"How much will that cost?"

Glen shrugged. Since he looked thirsty, Don bought a round. "You're a friend of mine," Glen said, shrugging like he had just lost his last dollar playing cards.

Don figured it would cost him fifty dollars. It cost fifty more. But he was in a hurry. Two days later, he met Fred Angelo in a downtown bar.

In appearance, Don and Fred were mirror images of each other. Don's year at American State had taught him to have his hair cut Princeton-style and to dress in tweed sports coats. With his fair complexion and freckled nose, he looked like a skinny Iowa farm boy, although a dormitory at college was the closest he had ever come to nature. Fred Angelo, at 22, affected a sharkskin suit and pointed black shoes, dark shades and long black hair that just escaped being combed into a pompadour. But they thought alike, which meant they each thought about money most of the time.

"I want to be an investor," Don explained while Fred held his face in profile to the plump waitress. "Glen said you could tell me about FHA."

"I'm just a fee appraiser," Fred said. "It costs money to be an investor."

"I've got enough," Don said, wondering how he was going to make it with only $400 left of his nut. "How much do you get a job?" He tried to keep the tone ambiguous.

Fred's dark eyes examined the corn boy from behind their dark glasses. "Who are you dealing with?"

"Uncle Max," Don said. "He's Blessings Real Estate."

"I never done business with him," Fred said. "He's not FHA."

"But he's got property for sale," Don said. "I just want to know how it works."

Fred was very nervous, because he had just gotten on with FHA, and he didn't want to screw himself up. But he could see the possibilities in his job because everybody over there was yelling about production and they didn't know how to get started. They didn't keep track of anything in the FHA offices either, and the files were in chaos. Appraisal requests were kept in a cardboard box on the floor beside the desks. Each one, for a fee appraiser like himself, was worth thirty dollars. Outside of some talk about "comparables," nobody had ever explained to him or to anybody else how the appraisals were to be made.

"You know what FHA is?" Fred began. "It's mortgage insurance for the guy who loans the money. Well, because of the riots, they got new programs like this 221 program where the people only have to put down $200 to get a house. A big family can get a house up to $21,000 with only $200 down."

Don marveled and wanted to know how a fee appraiser knew what a house was worth.

"It's worth whatever I say it's worth," Fred boasted.

"Nobody knows what the places in the ghetto are supposed to sell for. Some of them you couldn't sell for any price."

"Then how do you decide?" Don wanted to know.

"There is supposed to be this thing called comparables," Fred answered. "A comparable is how much a house like it in the same neighborhood sold for. But a lot of times you don't have that, so you use offers on the printout from the real estate listings. Or you might have to use the printouts on the photo index listing cards."

"But that's just a talking price," Don exclaimed.

"Besides that," Fred confided, "nobody even checks up on the comparable sales prices."

Despite his callow appearance, Fred's mind was quick and thorough, and he had gone through many of the laws and all of the documents relating to the new low-income FHA programs, with more than half an eye out for eventually using it for his own business. He also was anxious to please. Don's rapt attention began to draw him out, and he carefully explained how the appraisals were good for six months, how repairs to the property were spelled out in the appraisal form but not inspected by the FHA at the time of sale and how it seemed the government didn't care what went on as long as black people were sold houses.

When the two parted, Don's hands were shaking with greed. For a second time he went to see Uncle Max.

This time he told the old man he had a deal that would make it worth his time.

"Give me one of the houses like the gray frame one condemned on Madison, for $3,500," he pleaded. "I don't have anything to give you now. But I promise, I'll give you 2 percent a month or whatever you want and give you your money in two months plus $1,000 over. The house is your collateral, so what can you lose?"

"It's already my property," Max grumbled. "Why should I give it away?"

"Two thousand additional," Don said. "You got to move your houses. It's worth the chance."

The old man liked a bet. "Do you have a contract lined up?" he asked.

"No, no," Don said. "It's something new. FHA."

"It's hard to deal with the government," Max stated.

"This is something different," Don said. "Besides, I got a friend inside."

"Ah, well, I like to see a young man better himself," Uncle Max said sentimentally. "Two thousand, 2 percent and two months. If not?"

To Don, the fat old man sitting behind his desk looked like a hawk. His heart was pounding, although he was uncertain whether it was with greed or fear. "OK," he said. "It's a deal."

Instead of going home for dinner, he went out to a good bar and drank scotch.

At seven the next morning, after a restless night, Don called Fred Angelo at home and told him to watch for his appraisal request at the office. Angelo promised that a friendly appraiser would examine the house. Then Don went to the Blessings office to sign the papers and get the keys. He called the FHA at 11 A.M. At noon, for the first time, he went to visit his new house on Madison.

He started feeling worried when he looked at its weathered siding and falling gutters, but when he went inside he wanted to weep. The interior walls hadn't been painted for ten years and five tenants; the wallpaper hung and the paint was dark with soot and grease. Worse, the bathroom floor was rotted through in front of the toilet, the water heater in the damp basement had apparently been stolen and the furnace was in disrepair. When he tried the faucets he got no pressure due to lime deposits in the pipes. The floors were worn and pitted, the lights flickered, the wooden back steps had been turned into sawdust by termites and dry rot. The house was unlivable and unsellable. Like everybody else, he thought, Uncle Max had taken him, too. But there was no backing out of a deal with the Armenian.

He spent the weekend cleaning floors and picking debris out of the yard to the mild curiosity of his black neighbors, who wondered what that white boy was up to. Monday, he rented a sander and started to work on the floors. Sweating, his clothes caked with sawdust and powdered varnish and a handkerchief tied over his nose and mouth, he had finished the living room when there was a knock at the front door.

He opened it, and a big man with a hat on walked into the hallway and said, "I'm the appraiser from the FHA."

"How did you get here so fast?" Don mumbled. "I mean, this place isn't ready yet."

Very casually, the man walked through the rooms on the first floor and down the basement stairs where he halted when he saw the water on the basement floor and trod back up again. He went outside and walked once around the house, noting the rusted gutters and peeling roof. He stepped over the back stairs rather than trust his weight on them.

"Jeesus," the appraiser said. "Who the hell owns this place?"

"I do," Don said. "Actually, it's in pretty good shape."

The man looked at him and made a sour face and opened his briefcase. "You know, I got to make out a 2800 form on this," he said. "That says what it's worth, and what has to be done to it. How much are you asking?"

Don had never thought that far. "What's your comparable?" he asked.

"My comparable!" the appraiser exclaimed. "I'm supposed to get that, too? I've never been in this neighborhood before."

He glanced nervously out the front window. "Those kids better not touch my car."

Don opened the front door and glared at the kids in the street. "I was going to ask $15,000 for it when it's all fixed," he said. "Is that a comparable?"

The appraiser took out an official looking book filled with addresses and undecipherable figures and leafed through it.

"There's a house three blocks away that went for $13,000 last fall," he said finally.

"That's about what I wanted," Don said.

The appraiser's ball-point pen hesitated and then he wrote in the proper blank.

"I'm supposed to write down on here everything that's wrong with it," the appraiser said without looking up. "You know, this house is a piece of shit."

"How much do you think it will cost me to fix it up?" Don asked.

"Five thousand," the appraiser mumbled.

"How much?" Don asked.

"Five thousand!" he exclaimed.

"I never had that much money in my life," Don exploded. "Why the hell don't you just take the key with you?"

"It could be less," the appraiser said tentatively.

"I've got $300," Don said. "That's all. It. Everything. My cash."

The man from the FHA looked pained. "I understand

how it is with you guys in business," he said. "I know you got to make a living."

"Yes," Don said.

"I like to keep on friendly terms," the man explained.

Don reached into his overall's pocket where he had his money in a roll wrapped in a rubber band. The appraiser's hat, he noticed, was resting upside down on the ladder. As unobtrusively as possible, he dropped the money in it while the appraiser discreetly looked away.

"To get down to business," the appraiser said, "I'm going to mark down paint inside and out and a new water heater and sand floors and gutters."

He made the appropriate marks and handed Don a copy of the form.

"Here's your appraisal," he said. "If you want my advice, I'd put something over the bathroom floor."

The FHA man lowered his head and quickly put the hat on. When he was outside in the car, Don saw him remove the hat and put something in his suit pocket before he drove away.

"Goddammit, goddammit, goddammit," he thought, looking at the $13,000 written on the form. "I'm going to be rich!"

Three miles away in downtown Romney City, in the same skyscraper that housed the HUD-FHA offices but down a couple of floors, the men who ran the American Eagle Mortgage Company had gathered in the big office of president Sammy Goldstein. There were five people present. Mr. Goldstein, a large-cigar chewing man of sixty, who had started the firm three years earlier with $10,000 cash, a line of credit from the Romney Trust Bank, and $90,000 in what was described to the government as "assets," but was actually the inflated appraisal value of two moldering apartment buildings and some suburban farmland located near where a department store had plans to build. The only other thing Sammy had to prove to the government was that he was not a part of organized crime. "I'm just a part of unorganized crime," he quipped at the time, and vowed that he was clean. His son, Myron, a 27-year-old graduate of Harvard Law School, sat across from his old man's desk. On the leather sofa were Jayson Penny, the firm's mortgage solicitor, a thin, nervous man of about 45; David

Cohen, American Eagle's general counsel; and executive vice-president Max Stein. Stein and Myron had just returned from a conference with the local HUD director, William Mix.

"As far as I can see, we have read the law right," Myron told his father. "We went all through it with Mix. Basically, as far as we're concerned, it operates just the same as the Section 203 program, except the government wants as much production as we can deliver."

"But how much production can we deliver?" Sammy complained. "These *schwartzes* never live any place. They don't have regular jobs. How do you ever get a credit check that holds up for them?"

"Will you go through it again, David?" Myron asked.

Cohen, who had been sitting with his elbows on his knees, opened his hands in supplication. "Sammy, it's not our responsibility," he said. "There is nothing in the law as far as any of us can see that says we have to be able to guarantee credit, job or anything. It's not even our job— it's up to the investor or the seller or whoever he is. We just have to process the paper. We're not being asked to go behind the face of the documents. If somebody's going to do that, it would be the FHA, I suppose. Not that I think they're going to do that because, first of all, they don't have the manpower. Second of all, they don't know what they're in for. But that's not our business."

"What is our business?" Sammy wondered.

Jayson Penny, the solicitor, raised his hand like a child in school. "Check out the 2800s as usual," he volunteered. "There's got to be a house there, for Chrissake. It's up to us to find out if the repairs are done."

"That's old housing," Sammy said.

"We don't care if the walls are falling down, as long as there's a new sink if the appraiser wants a new sink," Jayson reminded him. "Where we are going to be in trouble is if we don't get into the 221 and 235 and 236 business fast. The other mortgage companies are already out on the street with short-term money, tying everybody up. What I think we oughta do is find our own boys. We should finance some of the new guys who are getting into it. It'll cost a lot less than trying to pry the big operators away from their present contacts."

"I think you're right," Max Stein said. "I've also been looking into some of the short-term possibilities, Sammy, that I'll want to talk to you about." He caught the eye of the old man who acknowledged him and grunted. Sammy took a thick Corona from the silver humidor on the desk and studied its possibilities.

"You give me a list of speculators, Jayson. Now I want to think about this a while. I think we're done, unless somebody has something else to add."

"One thing," Jayson said. "Will American Eagle make mortgages on my properties?"

"You want to be on both ends?" Sammy inquired.

"There's a lot of profit in this business," Jayson said. "It wouldn't look good for me to go down the street to International, would it?"

"This whole thing is new to me," Sammy said. "Let me think about it for twenty-four hours. Is that soon enough?"

Jayson nodded that it was, and the four men stood to leave the president's office. Sammy asked Max Stein to stay for a moment as the others left. Max closed the door behind them and sat on the edge of Sammy's desk, removing for himself one of the Coronas.

"We can do for ourselves some good," Max said, "with this short-term money."

Sammy had done well for himself by listening to other men, and he waited impassively while Max lit the cigar and blew out a long stream of smoke.

"Short-term money is going on the street right now for about 2 percent, sometimes up to 2½ percent, depending on how hungry the buyer is," Max said. "Once there is an FHA appraisal on the property, it is a certain loan, because you can always call the guy's collateral and sell it yourself if you have to. But I don't even think that'll come up because the profit's so big."

"How big?" Sammy asked.

"They tell me the speculators are buying for $3,000 to $6,000 tops, and FHA is appraising the property at $12,000 to $15,000. The spread is at least 100 percent, sometimes more. They are turning over the property in sixty to ninety days."

"Where in the hell did the Negroes get so much money all of a sudden?" Sammy wondered.

"No money," Max said. "It's $200 down. They're selling to welfare mothers, even, Sam. Thirty-year mortgages."

"But they'll never have any equity," Sammy observed.

Max shrugged. "That's going to be Romney's problem.

But here's what I wanted to point out to you. That short-term money can come from anyplace, as long as it brings the investors back to American Eagle with the mortgage. Right? So it seems to me that we can pick up some of that 2 percent a month on our own."

"That wouldn't look good," Sammy said.

"Who looks? If we set up a subsidiary we put in our own money and just keep track. As far as the investor knows, it's all American Eagle. The protection is, we have demand payout, for you, for me. My brother wants to get into it, too. He's got $100,000. I've got that much. You do, too. We could do right by a lot of investors, do good by ourselves, and bring a lot of money into American."

"What about Jayson's side business?" Sammy asked.

"He's the best street man in the city," Max said. "You taught him good, Sammy. He's not that dumb hillbilly anymore. If we don't let him, he'll go someplace else, and we can't afford to let him go. Besides, his business will be just like anybody else's, except he'll try to beat us a little bit harder on points. Which is another thing I wanted to tell you."

"What's that?"

"They aren't regulated in any way except on the selling end due to FNMA [Federal National Mortgage Association]. With money as tight as it is, FNMA is buying at ninety-three but think about this, Max. International has been selling mortgages to speculators at ninety-one. That's two points up front in addition to the short-term money and the closing costs and everything else. Then there's the servicing for a half a percent which is what we're about, anyway."

"The mortgage investors aren't going to like all of that garbage," Sammy said. "There's going to be more bad paper coming out of this than anybody ever saw before."

"FNMA gets the garbage," Max said. "The investors get the good stuff. FNMA is supposed to help the public. Anyway, with that many points, they'll cash in even with the foreclosures."

"Everybody can't make money," Sammy said.

"So the government's gonna take a bath," Max told him. "Can't they afford it?"

"The FHA isn't like it used to be," Sammy murmured. "I guess I'm getting to be an old man."

As far as Jayson was concerned, the old man had given him the green light to line up the speculators and FHA. The first thing he did was set about renewing two old acquaintances: Uncle Max Haberol and Harry Breen, the Alsatian-born Canadian national who did a lot of unlicensed real estate business in Romney City. Breen was an enigmatic personality whom nobody knew well but frequently found themselves doing business with through one or another of Breen's many front companies. The last Jayson had heard, Breen and his sister, Mrs. Maximillian Koslow, were operating out of a store front on Twelfth Street near where they were milking half a dozen tenement apartment buildings.

He called Uncle Max and made an appointment with him for the following day, but the only way to get Breen was to find him in person. The Alsatian never talked on the phone.

Jayson parked his Continental in a no-parking zone in front of Breen's Charity Real Estate where he could keep an eye on it because of his usual qualms about being in such a black and dangerous neighborhood. He rang the buzzer at the door for admittance without trying it to see if it was open. It wasn't. A scowling black man with a scar on his cheek let him in and examined him with haughty suspicion. No, Breen didn't work here, never heard of him, what can I do for you, what do you want?

"No, I'm not the man," Jayson said. "I'm from American Eagle Mortgage. I want to talk with him about some business."

He handed the man, who couldn't read, his business card. Leaving him standing there in the cluttered, filthy office, the man disappeared behind a soiled tapestry curtain in the back of the store front, returned briefly to ask for his name again and ambled away. He reappeared with an address written in a shaky hand on the back of Jayson's business card.

"He at this place," the man said. "You want to see him, you go there."

Without further ceremony, he opened the door for Jayson to leave. The jittery solicitor gunned the Lincoln out of the neighborhood to Wimple Street on Romney City's northwest side where a Polish enclave existed amid blocks of frame two-flats. Breen's address was indistinguishable from all the rest of the houses with their low wooden stair-

ways and short porches, except that all of the windows
were protected with ornamental iron bars. A haggard,
middle-aged woman peeked through the curtain inside of
the front door and opened the door a crack with the chain
attached to ask him what he wanted.

"I'm Jayson Penny," he said. "I'm looking for Harry
Breen."

The woman let him in, locking and chaining the door
behind him. "He's in the study," she said with a heavy
European accent, and pointed down the dark hallway pa-
pered with an aging Victorian design in faded green and
yellow. The setup gave Jayson the creeps.

Breen's study, however, was brightly lighted with fluo-
rescent lights and was clean and empty except for several
large file cabinets, a long gray metal desk and, of course,
Breen. The light bounced off the top of Breen's completely
bald head as the short, stocky man with a strong forehead,
sea blue eyes and full, pink lips leaned back in his swivel
chair to welcome him.

"My good friend," Breen said, extending a powerful arm
decorated with a gold link identification bracelet. "What
brings you to my poor neighborhood?"

"Harry, Harry, what kind of a setup do you have?" Jayson asked, taking his hand. "This is a long way from the
suite at the Hilton."

"My sister and I are simple people," Breen said with his
faint, melodious accent. "We don't have the advantages
of you banking people downtown."

Jayson laughed. "Do you have any place where a wealthy
banker could sit down?"

"Certainly," Harry said. He motioned to his sister who
stood at the doorway and told her to bring them some
coffee. "Take my chair," he offered, getting up and taking
a white-painted kitchen chair from the woman. "It's the
only luxury we have to offer."

He seated himself on the chair backwards. "Liquor?
Brandy?"

"I'm off the sauce," Jayson said. "I'm getting ulcers,
Harry."

"It's a difficult business," Harry said. "You have my
sympathies."

"Well, it's looking up," Jayson said. "How's it going for
you, Harry?"

"We get along," Harry said. "It's a struggle nowadays,

with the people tearing out the toilets and selling them. I
suppose it's the same for everybody else."

"Yeah," Jayson said. "Harry, I want to talk to you about
some business. Do you want to have your sister in here, or
are you enough?"

"It makes no difference," Harry said. "What do you have
in mind?"

"FHA," Jayson said. "American Eagle is going to get into
the low-income programs in a big way. We've been looking
at it while everybody else got a head start. Now we're looking for customers."

"I have no single-families," Harry said. "I'm entirely
into multi-family."

"But we can make it easy for you to get in," Jayson said.
"I can give you a line of credit up to $100,000 right now.
The only condition is, we get the mortgages."

"What is this, the 221s?" Harry inquired.

"And probably some Section 235," Jayson said. "Maybe
even some 203s if you want to go through all of that, although I personally wouldn't bother. What we want is
volume."

"How much will I have to pay for the money?" Harry
wondered. "What kind of collateral?"

"That hasn't been completely decided," Jayson said. "I
think about 2 percent a month. What I think we'll do is
extend you a line of credit against the titles and FHA appraisals. Probably not the whole thing, but 50 percent or
two-thirds. It'll more than cover what you have into the
properties and give you working capital, too."

Harry removed a yellow legal pad from one of the file
cabinets to make notes on. He wanted to know how long it
took to get mortgages through the FHA.

"I think I can get them through in a week," Jayson said.
"I've got good connections."

"And the repair inspections?" Harry asked.

"I handle them for American," Jayson said. "Of course,
it's easier for friends."

"Of course," Harry agreed. "What do I do about the
appraisals?"

"That's up to you," Jayson said. "We just handle our end.
You've got to take care of the buying and selling. But we'll
deliver the mortgages."

"I'll investigate it," Harry said. "I'll tell you next week
what I want to do."

5

We Buy Houses for Cash

"There was a solicitor from American Eagle came to see me about this FHA business," Uncle Max told Giovanni the next time the young operator came to see him. "You are right, perhaps, about the potential here. I told him about you, and I want you to go and see him."

"The house is ready to sell," Don said. "Do you have any buyers for me, Max?"

"How can it be ready?" Max asked. "It's condemned."

"Nobody expects it to be a new house," Don said. "I painted it inside and out. I sanded the floors and put tile on the bathroom floor. I put new boards on the back steps."

"The wiring and the plumbing is bad," Max recalled. "Does the furnace work?"

"It's too warm to turn on the furnace," Don said. "If it doesn't work, I can fix it later. I put in a new water heater, though. I put up some new gutters, too. I put more than $1,000 in materials into it. What do you want?"

"I am just curious about how you can do a cosmetic job on a condemned house and sell it for the government," Max said. "What kind of a price do you want?"

"It's appraised for $13,000," Don said.

Max was surprised. "How did you arrange that?"

"The appraiser and I got to be friends," Don said.

"How much does that cost?"

"I gave him a tip," Don said. "Three hundred dollars."

"So you are learning the business," Max said fondly. "What kind of a buyer do you want me to find for you?"

"He should be alive," Don said. "Where is this mortgage company?"

Don went off for his introductory meeting with Jayson Penny. Max remained in his offices where he methodically reviewed his inventory of properties: 112 houses, a dozen of them condemned and three dozen others that he knew should be condemned if the city ever got around to it. He had acquired them singly and in groups from the estates of other slum operators over the past twenty-five years—keeping some to rent out or sell on contract and disposing of others. But the list had always grown. Some he had purchased for as little as $1,500, and a few had cost as much as $8,000, but most of them he valued at $4,000 to $5,000, about four times their average rental income of $1,200 a year, or $100 a month. Whenever Max went over his holdings like this he was amazed to rediscover that he was a man of substantial means. But now, for the first time, he was considering how he could become a millionaire.

About four that afternoon a heavy black woman with three small children in tow entered the Blessings Real Estate office. She had the anxious look Max knew so well, the look of a poor woman with a houseful of kids and no place to live.

"Is you Mr. Blessings?" she inquired.

"Mr. Blessings isn't here," Max said, "but I work for Mr. Blessings. Can I help you?"

"I'm looking for someplace to rent," she said. "I've got four kids, and I need someplace big enough."

"How much do you want to pay?"

In his best grandfatherly way, Max motioned for her to take the seat beside his desk and handed the children pieces of hard candy to keep them quiet.

"I don't have too much money," the woman said. "I'm ADC."

Max began writing down her financial statement. The state gave Dorothy Ann Green $326 a month, including a housing allowance of $100.

"Other income?" Max asked.

"I does some housework and get another forty dollars a week," Mrs. Green said.

"Savings?"

She shook her head, "No."

"Age?"

"Thirty-five."

"Married?"

Again she shook her head.

"Listen," Max said, "would you like to own your own house?"

For the first time, she smiled. "Yaas, I would. But I don't have any money."

"There's a new thing called the FHA," Max said. "Have you ever heard of that? It's the government. The government has said that good people like you are going to get their own houses. Does that sound like a good idea to you?"

"Yes, it does," she said. "But what kind of houses?"

"Good houses," Max said. "They're all United States government guaranteed. It won't cost you any more than rent."

"This is some thing," Mrs. Green marveled. "You got one of them houses I can look at?"

"Right now I got just one," Uncle Max said. "You want to come look at it now?"

"What'll I do with the kids?" she wondered.

"We just take them along."

Max piled the woman and kids into the old Chevrolet he used for this kind of business, leaving the black Cadillac behind the office, and drove her to Don's property. With a professional eye and a feeling of aesthetic distaste, he noted that Don had coated the outside of the property with a bright yellow, cheaply glistening enamel, without having scraped away the original flaking paint or replacing rotting boards. He found only two sections of new gutters and assumed that Don had patched the others with wire mesh and tar. But Mrs. Green was very impressed.

"Oh, my, what a pretty color," she said.

"Yellow is very cheerful," Max said as they walked to the front door. "As you can see, it's all been freshly repainted the way the government wants."

Inside, he found that Don had continued the same pattern of bright, cheap paints. The living room and dining room were painted bright blue, in latex, thank heavens, not lead-based paint (although he suspected that undercoats of lead-based paint still remained, to eventually flake and poison children). The kitchen was green, and Don had installed a cheap, secondhand stove and refrigerator. The bathroom was canary yellow, with new, badly fitted black-and-white tile squares on the floor. When Max stood by the toilet bowl to flush it to show how well it worked, he felt the floor give under his weight and realized that Don hadn't repaired any of the rotted floorboards. He had sanded the floors and put a single coat of thin varnish over them that would hold up under the running feet of four children for perhaps, six months. The blue, green and yellow paints were repeated on the second floor in the three bedrooms. None of the window frames or sashes had been repaired, but at least the dry rot was hidden under the paint. On the ceilings he saw that Don had replastered where the leaking roof let in rainwater and melting snow, but unless the roof had been patched, the repair would last only until the next storm.

The basement was still wet from the cracked foundation, but Max told Mrs. Green that the water came from pipes when the new (actually used) water heater had been installed. The huge old coal furnace with its gas conversion unit appeared to be so foreboding that Mrs. Green didn't even ask if it worked. She seemed to be pleased that there was any furnace at all.

"My, my," she said. "I can actually buy this house?"

"Yes, you can," Max reassured her. "Let's go fill out the papers. Do you have $200 down?"

For the first time, Mrs. Green disengaged. "I don't have $200," she wailed.

"You must be able to get $200," Max said. "Can you borrow it from your family? From friends?"

She shook her head stubbornly. "I got no family here. All my people are in Philadelphia. You tole me I didn't have to have any money."

"Two hundred dollars isn't very much," Max observed, as much to himself as to the potential buyer. In fact, he thought, his profit from the deal, if he could sell it to her, was $2,946—2 percent a month for two months on the original $3,500 price he had sold it to Giovanni for; the $2,000 Giovanni so recklessly promised him in return for selling him the house without any money passing hands at the time; and $780 as his 6 percent sales commission on $13,000.

"I'll tell you what I'll do," Max said. "I'll lend you the $200 because I appreciate the position that you're in."

"You'll lend me the money?" she demanded. "Now, why would you do that?"

"Because I'll get it back from the government," Max said, thinking that it wasn't far from the truth. "You can pay me back whenever you want."

At the time, Max didn't know that giving the woman the $200 down was illegal and by the time he did know, it didn't make any difference because he didn't care.

"Oh my, children, this is going to be our house," Mrs. Green cried out. "This is our lucky day."

But even after Max had Mrs. Green's signature on the purchase order and her FHA application filled out he didn't feel the normal jolt that came from making money by his wits. If he were more sensitive to his own feelings, he would have recognized that the disquietude and flashes of temper that made it hard for him to work were jealousy. If his profit was $3,000 for extending a loan and making the sale, the kid had made about $5,500 in a couple of weeks by simply persuading Max to give away the property and then letting him sell it. Max was working himself into a rage when Don rang the buzzer at the door and sauntered in.

"Big shot, you've been drinking," Max charged, "while an old man like me is working all day and night doing your dirty work."

"Huh?" Don said.

"What thanks do I get from you," Max said. "A lousy 6 percent. It's a crime. That house. I never saw such bad workmanship. Rotting floors. Bad wiring. A broken furnace. That poor woman's going to have to live in that place with her four little children."

"What are you saying, Max?" Don wondered. "Did you find a buyer for it already?"

Max held up a sheaf of papers. "Offer. FHA application. Credit report. Everything. I even advanced the lady $200 out of my own pocket for you. Why? What do I get out of it?"

"You didn't give a buyer $200 cash, did you?" Don asked, shocked by the idea. "How do you know she'll ever come back?"

Max glowered and threw the papers on the desk. "You

are going to give me the down payment money," he threatened. "I want my money for that house, now."

"We agreed two months," Don said. He did not seem to be at all flustered by Max's unexpected change of mood. If Max was cooler, he would have noticed that Don wore a new English tweed sports coat, and would have started to figure out what had happened at that mortgage company.

"I know how to deal with fucking punks like you," Max said. "How do you drink when you can't even pay me the money you owe?"

"Go away from me, Max," Don said. "All I ever did to you was make a legitimate deal, to get you out of a bind. I don't need your threats."

"I've killed men like you," Max said harshly. "When do I see my money?"

"You are really some goddam operator," Don told him. "No wonder you never made it, but laid back here with your damn rents and runners and milking operators. What do you want, Max? You'd better tell me, so I can get the hell out of here."

"Pay me for my house," Max demanded. "And the action money, too."

"But that's not fair," Don said. "I only had the credit for two weeks. The deal was eight weeks. So I would owe you only $500 if I paid you off now."

"Five hundred dollars, $10,000, what difference does it make?" Max asked him.

Don dropped into a swivel chair and propped his feet on Max's desk. "Are we playing housewife, or doing business?" he asked. "Let me put it this way, Max. If I paid you for the house now, would you settle for $500 for the loan?"

"I pray at night I get at least $500," Max said.

"So that's $4,000," Don said. "Is that right?"

"That's right," Max said flatly.

Don took out his checkbook and wrote out two checks, one for $500 and the other for $3,500, which he signed and handed to the surprised old man.

"Where'd you get the money?" Max wondered.

"My business," Don said. "The checks are good. You can deposit them tomorrow. About the sale—you can complete it and get your 6 percent or you can fold it in, I don't care. I just want fast results."

"Where did you get the money?" Max cried.

"When you figure that out, you'll know what the real estate business is all about," Don said.

He walked out of the office, leaving Max cursing to himself. When he calmed down, Max took a bottle of ouzo from a desk drawer and poured himself a drink in the bottom of a dirty coffee cup. There was only one possible place for Don to have gotten the money—American Eagle. But on what basis? Why? All the kid had was one junk house that the city wanted torn down.

Because there is a great deal of honor among thieves who do business together, Max went ahead and closed the sale, going to Jayson for the help he needed to make the mortgage. It took less than two weeks for Jayson to get the FHA loan approval through the local HUD office because, as he explained it, he "walked it through." That meant he took the paper work to the HUD officials with whom he had made arrangements for fast service. Since American Eagle had an obligation to make sure the repairs that had been ordered were done, Jayson stopped by the house to check off the appropriate specifications. He discovered that the first floor timbers had been eaten through by termites, but because the FHA hadn't noted it, it wasn't his concern. In fact, he felt proud of Don for being able to sell such a piece of trash for $13,000. He also appreciated the fact that the kid didn't have to be reminded to give him a gratuity for his quick service in making the inspection. The customary tip for that was only twenty-five or fifty dollars. On a good day, however, he could inspect eight or ten houses for the mortgage company. That extra $200 or $250 a day added up.

When he handed Jayson the tip money after the inspection, Don told him that he would be coming by the mortgage company the following week to arrange a second loan. Jayson could see that Don was going to be one hell of a customer for American Eagle's short-term money as well as be a good mortgage market.

Although Don still hadn't gotten his money out of the deal—he couldn't until the sale was closed—he had already gone out on the street and found a seller of his own for a house at $4,000. With $100, he had closed an option to purchase from an elderly woman with cataracts who wanted out of her house on the edge of the ghetto with a ferocity that bordered on fanaticism. He had also called the FHA and talked to the appraiser who had come by the first time in place of Fred Angelo, the heavy man he came to call Windshield Willie, William Nefretti, who was a ten-year man with the feds. That cost another $300, but he got an appraisal for $13,500.

Don's finances, which had been virtually nonexistent when he entered the FHA business, showed signs of healthy improvement. Uncle Max had given him the first house for no cash up front. Don sunk $1,000 in repairs to the house, which he put on the cuff with suppliers and hardware stores. American Eagle had given him a loan of two-thirds the FHA appraised price, knowing that the appraisal was like a guaranteed price tag. When he walked into Uncle Max's office, he had just deposited about $8,600 into his checking account. Four thousand dollars went to Max, and $500 went to the suppliers to keep his credit with them good, and $400 had already gone toward buying a second property. Don knew that he would have to swallow the first buyer's $200 down payment and that he would have to pay points for the mortgage, although he still wasn't clear what points were and how much they would run.

But he expected to clear a minimum of $6,000 from the sale of the house, which was damn good money for less than a month's work. He could make that much from the second house, too. But he realized that one-shot profits could make him a good living, not a fortune. If he wanted to grow, he had to hire help.

Back at American Eagle things were also looking up. Breen had come in and walked away with an initial $50,000 line of credit, and Uncle Max, who didn't need any working capital, stopped by almost every day to reassure himself the low-income FHA programs worked the way he hoped they did. If he FHA'd all of his properties, it would represent about $1 million in mortgages and a hell of a lot of quick profit and servicing fees. Jayson had also made contacts with nearly two dozen other real estate firms and speculators, to let them know that American Eagle was ready to do business with the FHA.

Sammy Goldstein and Max Stein had created a second, subsidiary corporation called Commonwealth Properties,

Incorporated, which was funded entirely with money from themselves and their families. Speculators who came to American Eagle for short-term loans were getting the money through Commonwealth from the persons who ran the firm. Naturally, they didn't know that, and they wouldn't have cared very much if they did. The American Eagle bookkeeper was puzzled by the notations he had to make for these loans. The one to Breen was shown as

	SS	MS	GS	TR
Breen:	$50,000	$25,000	$5,000	$15,000	$5,000

The initials SS and MS stood for Sammy and Max Stein. The initials of Max's wife, Gloria, were GS. Terry Sheridan Rojecki, TR, was his son-in-law, a lousy Pole who got his daughter knocked up at college.

What tickled Sammy wasn't only the tremendous growth opportunities he saw in the new FHA business, but the way his boy had gotten into it. For Harvard Law School, Myron Goldstein wasn't a bad kid, and Sammy didn't even resent how the boy slept around with *shiksas*, although, God knows, his wife did. Sports cars he appreciated, too. What had gotten under his skin about Myron was how that great big *schmuck* didn't appreciate that to spend money you had to make it first. Well, now he saw that Myron just hadn't understood how money was made. The FHA business had opened his eyes.

Take what Myron had just come back with from upstate. On a goodwill mission to explore American Eagle's relations with its correspondent banks and mortgage buyers, Myron discovered that every banker, down to the last white WASP hair on his head, wanted to get his conventional mortgages out of the core city. The bankers saw their urban mortgage investments as liabilities, which far too many of them were and guaranteed to only get worse. In addition, they hated to have their money tied up in old, low-paying mortgages when present interest rates were so much higher. The suburban markets represented much safer loans and higher yields, and the bankers wanted to unload their city portfolios.

Myron, bless that Harvard Law School in his soul, immediately saw what an opportunity this presented for American Eagle. He came back and sat in the president's office like a businessman his father could be proud of and explained what he had found out.

"The correspondent banks are unhappy with their conventional paper," he said. "Not all of it, but an awful lot of the mortgages they've bought from us in the inner city area have been starting to go bad. Hell, we know that better than they do—that's why I went out to mend fences with them. But what they're worried about is the same thing that concerns us: Those houses aren't worth the money that's been loaned on them. The neighborhoods are going bad. The investors are overextended. The old buyers want to get out, bad. The new ones are all black and Puerto Rican —their mortgages aren't worth anything. Everybody's afraid that the foreclosures are going to keep compounding, and they'll have to take a bath. They're right, too."

"I know," Sammy said impatiently. "I know it, I know it."

"Then there's the other part to this," Myron continued. "Suburban housing is starting to pick up again. The federal money will heat it up more. There are good new mortgages to be made, at present rates, which are a hell of a lot higher than the return coming from the old paper. So I've worked up an answer to everybody's problem, ours included, which will give us more business than we can handle. You ready for this?"

Sammy watched his eldest son presenting his plan to him with mixed fondness and greed. He nodded his head and snapped open a silver-plated ball-point pen to take notes in his careful hand.

"What I suggest we do is convert the risky and defaulted mortgages over to FHA," Myron said. "If we make arrangements to resell the houses and pay off the conventional mortgages, we can then get new buyers for them at much higher prices and higher rates, and sell them to the poor under the new FHA programs at the price that we want to get. That will immediately do several things. First of all, it will make our correspondent banks much happier with us, and we've got to keep them happy to stay in business. They provide our raw material, which is money, as you taught me when I first came into this business.

"Besides an immediate improvement in our track record, it will generate a lot of new business—the FHA mortgages. Every house sold out of the conventional way will give us a new deal. Points, I noticed this morning, are going at eight or nine. That represents one hell of a spread between what we buy a mortgage for and what we can get for it from anybody, including FNMA. With fees and other costs, we should make out like bandits.

"Then for a third thing, every one of those Poles and Italians and Jews who get converted have to move someplace, and the suburbs are where they want to go. All we have to do is supply the mortgages out there with the fields and trees, and we've got a second deal all tied up waiting for us to put a bow on it. Nice, huh?"

Myron was obviously pleased with himself, but his father scowled.

"How do we work all those deals?" he asked. "Our staff is very short. We know nothing about buying. I don't even want to get involved in the real estate business with those crooks. And besides, where do we get the money to make all of these loans? We have a hard enough time now getting enough money to make our regular mortgage business."

"That's the beauty of it," Myron said. "The correspondent bankers told me that they would finance the whole thing. See, their first interest is to get out from under. They're willing to do that without even making any money—although that would be nice. They just don't want to swallow all of those losses. They will extend the money to us on lines of credit against the new mortgages at a prime rate. They will also buy the suburban mortgages if we want to sell them that way, because they are safe.

"In fact," Myron said a bit arrogantly, "it's the same kind of a business we have always been in, except that this time we are doing a very particular favor for our correspondents —we are saving their portfolios. We don't have to do any of the actual buying and selling ourselves, either. The speculators are only too willing to do it for us because they'll get rich in the process, too. There isn't one thing wrong with the idea."

Sammy thought about it. "There's got to be a flaw someplace," he decided. "Things don't work out that perfectly, except on paper. Where will we get stung?"

"No place," Myron assured him. "The only thing that I can see is we have to keep quiet about what's going on because those neighborhood groups are going to start to yell if they think their areas are being converted. But they won't suspect what's going on because they don't know anything about business."

"There are laws about blockbusting," Sammy said. "What if the state's attorney doesn't like it?"

"Blockbusting!" Myron exclaimed. "How is this block-busting? I know how all those people talk, but they're a bunch of damned prejudiced factory workers. You know that. The federal law is that you can't discriminate, right? So we don't discriminate. What they call blockbusting is only black people having an equal right to buy a house. The federal government wants that to happen. So it's not that we are breaking the law. We are going along with the law. We cannot *not* lend to black people. That's our defense, if anybody ever asks about it. We've got to obey the civil rights laws.

"So I'm willing, dad. And the people who get moved around a little bit, they want to move, anyway. Even if they don't, they'll be happier out in the suburbs without all the crime and drugs to worry about."

"How do you get the speculators going on it?" Sammy wondered.

"We get the addresses and the lines of credit from the correspondent banks," Myron answered. "Then we talk to a few people whom we trust and we give them the address-es and make the short-term loans. They know how to get into a neighborhood and turn it over, fast. We just have to make sure we are dealing with people who can be trusted, people who understand how important all of this is when there is money tied up in it."

"We know who those people are," Sammy said. "But do we have enough of them?"

"There are some new ones that can be checked out," Myron said. "I've been impressed with this kid named Don Giovanni. He's a protégé of old Uncle Max, but a lot sharper in my opinion. No education, but he really seems to know a lot about the business. In fact, I gave him a $15,000 line of credit the other day. Maybe I should have told you about it."

"You gave him the line against what?" Sammy de-manded.

"One broken-down piece of property he got for $3,000 and has sold for $13,000," Myron said. "The way he oper-ates, he'll be our biggest customer. Mark my words."

"But an Italian," Sammy fumed. "Why take the chance?"

"Don't get all tied up in that," Myron said. "Even that business seems to be changing. I heard that the First

Romney City Bank has more than $2 million into Jack Black's New Suburban Homes development out by Seventeen Mile Road in Nixon Township."

"Never heard of him," Sammy said.

"Just a kid," Myron told him. "His father is Black Jack Mirro."

"That's Mafia," Sammy said. "You mean to tell me that First Romney City is doing business with the Mob?"

"There are your prejudices again, dad," Myron said disapprovingly. "The grandfather and the father may be involved in some things they shouldn't. But they're substantial people, really rich, and they've had to branch out into legitimate business. Besides, the kid has no record. He even went to Yale. You can't deny him the right to make a living because of his ancestors, can you?"

"It's not your average pushcart kind of operation," Sammy said. "How does a kid—how old is he?—get $2 million for a development?"

"His credit is good," Myron said. "The land alone is appraised at more than $1 million. There are buyers for that new tract housing everyplace. It's all FHA, remember? That's the world we're dealing in—it's all government now. Everybody gets a piece of the pie."

"The government is now a businessman," Sammy exclaimed. "What is this, Republican business?"

"You going to vote for Nixon the next time around now?" the son said, laughing. "Done with the Democrats?"

"They're all crooked," the old man said. "Contribute equally to both parties and take the gravy." He reached out a hand and patted his son on the shoulder. "Good work, son. I want to call in the others now, to see what they think about this."

Sammy punched the red button on the intercom and told the secretary to call in Jayson Penny and Max Stein. As usual, they arrayed themselves in a row on the sofa, while the president explained his new plans to them. Both agreed that the conversion business promised to be a good one. Jayson, in fact, because of his close dealings with speculators, began to expand on the idea of how they could turn over whole neighborhoods from conventional mortgages to FHA, but Sammy stopped him.

"I don't want to hear about the details," he said. "There are some things I shouldn't know too much about. You have a free hand, Jayson, just keep us out of court."

Max had a new concern he wanted Sammy to consider
—236 multi-family apartment investments.

"These are just unbelievable," he said, lighting another
of Sammy's big cigars. "The way this is, Sammy, is we
have to put up only 10 percent equity in the limited divi-
dends partnership program to get 100 percent write-off,
instead of 25 percent like in a normal building to write it
down. It comes out at nine-to-one depreciation for investment, instead of three-to-one conventional. On rehabs, you
get to knock down the whole thing in five years.

"Better than that, the 10 percent doesn't have to be in
our cash—it just has to represent 10 percent of the total
cost.

"Take a $1 million project. We buy the land for $10,000,
and the government appraiser says that it's worth $100,000.
That's our 10 percent investment. We get 6 percent back on
it, plus the entire $1 million depreciation. If we have the
money in a rehab project, we can write the total off in five
years."

"Why does the government appraise the land for
$100,000?" Sammy wondered reasonably.

"The government estimators don't know what they are
doing," Max said. "We are getting enough experience with
the FHA to know that it does not know, in any part, what is
going on. The appraisers, they are usually *friendly* people,
anyway. Then, the land is worth only $10,000 to us, but if a
$1 million project is being built on it, it is worth $100,000
—right? The government doesn't care what you pay. Only
what it would be worth with $1 million worth of apart-
ments on it. So it's nice to see your investments grow. But
the depreciation is the thing."

"Say that my income for the year is $200,000," Sammy
said, writing down the figure. "What does the depreciation
mean to me?"

"On rehabs, about $100,000 a year," Max said. "Your
depreciation is $200,000 a year, so you pay no income
taxes for five years. You are half a million ahead, cash
money. On a new 236, your $20,000 cash will clear you
about $12,500, or $375,000 over thirty years, should you
live so long, Max. But you can make out by selling after
ten years. Plus, you get your 6 percent."

"It is better than oil depreciation," Sammy observed.
"Don't talk about my death. Why does the government do
this?"

"They want housing starts," Myron interjected. "They are willing to pay for them."

"Planting money itself is a cheaper way for the government to go," Max sneered. "There's a better reason. My cousin Angelo, Winnie's boy, a Ph.D. from the University of Chicago, was part of the Johnson brain trust in the White House after Kennedy was shot. He told me the depreciation business was written by the home builders and our own national mortgage association. The Johnson boys bought it, to hold budget cuts. Interest and tax credits seemed cheaper. The House Banking and Currency Committee, which writes the legislation in Congress, is filled with people who have ties to the industry. Nobody protested when the idea came up because the Great Society people wanted housing more than anything. They wanted a big program, fast, and they weren't about to quarrel with how it came about."

"I used to worry about the government getting involved with housing," Sammy said, "but it seems they are more interested in helping us out than I thought."

"It's like the industrial-military complex," Max observed. "Except it is the housing-banking complex. The lobbyists have done a good job for us."

"We are important to America," Sammy said. "The government can't put roofs over the heads of the population without us. We deserve something for taking the risk."

"That's why free enterprise is so important," Max said sentimentally.

Myron laughed. He thought Max had a hell of a sense of humor.

6

The Sacred Trust

While the speculators and mortgage companies got their acts together, another kind of reality was being enacted in the private offices and large open working spaces of the HUD area offices in Romney City. There, career bureaucrats and high level appointed officials waged a war for control of the HUD-FHA operations, advancement and easy money. The office operated on a crisis-a-day program.

There were two main reasons why daily operations were so confused. One of them had to do with a new decision by President Nixon to merge the traditional FHA operations with those of the Department of Housing and Urban Development, under the direction of new HUD Secretary George Romney. Two philosophies stood behind this move. The first was to save money by consolidating operations and making the sprawling HUD bureaucracy more comprehensible, at least on the flow charts. The second reason had to do with the mandate of the 1968 National Housing Act passed by Congress which was supposed to vastly increase housing production and home ownership for the poor.

In addition to the simple trauma of forcing two different operations together into the same office, the FHA bureaucrats and HUD workers came with differing philosophies— conservative and socially liberal. The FHA employees, with few exceptions, thought like traditional bankers. Their job had always been to protect the money loaned by the lending institutions and to deliver houses to buyers only if they were good enough to make payments and take care of the property. But the HUD employees were more geared to the ideals of the Great Society; they were generally younger, blacker, and less concerned with the bank balances of the buying public. For the most part, HUD workers were not expected to take on the specific and complicated jobs of the old-time FHA clerks and functionaries, or the other way around, but the people eyed each other suspiciously, each jealous of the prerogatives of place and hierarchy. The duties of higher level supervisory personnel were so expanded, or changed, however, that a man familiar with FHA operations often had little touch with his area of expertise.

On the highest level, where Rodney Morton, the area director, had just taken charge, confusion was the worst. Morton knew about working for the Republican party, and about law, and about how nice it was to get a top level government job as a reward for his loyalty, but he knew nothing about housing, nothing about cities, nothing about mortgages, nothing about appraisals, nothing about repairs, and nothing about the jungle in Romney City called the real estate industry. But Morton knew that he wanted to do well in his job and keep the good favor of Mr. Romney.

Nobody knew everything there was to know about FHA because the laws and regulations and department judgments and policies since 1934 filled a row of books jokingly called "the seven-foot shelf." The books contained classes, subclasses, and qualifications, new laws, old laws, outdated policies and new ones, and simultaneously allowed and denied almost anything an FHA employee decided to do. The ones who lasted knew the regulation that covered their action and ignored those that forbade it. The art of buck-passing was a style of life.

Every one of the 150 people who worked in the HUD office, excepting the secretaries of the big shots, knew the word was mortgage production and that former standards no longer applied. Other than that, they were mostly in the dark about what the President and the Congress wanted them to do.

A typical example was William Nefretti, the 45-year-old FHA appraiser who was to become known to the speculators as Windshield Willie. Nefretti had been an FHA appraiser for ten years, without straining very hard and without ever learning very much about houses. It wasn't Willie's fault, however: Nobody in the government ever taught him what he should look for in a house. He just followed the rules and tried to make things difficult for people.

Not that that was necessarily bad. The rules were fairly clear-cut. He wouldn't put an FHA value on a house in a bad neighborhood. He would always specify that the roof had to appear to be sound, and he demanded that sellers paint walls that were dirty and discolored. The electricity was supposed to be up to city code, and the furnace had to work properly. When Willie had gone down his list the traditional way, the house was supposed to be economically viable, and it usually was.

The new regulations, however, called not for economic viability but "acceptable risk." Willie didn't know what that meant, although he supposed at first that the houses he appraised were supposed to match the old standards, the difference being their location. His supervisor soon let him know that applying the old standards slowed down production and made the real estate speculators angry. So he got the word and started to figure that if a place looked OK, if it was standing there at all, it met the new standards.

That was OK with Willie. He suffered acute discomfort while appraising houses in black and changing neighborhoods because he was convinced that his car would be stolen, or he would be assaulted and robbed any minute. The harrassment of one of his co-workers by a gang of youths convinced him that his suspicions were based on fact, and they may well have been. It quickly became Willie's technique to appraise houses on the basis of a drive past them, sometimes including a quick, furtive dash inside and out. The value he set on a property was based on comparative values—how much a house like the one he was working with had recently been sold for. Willie knew that the comparative values were so much hot air because as often as not the government list he was handed was based not on actual *sales* prices but on real estate *asking* prices on the photo index listing cards, or on offers and not final sales. Any real estate operator could arrange to make a high offer for one of his houses, knowing it would be listed in the government figures. That established the value of his other houses.

In addition, Willie usually didn't know if houses were comparable or not, because in the older neighborhoods few of the houses were exactly like one another. A house could be compared to another on the basis of construction, number of bedrooms, type of heat and that sort of thing, but to really know that, an appraiser would have to count rooms, and measure the size of them, and thoroughly examine a place. As the number of houses Willie was called upon to inspect increased from two a day to six, he certainly didn't have time for that kind of fussiness.

The main reason why he grew more and more lax about his job was due to another factor. Money. Like any government employee who deals with housing and building codes, he was constantly tempted to bend a rule or make an exception for an owner in return for a payoff. He had long since stopped refusing money in return for his favors, because he needed the cash, and it was everyplace. What was astonishing about the new FHA business was how much the speculators would pay for a favor. The going price was $300 to give a favorable appraisal, or to ignore blatant violations, or to just be a regular fellow. He knew that if he enforced the rules he would be in trouble with his supervisor, who was thick with the real estate guys; and if he didn't, he made money hand over fist. A reasonable man took the path of least resistance.

Willie's supervisor was Glenn Cavern, a thin, bad-tempered man the same age as Willie, who had less interest in cash and a passion for girls. He usually didn't expect to be paid for his favors. Only laid. The speculators were glad to oblige.

It soon developed that no department in the FHA offices was free of graft, of several kinds. In the appraisal office, men like Willie got paid for inflating values and ignoring defects. They appraised the houses the speculators paid them to appraise. Fee appraisers, whom the government hired to assist the regular men, frequently worked for the same mortgage companies or real estate firms the houses were being sold by. Comparables weren't established. The supervisors got paid to allow the graft to continue and to ignore complaints when they came in from bilked buyers.

In the departments that dealt with paper—credit reports, job verifications and the like—the payoffs were from the mortgage companies, to ignore obvious inconsistencies and blatant fraud. They were also paid to hurry up processing or to go ahead with approvals before any documents arrived at all.

The department of property management had almost endless opportunities for graft. It was built into the structure. The repossessed houses were given to real estate companies that had been designated as property managers. For a fee of a few dollars a month, a real estate company was charged with protecting an FHA-owned house. Some firms ended up with hundreds of properties under their control. The same property managers were supposed to solicit bids for repairs when HUD decided to sell off the inventory. Their procedure was to rotate the winning low bid from a stable of kept repair contractors, telling this one to bid high this time and this one to bid low. The property manager was well paid by contractors for his favors because he arranged for the work to be done and also was supposed to make sure that it was done as ordered. The FHA officials who ran this department knew what was going on and were well paid to allow it to continue.

Those officials who handled the paper when a house was in default or foreclosure were also rewarded—for not asking questions, and to hurry a foreclosure when a mortgagee wanted it to be done.

In Romney City, the corruption went on up the line, through the department heads and through the deputy directors to the director himself, who belatedly learned that the big speculators and mortgage companies had profitable deals for him in kickbacks and land schemes in return for keeping the heat off. Windshield Willie thought that he was only as honest as he had to be, but he kept his arrangements to himself. Even he would have been shocked to learn everybody else was in on the deal. He never stopped to think that if he was the only crook, he would have been quickly stopped.

The area office was under the jurisdiction of the regional office, and the regional office reported to the HUD national headquarters in Washington, D.C. Corruption at these rarified heights operated a bit differently because it was linked to politics, power and real wealth. It was not in the interest of regional officials to forward on to headquarters bad news about rising defaults and foreclosures because it made them look bad. Regional officials regularly downplayed the seriousness of troubles in district offices when district heads were rash enough to forward that information on. Because the regional heads had their jobs, too, in reward for tilling the electorate, they were well-connected to the large real estate and mortgage companies on a social basis and had no desire to rock the boat. A word to a zealous prosecutor that HUD was taking care of its own problems was enough to call off the dogs.

Nationally, the FHA and the building industry are almost indistinguishable at the highest levels. The real estate interests and banking concerns make it a regular practice to make their own officials available to the government for a stint of public service. They also hire those who are bright enough and compliant enough at the FHA to act as vice-presidents and lobbyists, to maintain their good relations with the Capitol and the Hill and the big building which houses HUD. Many of these men find personal graft unthinkable—it's beneath their station. They benefit by going from a $35,000-a-year job with the FHA to $75,000 a year with the firms the FHA is supposed to work with and supervise. The process is inevitable.

As it happened, the whole chain for profiteering, fraud, payoffs, corruption, default, foreclosure, individual ruin, political pressure and coverup nicely fit into Don Giovanni's premier deal.

After his initial purchase from Uncle Max and the subsequent payoff to Windshield Willie, and after the cosmetic repairs and hoodwinking of poor Mrs. Dorothy Ann Green, the papers were forwarded to American Eagle Mortgage Company for a mortgage. Jayson Penny scanned Mrs. Green's financial information and determined that she didn't make enough money to qualify for the purchase of a washing machine, much less a house. He placed a call to Uncle Max, who wrote out a brief note saying that she also did part-time work for Handimaid, a wholly imaginary daywork service, and earned an additional, and imaginary, fifty dollars a week.

Letters from American Eagle to her other job references disclosed that Mrs. Green had exaggerated, to put it mildly, her work record and income, since she worked for nobody and hadn't since she was fired from her last part-time job. This information was deleted from the forms which would be sent to the FHA.

Jayson himself carried the papers over to the FHA where he sat down with an old friend, an "inside man" named Burton McKean, who got the application for FHA insurance through the system and approved in three days' time. Of course, the process could have gone even faster because the FHA never checked to make sure that any of the statements on the application forms were true—the government relies on the intrinsic honesty of the mortgage companies to do this.

McKean did request Penny to certify that the repairs specified by the appraiser had been made, which Penny was glad to do. In return for making the certification, Giovanni slipped him fifty dollars.

In a week's time, the deal was ready to be closed. Present at the closing were Mrs. Green, Giovanni, Penny, the man from the title company, a lawyer for American Eagle and another lawyer, selected by Penny, to represent Mrs. Green. First the title company man made his guarantee that the property had a clean title with no liens against it. Then Penny told Giovanni that he was being charged twelve points on the sale, and Giovanni clenched his teeth and said, "No way," and "What in the hell is going on?"

That dispute slowed things for a minute, and Mrs. Green, who knew nothing about the machinations of high finance, watched in mild interest when Giovanni stormed out to the office of Sammy Goldstein, American Eagle president, to find out what that fat sumbitch was trying to do to him.

What Sammy was trying to do was take a little advantage of Don's greenness and anxiousness to close the sale. That day he was selling mortgages at ninety-three, or a discount of seven points, and he had decided just for the hell of it to pick up five points on the top for himself. But Don yelled, and Sammy argued, and they settled at a discount of ten points for the deal, with a little gift so that Sammy could buy his wife a nice dinner that evening.

When Don got back to the conference room where the closing was taking place, he found that Uncle Max had appeared, to watch over his customer and make sure that he got his 6 percent for making the sale right away, as a reasonable man would.

With a great deal of formal ceremony, the lawyers checked all of the papers, and then Giovanni signed and Mrs. Green signed and the mortgage company signed, and a beaming Mrs. Green was told she had bought herself a house. When she left, with a payment book and more confidence in her future than the circumstances warranted, the other participants started signing checks back and forth to each other.

The title company man got twenty-five dollars for his customary tip from the seller. Uncle Max got his check for 6 percent from Giovanni. Penny got a little tip from Uncle Max and from Giovanni, for all of his help. Giovanni got $200 from the mortgage company for bringing the business into the house. And "Fast Pencil" Maxwell Wacher, the almost invisible clerk who had written up everything, got $100 for his trouble, because he had added in closing costs twice, bringing the total sales price to Mrs. Green up to $14,300—$13,000 for the house, plus title costs (twice), lawyers' costs (twice) and a few other charges nobody could make any sense out of. Both lawyers got paid $200 apiece, and each of them gave a little bit to Penny and Giovanni, to insure their continued goodwill in future transactions. American Eagle, of course, got its ten points, or $1,300 in mortgage discount, out of the deal, plus its own fees.

Jayson opened the cabinet in the bookcase, removed glasses and brandy, and poured everybody a drink.

Mrs. Green hailed a cab and went directly to her new house, where her brother was expected with a U-Haul truck and her battered furniture. When she entered she found that something didn't smell right and discovered that the basement was flooded. She went down to the corner store to tell Uncle Max about it, but he wasn't in. "Stay out of the basement," she told the kids when they arrived. But she didn't know what to tell them about the kitchen when the electricity wouldn't work. Uncle Max would make it right.

Mrs. Green spoke with Uncle Max the next day, and he was sympathetic. He hadn't owned the house, however—it wasn't his responsibility. Here was the number of Don

Giovanni, a nice young man. Mrs. Green called this Italian fellow, but he didn't seem very nice on the phone. He didn't know about the basement. He didn't know about the lights. Everything had been fine before she moved in. What had the kids been up to?

Mrs. Green called for two weeks. One day a workman came and fixed the lights. They worked properly for the next three months. Nobody ever came out about the basement. That bothered her a lot, because her brother told her there was something wrong with the sewage pipe.

While Giovanni, American Eagle and the other operators went about making their FHA business bigger and bigger, Mrs. Green stayed home, cleaned house, and worried a lot. A couple of things make it hard to sleep at night. One was money. She made her first two payments right on the dot and found that she didn't have anything left of the welfare checks for shoes and clothes for the kids. The yard needed seed, the roof began to leak, she had to make repairs. But the welfare people had only five dollars a month for home maintenance. The man said the roof would cost $600 to do it right. Nobody knew what it would cost to fix the water in the basement. It would cost $200 to run a snake through the drain and find out.

What else bothered her dreams was the neighborhood. It was no damn good. She didn't know anybody. The people here weren't friendly like at the other place. The kids were running wild. There was a dope house right down the street. What's a woman going to do?

She would tell the government about what was wrong with the house, first off. It was a government house, and if that Giovanni fellow wasn't going to fix things right, she would get him in trouble. She called the FHA, and the girl there told her just a minute, and then lost the call. Mrs. Green called back and finally got through to somebody who took her complaint. But the man said the house wasn't FHA guaranteed, only the mortgage was. She didn't know what that meant. She wanted the house fixed. The FHA doesn't repair houses. But the house is FHA. That's right, go to the man you bought it from. Click.

The next day Mrs. Green went right down to the offices and sat herself down, demanding to find relief. She talked to a man who asked her why she didn't have enough money for repairs, since she was making so much, like fifty dollars a week extra from Handimaid. Mrs. Green shut right up because she didn't want to get in any trouble. However, she didn't know about that fifty dollars a week, and she didn't know what was going on.

Mrs. Green's girl friend had a brother who worked for the Romney City building department, and she suggested to the new homeowner that the city could help her out. Mrs. Green called the city and told the man in the building department that her roof leaked and the basement was flooded. The city sent a man out right away, and he said, "Yep, sure is a mess."

"What are you going to do about it?" Mrs. Green demanded.

"I've got to cite you," the man said, "for all the violations. The electricity is bad, too."

"You gonna cite me?" Mrs. Green cried in anguish. "This here is a government house. I want that damn real estate fellow to be arrested."

"It's your house now," the inspector said reasonably. "You're responsible."

They argued back and forth for a long time. The inspector seemed to want something from Mrs. Green, but she didn't know what. Finally he threw up his hands and wrote out the citations, even putting down the date she was supposed to appear in court for having such a bad house in Romney City.

"It was a bad house before," she said.

However, she was starting to suspect it wouldn't make any difference to a judge.

The mortgage company, she thought, was her last resort. Since they took her payments, they must have an interest in the house. There was no way for Mrs. Green to know that the mortgage company no longer had any interest in the house except for the one-half percent a month it got for servicing her account. It had long since sold her mortgage, along with a batch of 150 others, to FNMA at a discount price of ninety-three cents on the dollar, and now only acted as an agent for the secondary mortgagee. Mrs. Green was so angry to find out that American Eagle wouldn't help, she decided to show everybody and not pay for the house.

American Eagle sent her letters asking for the money, then told her she was in default and in danger of losing the house. Mrs. Green didn't care. She would stay there until they threw her out, but she actually moved out when September came because the furnace didn't work, either, and it was getting cold. Mrs. Green took her possessions away in another U-Haul, her things and her kids, and moved in with her brother's family in a cramped six-flat.

It took six months from the time of Mrs. Green's first defaulted payment for FNMA and the mortgage company to get foreclosure proceedings moving toward a payoff by the FHA. But it only took twenty-four hours after Mrs. Green moved out of the house for the enterprising operators in the neighborhood to move in and remove the stove, refrigerator, interior doors, water heater, curtain rods and usable furnace parts. The door swung open in the wind. The sheriff fixed a notice to the front. A group of youths used the house for a wine party and a little loving. A pair of junkies stopped in to live for a week and do some dealing. A wino stopped by to escape the wind, lit himself a little fire on the floor to keep warm, and burned down the kitchen.

When foreclosure was completed and the house turned over to the property manager, Blessings Real Estate, a carpenter came out and nailed plywood over the windows and doors. A man from the government put up the notices that said the property was owned by the United States government, stay out, this means you. By spring, the mortgage had been paid off to FNMA at 100 cents on the dollar, with all interest due, and legal fees. Since FNMA had bought the house for 92 cents on the dollar and got its 7 percent interest for the year, its rate of return on the mortgage had been 15 percent, which isn't bad considering the house was lived in for only four months.

American Eagle had a minor problem to solve when its reported number of defaulted FHA mortgages rose to 10 percent. Its actual number of defaults was 14 percent. The FNMA complained to American Eagle, and American Eagle said that things were being rectified, and they were, substantially. Three hundred of the defaulted houses were finally foreclosed, and FNMA was paid off. Then American Eagle, too, could write the house off its books.

The FHA couldn't, however. The FHA was adding thousands of foreclosed houses to its inventory every month, and the local newspapers were getting onto the story and starting to make the local director look bad. Meeting after meeting was called, and a series of plans was developed to reduce the inventory. The first way was to fix the foreclosed houses up and resell them.

The word went out to Uncle Max to get quotes for the repair of what had been Mrs. Green's house. Max did business with a dozen repair contractors, and he decided that this time the job would go to Steady Service, which belonged to an old friend. He got on the telephone and had an estimator from Steady Service go out to look at the house. Then he made arrangements for three bids, the way the government demands. Fly-By-Nite's repair bid was $8,700. Destruction Corporation bid $8,400, and Steady Service came in at $8,250. The FHA man in property repairs had no trouble identifying all three bids in the hand of Uncle Max and marked the fact down in his notebook. He always noted things like that because when he went to Blessings Real Estate, as he did every Saturday, he wanted to be able to point out to Uncle Max every favor he had done for him over the preceding seven days. His retainer from Max was $500 per week.

Max let the contract to repair Mrs. Green's house and submitted to the FHA regular progress reports so the contractor could get paid. He was so dutiful about this that Steady Service was paid in full before anything had been done to repair the house. As it developed, it didn't make any difference, because a man from the FHA came out, looked at the house, and determined that it was one of those that the FHA would tear down. The government had decided that it would destroy 10 to 20 percent of its inventory and get those damned, no-good houses off its books. As Romney himself frequently put it, the government doesn't abandon any houses. It either repairs and resells them, or it tears them down.

Mrs. Green's house was bulldozed down. The firm that did it got paid $1,000. The vacant lot was sold at a token fee to the homeowners on either side.

Before the house disappeared, a Romney City councilman got wind of what had happened to Mrs. Green, talked to her and visited the property. He was so angry he called the newspaper which in turn investigated and did a story about it. District director Rodney Morton said he would do something about it, and he wrote down the address on a

long list of FHA property with questionable backgrounds.
He told the deputy district director to get the case file
from Washington, where the records of foreclosed property
are sent, but he eventually reported back that Washington
had evidently misplaced the file. Morton told the newspaper, "We are still working on it."

The city councilman wasn't satisfied with that explanation, so he went to Tim Savage, the prosecutor, and demanded an investigation. "So what?" Savage asked.
"This is white-collar crime, if you can prove anything at
all. I don't have the manpower for it. I've got rapes and
murders and drug dealers, and two men available for
consumer stuff. Give me a break. Let's wait until we have
a good one."

The councilman was adamant, so he went to the U.S.
Attorney in Romney City and presented him with an extended list of complaints and allegations of criminal
conspiracy, fraud, and other mischief. The U.S. Attorney
explained that he was working on it already, that HUD's
own investigators were looking into dozens of these things,
but they were overworked and understaffed, and this is
very low priority stuff, you have to understand.

When the councilman stomped out of the office, the
federal prosecutor called Morton to complain.

"You've got to do something to clean up this mess, Rod,"
he said. "The administration doesn't want to go very far
into this before the election, and I can understand why.
Isn't there some program you can announce, to fix things
up?"

Morton had been talking to the Washington office and
had some new plans. One of them was to sell the houses
in the inventory to nonprofit groups for $100 or so apiece,
pay them to fix the houses up, and get them resold. The
program worked until it was tried. The nonprofit groups
generally were backed by the contractors who did the work,
and repair costs ran up to the cost of the house. Sometimes more. Some of the nonprofit groups made $100,000
or $200,000, and disappeared into the night.

If anybody was at fault, Morton supposed that Giovanni
was the guy behind the fall of Mrs. Green's house, but
Giovanni was a pretty decent guy. They knew each other
from the University Club, and Giovanni occasionally had
him up to his summer place on the island. Giovanni was

also a good real estate operator who had allowed Morton to invest with him in some farmland that was being sold in parcels near a recreational area. Morton didn't plan to stay with the government forever, and it was good to build up savings now while he was still a young man.

Finally, Mrs. Green's case was only one of a quarter million or so cases. It was up to men like Morton and his superiors in Washington to look at the big picture, the overall plan, the underlying social causes of the problem, to determine a solution. You couldn't fix blame when something this big happened. It was a natural disaster, to be expected when you have a large area populated with the poor and uneducated. Deep economic forces were at work, figured Morton and Romney. The program itself was at fault. Welfare state programs like this led to social destruction.

Some people, like Don Giovanni, knew how to take care of themselves. Don made more than $3 million clear from 1968 to 1972, invested his money in land development in Mexico and Central America, and retired from Romney City. Uncle Max had cleared out all of his condemned and slum properties when he finally decided to go into the FHA business without reservation, then consolidated his cash and launched half a dozen other speculators in the business, acting himself as a mortgage company. American Eagle did more business in Romney City than any other mortgage company, and also had more foreclosures than any other firm, both in total numbers and by percentages. The company yelled like hell when the government finally cut back on the FHA program and announced that the FHA had a responsibility to the poor to maintain the program. Privately, the officers complained that the savings and loan people had the ear of Washington and were trying to cut them out of the business. American Eagle still did some business, but it was with Mortgage Guarantee Insurance Company (MGIC), which meant that the salad days were about over.

Morton considered a variety of job offers, including a vice-presidency with FNMA, but decided that his future lay with one of the new home developers who had built thousands of new houses sold FHA in the suburbs. Windshield Willie paid off his own mortgage and went plugging away with the FHA, working toward his retirement.

Nobody ever knew what happened to Mrs. Green, including the poor woman herself. It didn't work out for her to live with her brother's family, so she decided to buy another house. But the man at the bank told her that she could never again buy a house because she had foreclosed on one, and her credit was ruined forever. With all the moving around, her kids got wilder and wilder, and the oldest boy fell in with a bad crowd and started to get on drugs. The next boy stayed in school, but he was a hot-headed, bitter boy who spoke of being a revolutionary. When he was seventeen, he murdered a man who owned a party store and he was sent to prison. The other two children just went on like their mother, surviving as poor and decent people trying to get by.

Mrs. Green's opinion of the FHA wasn't too high. "That's just a trick bag," she decided. "A damn jive trick bag."

Her counterparts were ethnic whites like Mrs. Irene Wichkowski, who had once lived near Mrs. Green's FHA house, and who had been "converted" out of it by the machinations of American Eagle and Don Giovanni as they "changed blocks."

"What a neighborhood that was," Mrs. Wichkowski would remember. "All Polish, with the bakeries, the music, the church where all the children were baptized. It was our neighborhood until those black people came, moved in and ruined everything. I drove through there just last week. You should see it. All of the houses are ruined and boarded up. There's garbage everywhere. It's just a shame."

Mrs. Green is convinced that Mrs. Wichkowski is responsible for her poverty and plight, because she is white. Mrs. Wichkowski is certain that Mrs. Green is a savage who destroys whole cities in a few short years.

But at heart, both believe in the system, the American system, that they think will both house them and keep the city alive.

For them, they believe, the government has a sacred trust. But that trust has been betrayed, to benefit the sources of capital and the well-to-do. If there has been any "sacred trust" it has been governmental devotion to the mortgage banking industry—the least regulated big business in the United States.

7

The Mortgage Bankers: the Mystery Unmasked

Since August 1972, I have had as a cumbersome companion a twelve-inch pile of sworn congressional testimony about the operations of New York's largest mortgage bankers and the industry nationwide. The 2,000 or 3,000 Xeroxed sheets I ran off myself from the original copies surreptitiously given me by Jack Blum, majority counsel for Sen. Philip A. Hart's Subcommittee on Antitrust and Monopoly. Just pushing the damned pages through the copier took me two sweltering August days. Reading and rereading the more than 500,000 words of testimony were my bedtime and breakfast occupations for five months. As I grew to understand what all the extraordinary, sometimes bizarre, testimony meant, I started to think of those pages as a microscope which allowed me to see and understand the pathology of urban blight and the Federal Housing Authority (FHA) scandal.

The proper—and unreadable—way to present this dissection of the mortgage banking industry would be in a scholarly tome replete with footnotes. A better way, however, is to go charging through with my own interpretation, with the admonition to my critics and any skeptics that I can document both facts and charges.

First, let me retell a little story related to me by one of Secretary Romney's aides about a powerful HUD undersecretary and the undersecretary's attempts not to discipline a mortgage company that had been publicly caught with its hand in the honey pot. The aide had argued for strong measures against the firm, including long-term or permanent suspension.

"Listen, you son-of-a-bitch," the undersecretary told the aide. "You can be righteous, because your future is open to you. But I have to go back to the industry."

The FHA is a government insurance company. It doesn't make your mortgage and it doesn't loan the money for mine. Instead, it insures the institution that loaned the money to pay for the house against losing any money if I decide I don't want to make my monthly payments any longer. I might be a bit resentful that one-half of 1 percent interest a month on my mortgage is really an FHA insurance payment to protect the money guy, but that's the way it's always been since the FHA was formed.

The FHA was a product of the nation's Great Depression, and was created after traditional economics had crashed along with the stock market, the banks and the mortgage market. Persons who wanted to buy homes couldn't get any mortgage money because institutions with capital—money —were afraid to take the chance after tens of thousands of houses foreclosed when homeowners no longer had the income to pay for them.

It was decided that the way to build investor confidence in the housing market was to protect the lender. The FHA was designed from its very inception as an insurance plan that covered the mortgage maker, albeit one that was paid for by the homebuyer. It was a socially progressive program, one must suppose, compared with the mortgage market that existed before that had demanded down payments of one-quarter, 50 percent, and more of the sales price, but it wasn't all *that* socially progressive.

As usual in the United States, when a socialized economic program is created it benefits the wealthy while the poor are required to pay for it.

The FHA was designed to pay its own way from the proceeds it got out of the one-half of 1 percent "insurance" money, and it not only paid the salaries of its employees out of that money, it created great reserves. Over the years, the FHA became known as the most successful social welfare program in the nation's history.

You may be surprised to learn, however, that the mortgage company or bank that loaned me the money to buy the house is usually not the final mortgagee, or the guy I owe the money to. That's because the mortgage banker sells my mortgage to somebody else, usually to FNMA (Federal National Mortgage Association) or to large banks, insurance companies, pension funds, and the like.

I would like to think that my mortgage was worth 100 cents on the dollar to whoever held it, but that's not the case. Instead, the secondary mortgagee paid anywhere from 92 cents to 96 cents a dollar for it, because that's the way the mortgage industry works. If my FHA mortgage costs me 7½ percent, one-half of 1 percent goes to the FHA for the insurance, and another one-half percent is paid by the mortgage holder to the mortgage company that made me the loan in the first place. He gets that money for servicing my loan—collecting the payments and sending me nasty letters when I fall behind.

That doesn't sound like very much money in return for sending letters and making payments, at least not at first blush. But one-half of 1 percent of $10 million in mortgage loans is $50,000 a year. You can start to understand why the mortgage bankers you know drive big cars and live in nice houses on the hill.

The matter of the discount price for which my mortgage was bought leads to several interesting questions and answers. One of the questions is, who determines the discount? The answer is, FNMA does. Why? Because Fannie Mae, as the corporation is affectionately called, buys about half of all FHA mortgages. It presently holds about $18 billion worth of FHA mortgages and occupies so much of the market that it effectively fixes prices.

How is the discount determined? The people who run Fannie Mae decide it, based on how much they can buy their money for and other complicated factors. Fannie Mae exists to make money, so you can rest assured that its calculations include a healthy profit on the discount as well as on the interest payments that I make each month.

It's easier to speak of the discount in terms of points instead of a percent figure. One point equals a 1 percent discount. Mortgage people will speak of an investor taking four points, or buying the loan for ninety-six cents on the dollar. A point equals one-eighth of 1 percent difference between the going FHA allowed interest rate and what conventional mortgages bring. For instance, if the going FHA interest rate is 7½ percent and the going interest rate on the open market is 8½ percent, the mortgage banker will want to get eight points on the deal.

Do I mean to say that the mortgage banker does not make the loan at 100 cents on the dollar, either? Yep. But in FHA transactions, the seller pays the points, not the buyer. That's one of the reasons why private sellers don't like FHA deals, because it costs them money.

Let's look at an example. My house has been sold to you for $10,000. The FHA-controlled interest rate is 7½ percent and the going market rate is 8½ percent. That spread of eight points, or 8 percent, is paid for by me. I don't get $10,000 from the mortgage company. I only get $9,200. You, of course, owe $10,000.

The Fastback Mortgage Company with whom we have been dealing will make up a package of loans, say $100,000 worth. Fannie Mae has offered to buy FHA mortgages at a six-point discount. Fastback accepts the offer and sells the mortgage package for $94,000. Because it charged the sellers eight points, it only spent $92,000 to get the $100,000 worth of mortgages. Its profit on the sale to Fannie Mae was $2,000.

Now one of the curious things about all this is that no-body—not the FHA, not any government agency at any level, and certainly not Fannie Mae—has any way to control the number of points Fastback made me, as the seller, pay. If Fastback wanted to, and I was desperate enough to go along with it, it could charge me ten points, twenty points, fifty points. The seller has to pay the points requested by Fastback, or any real mortgage company.

Now here we are starting to get into some interesting waters. You think that Fastback is making a mortgage to you, but Fastback thinks that it is buying a mortgage. The principle is the same as in any business: buy cheap, sell dear. The mortgage company profits on the resale.

In order to make as much money as possible, Fastback wants to buy as many mortgages as possible. It's inconvenient as hell to have to deal with individuals all the time. It's much better to deal with volume operators, who are called real estate brokers or, as we know all too well, speculators.

You can't just throw open your doors and get business from these guys; you have to entice them to come to you. Fastback has several ways to accomplish this. One way is to promise the speculator that FHA mortgage applications will be processed and approved as quickly as possible. This naturally leads to Fastback hanging around the FHA insuring office to establish good relations and "walk a mortgage through." Sometimes, perhaps usually, this leads to having an "inside man," who helps Fastback for a price. Because the inside man speeds things along and ignores what may be suspicious flaws in the mortgage application, Fastback figures the payoff really pays for itself.

A second way Fastback gets speculators to bring in business is by hooking them with interim financing. A speculator needs money to conduct his business—a lot of it, because even houses bought at panic prices add up in cost. Fastback loans interim money to the speculator in exchange for 2 percent interest a month—that's 24 percent a year—and the promise from the speculator that he will bring the mortgage business to Fastback.

A third way Fastback can encourage business from the speculator is by not being very choosy about the houses the speculator has sold or about the people to whom he has sold them. In its infinite wisdom, the FHA has required the mortgage company to ascertain if required repairs have been made. At the same time, Fastback doesn't care if its inspector gets paid a gratuity or is even bribed by the speculator for ignoring repairs that are supposed to be made on the houses, because Fastback doesn't want to know about problems that would prevent a mortgage.

It is also up to Fastback to prepare the FHA mortgage insurance application form. Fastback is glad to let the speculator fill it out himself, or to write in the information about a buyer's credit and references. Fastback does not check to see if this information is true or not, as is done when money is loaned in conventional ways, because he cannot lose money—ever—on FHA loans. The FHA insurance protects him, as it is intended to do.

For its part, the FHA does not trouble itself to determine if the facts on the insurance application are true or not. It trusts the mortgage company.

But theory will only take us so far. Let's look at the tangled affairs of United Institutional Servicing Corporation (UISC), a major New York mortgage banker, as they were revealed to the Hart subcommittee on May 3, 1972. (Mortgage bankers in New York can't call themselves mortgage bankers. I wouldn't want to be called a mortgage banker either.)

The affairs of this troubled firm were presented in sworn testimony by John H. Payne, Jr., president and chief executive officer of the Empire National Bank, the 185th largest bank in the United States. Payne was called to testify because Empire purchased UISC and four other associated mortgage banking firms in 1971, after having done business with UISC for some eight years.

For what it's worth, UISC came to Empire with the expressed warranty that "operations of their respective businesses do not violate any law, ordinance, rule, regulation or decree of any governmental authority which is material to the operation of their business."

At the time, Empire was aware that UISC had been suspended as a seller-servicer by Fannie Mae and Ginnie Mae (Government National Mortgage Association) because of high default rates in UISC's portfolio of about $114 million in FHA loans. The suspension, in fact, was why UISC was being sold.

One of the first things Payne learned was that UISC had no internal procedures of any kind for approval of FHA mortgage loans.

"In other words," Payne said, "any mortgage on which a firm commitment was issued by the FHA or VA [Veterans Administration] was automatically closed without any further internal investigation.

"Because these loans were government insured or guaranteed, it was apparently assumed that there would be no substantial loss to the company irrespective of whatever loss there might be to the government by virtue of its insurance or guarantee."

Payne called the nonreview policy used by his new acquisition "unique."

The next thing he discovered was "possible conflicts of interest" from the investment of personal funds of UISC's officers and their families in interim loans to speculators. And he learned that all inspections of FHA-required repairs were handled by a single individual, that UISC employees were accepting "gratuities" from speculators, buyers, and lawyers at the time of the closing, and that some of the speculators had rather impressive rates of defaulted and foreclosed mortgages.

These practices, he said, "were apparently common to the mortgage banking industry."

On May 6, some of these points were elaborated on by some UISC employees—Kiva Berwald, a solicitor or mortgage salesman, and Irving Roiter, the inspector. Both appeared in answer to subpoena.

Berwald had worked for UISC for fifteen years and had started when there was virtually no FHA business. The business in those good old days consisted of selling three-tiered mortgages, of which the second mortgage was sold at a 30 to 50 percent discount and the third mortgage was nearly worthless paper on the market.

Berwald said he discovered the FHA business, in Queens, about 1965. When he found it, speculators were foreign to FHA transactions and he admitted it was part of his job to show them how it operated. But, he cautioned, "I don't want you to think that I am the one that created the FHA mortgage business in Brooklyn. I just happened to be there at the time."

Berwald explained to real estate brokers how to know which buyers qualify for FHA insurance and how to fill out FHA application forms. The brokers learned quickly, and also came to appreciate that UISC had ample money to close mortgage loans. About the same time, Berwald got into the real estate business himself. He bought in partnership with people who brought him buildings; he supplied the financing and they had the houses. He did all of his business with his employer, UISC, which did not mind because he was bringing in mortgages—about $1 million worth a year. Berwald benefitted from these deals in several ways, because he was also a UISC stockholder as well as being an employee who got commissions on the business he generated. He also admitted that he was involved in personal interim loans to speculators through a UISC subsidiary.

Berwald, anything but an effusive witness, said he did not know how FHA appraisals worked but knew they increased over the years and "created a spiral." He heard "rumors" about FHA appraisers who were being paid to make favorable appraisal reports and also about brokers who sold homes under FHA mortgage to straw men who then rented the property.

He said he did not feel he was personally involved in any conflict of interest because "conflict connotes some devious thing that did not exist. It [his business] was wide open knowledge to everybody."

He said the rash of foreclosures in New York City was caused by unqualified buyers who "squandered the money or spent it and did not regard it as a part of their mortgage payment. Foreclosures resulted. As a result of the foreclosures, we had a lot of boarded up houses as a result of FHA policy. It resulted in vandalism and everything else."

He said he had no idea how many of the properties he sold on his own through United had since gone into foreclosure, and his testimony did not indicate he cared very much.

Following Berwald to the witness table was Irving Roiter, who was UISC's solitary inspector of FHA compliances. For this sensitive position he had received no training, either in inspections or in property appraisals. What he was, as he saw himself, was "just an average layman looking at a house to see if it was in good condition."

Good condition was a matter of judgment that Roiter never bore down on too hard, because if he was too tough, UISC officials and the brokers let him know about it. It seemed that one had to go along to get along.

Sooner or later, some of the low-income buyers who got the FHA houses complained about the condition they were in. ". . . When people complained bitterly," Roiter said, "I advised them to go to their broker that sold them the houses and please tell them what the story is, being they found these conditions where there was an oversight by the FHA inspector at the time he appraised the house."

At the committee's request, Roiter furnished records that showed he received "gratuities" from brokers who did business with UISC for "going out of my way for them. . . ."

Warren Light, who had been an assistant vice-president of United and executive vice-president for United's Delta Capital Corporation (the interim mortgaging arm of the huge mortgage banker), was in charge of interim financing records. He was given the job by Edwin Katz, one of

United's owners. Among those UISC officers, owners, and their families who loaned their personal money to speculators through Delta, Light said, were Bernard S. Roth, president of UISC; Larry Levy, an attorney who had his investment guaranteed by Roth; Jerome F. Katz, senior partner of the law firm Katz, Wittenberg, Silverman and Levine; Bea Katz, sister-in-law of Edwin Katz and mother of a UISC employee named Robert; and Hildreth Katz, Edwin's sister.

The investors were employees, their families, lawyers who knew the company, and other insiders with money to invest. Obviously, it seemed to be in their interest for United to make mortgages to the speculators who worked with this privately invested capital through Delta. When a deal was closed, these investors could take back their money and profit, or keep it in the revolving fund for future action.

When Light first came to United, he was assigned the job of figuring out what to do with some 500 conventional loans made by United, principally in East New York City, Brownsville, and East Flatbush. These mortgages had been sold to about twenty-five New York state banks, and many of them were unhappy with threatened foreclosures and delinquencies on the properties.

To mend fences, Light, Katz, and a third UISC employee went to visit these bankers. "I realized that certain people [bankers] must have had the impression that they got a raw deal [because of the foreclosures]," Light said, "where others were willing to look at it that they went into it with their eyes wide open and it [the endangered mortgages] was just an investment that didn't pan out correctly."

Neither Light nor the bankers involved wanted the properties to be foreclosed, because once a bank owned the property it was also liable for building code violations. One alternative to this, he said, was to "convert [the mortgages] to FHAs and VAs."

Light testified that about 10 percent of the troubled mortgages he dealt with were "converted" to FHA loans.

To accomplish this, Light would call a broker and tell him that a bank "was desirous of selling the following mortgages. They could go out and make a bona fide offer [to buy them], and I would forward it to the bank for their approval or disapproval or whatever." Meanwhile, Light was paid "gratuities" from brokers for the closings for interim loans, so that the speculators would have money to work with.

John G. Haskell, president of the Oneida Savings Bank in Oneida, New York, a small upstate bank, told the subcommittee that conversions of endangered conventional mortgages to FHA mortgages was "all originated from the United people.

"They would say that they had a conversion—not a conversion, maybe a buyer for this loan, which was a corporate loan, where we pay back an FHA loan of X amount, which we always had so much money invested in."

Haskell said he "absolutely" preferred to have FHA insured mortgages instead of conventional mortgages on high risk properties.

"They [UISC] would say, 'We have a mortgage,'" he continued. "Most of these were corporate mortgages, corporate conventional. 'You have a mortgage with this XYZ company. It is to be sold to Johnny Jones. Would you take back an FHA loan of X dollars?'"

In a typical transaction, United would arrange to have Oneida's endangered conventional mortgage sold and remade with FHA insurance. The first loan was satisfied in principal, interest, and arrears. "And then we [Oneida] would receive the papers with the FHA commitment and the guarantee certificate; or, if it is an FHA, the insurance certificate."

Another upstate bank, the City and County Savings Bank of Albany, New York, converted at least twenty-three shaky mortgages handled by UISC to FHA insured loans. Frank E. Cheeseman, the bank's vice-president, said City and County Savings did not inspect any of these houses when the FHA loan was made. The effect of the conversions, he admitted, was to relieve the bank of loss. In place of shaky conventional loans at 6 percent, the bank got government guaranteed mortgages yielding 7½ or 8 percent, for much higher mortgage amounts than the original loans.

Essentially, Cheeseman agreed that City and County Savings had only three choices of what to do with its endangered mortgages in New York City: convert them to FHA mortgages, thereby shifting the loss; bring the mortgages up to date; or simply write off the property and abandon it.

Bernard Roth, subpoenaed to appear before the Hart subcommittee, respectfully refused to testify, saying: "On the advice of counsel, I respectfully decline to answer on the grounds my answer may tend to incriminate me. I avail myself of my rights against self-incrimination under the Fifth Amendment of the Constitution of the United States."

A much more willing witness was John P. Lomenzo, New York's Secretary of State, and an early crusader against blockbusting and speculators' activities.

Lomenzo had seen it all. The roots of the FHA scandal, he observed, began with racial change on a middle-income level. The speculators, he said, "saw a complete turnover of homes and equated this, in their minds, with the commissions that are involved. So they realized the lucrative market that was available, that there was this kind of a complete change-over. As a result, they looked for other communities in which they could negotiate the sale of homes to this minority middle-income purchaser."

The next community selected in New York City was Bedford Stuyvesant. But as the community was integrated, the real estate brokers discovered there weren't many middle-income blacks. "They then conceived the idea of selling homes to the members of the low economic status groups. Their project became the poor without regard to race, creed or color," said Lomenzo.

Before the 1968 Housing Act, poor persons could not get mortgages from banks, or through the FHA. So the speculators, working with speculative investors who would later surface as mortgage bankers, created the "black tax" loan —the first, second, and third mortgage loan.

The procedure was this. The real estate speculator "panic peddled," broke the block, and purchased the house from a white owner for $10,000 or so, cash. Then he resold it to a low-income buyer for $24,000. He took back a first-purchase money mortgage for $12,000, which covered the cost of buying the house in the first place. He took a second-purchase money mortgage for 60 percent of the balance, or $8,000, and a third-purchase money mortgage for the remainder of the sales price.

All three mortgages were sold. The first one went at a 10 percent discount, so the speculator got his money back and a small profit. The second mortgage was sold at a 20 percent discount, and the third mortgage sold at a discount of

50 percent or more. The speculator ended up with an approximate profit of $9,000 on his $10,000 investment. The buyer owed $24,000 and usually had a hard time maintaining the mortgages and the property.

"Of course," Lomenzo said, "this led to a deterioration of the community, the eventual destruction of the area into a ghetto, which is what the people wanted to get away from in the first place."

Then one day in 1965, Lomenzo said, "As we are checking into blockbusting, we realized that there was some other type of activity, that there was a very important tool of blockbusting.

"And that had to do with the fraud that now all of us know about; relating to it, they changed certain mortgages."

What he discovered was that, as the amount of conventional mortgage money rose in 1965 and 1966, a new kind of mortgage service funding company began to take hold, a new financial middleman. It was the mortgage banker.

The speculators no longer needed the "black tax" mortgage system because they could apply for mortgages to the mortgage service funding companies "which would charge points at discount."

And, he said, "The tighter the money market, the more business was directed to the mortgage service funding companies, who, in a few years, were the only lenders accepting mortgage applications."

Lomenzo found that discounts on FHA insured mortgage loans ranged as high as 11 percent. "In order to meet the payment of the discounts, and other expenses, the real estate dealers and speculators, and licensed real estate brokers, began to speculate and flock to communities which were 10 percent to 15 percent integrated, and started a massive campaign of solicitation.

"And who were they looking for? The poor; white, black, English-speaking, Spanish-speaking. Of course, in the main, a substantial number of the victims in all of this were the black people, and the Spanish-speaking people because there are more of those, unfortunately, in the low economic groups."

What got Lomenzo so interested was a case of a family with no financial stability, income, or standing that qualified for a mortgage and bought a house for $28,000.

"We decided to look into that completely and specifically. We found that many of the purchasers in the low economic status, unqualified purchasers who were approved for mortgage loans, got them based upon the falsification of their employment and financial status.

"They were induced to purchase these homes because they were crying for housing, and we don't have enough housing anywhere, because the unscrupulous people would say to them, 'Never mind renting a house, buy one. It won't cost you anything. What have you got to lose?' And that's the way it went.

"The methods used by these individuals are incredible. In order to establish credit, they would actually pick up at some local IRS office blanks of income tax forms, would make them out, submit them as part of their application for mortgages.

"Under FHA regulations, a certain amount of money is required to be on hand. . . . These individuals would . . . deposit their own funds in the name of the purchaser: $1,500. So when the check was made, they qualified.

"The income tax form showed that they had an income. The credit reports, which were also falsified, indicated that they had good credit. And when they looked to see if they had the required funds to close the transaction, they found $1,500 in the bank. Of course, right after it was over, the individual who put in the money in the first place, would take it out. And this was the way it went.

"And this could not have been possible unless there was absolute complete specific cooperation from the top to the bottom in certain areas."

Then the same, tragic story of overcommitted people in FHA houses was told again. The buyer took in tenants to get their rent; he couldn't afford maintenance on the property; he would be foreclosed and thrown out on the street.

"And then," Lomenzo said, "you would have the consequence of that human reaction: frustration with the system and the establishment, and all of these things that have caused such disorder and such distrust of things."

Lomenzo testified that the irregularities in housing uncovered by his department would be removed "if the FHA personnel exerted closer scrutiny and controls over their mortgage-lending procedures."

Patrick Cea, counsel for Lomenzo's office, said many

speculators got into the FHA business at the suggestion of mortgage company representatives who came to appraise properties that were to be sold with the "black tax."

"And he spoke to the broker, and he says, 'What are you doing? You're selling these houses for $7,500. Why don't you get an FHA appraisal. Why don't you, for $35, get a pre-conditional commitment.'

"The broker says, 'What's that?' So, he explained it to him. He says, 'What you're doing here is selling the house for $9,000. Why don't you submit an application to the FHA for pre-conditional commitment and say that you're selling it for $20,000 . . . and see what happens?'

"So they did that and they got a commitment. . . . and once the broker saw that, he said, 'All you need is front money to put deposits down, pay appraisal fees and other expenses.'

"Now, once the broker got someone [the mortgage bank] to go in with him for the front money, some capital to start, he bought all the houses up in that area—every house that was up for sale—and [the broker] working for the funding company then assisted him in processing the applications, and he sent them in.

"And the way [one speculator] put it, and I quote: 'Once the person saw how they could get a mortgage commitment far in excess of the price that the person intended to sell [for in the first place], zoom, it was wide open.'"

The people committing fraud against the FHA and the poor apparently came to believe it was all justified. Lomenzo's observation was that brokers and mortgage bankers felt "everybody was doing it," and that's why they did.

This led to an incongruous situation that Lomenzo described as "moralistic larceny."

"If you do something long enough," he said, "it takes on this usage and custom in the trade. This is exactly what's been happening."

Lomenzo told the subcommittee he believed "there is a massive fraud condition" by mortgage companies and speculators "not only in New York but throughout the country."

One of the simplest manifestations of the con consists of the eagle symbol of the federal seal that FHA-approved mortgage companies are allowed to display. The eagle gives poor people—and many sophisticated people—the idea that they are dealing with a federally regulated or government agency.

But mortgage bankers, instead of being controlled and regulated, operate under no banking regulations at all. As a consequence, that poor eagle has been witness to billions of dollars of misrepresentation and fraud.

This is not to say all mortgage bankers and all mortgage banking are corrupt. I have found people in the industry who are honest and concerned about the jobs they do and the people to whom they make mortgages. In fact, some of my best friends are mortgage bankers, but I must confess they became my friends before I ever learned about their business.

Mortgage banking is a huge industry. In 1970, the last year I have statistics for, mortgage bankers originated about $13 billion in new mortgages, of which about 70 percent were FHA or VA insured. Of the total of $8.1 billion in FHA single-family (one- to four-unit) mortgages made in 1970, mortgage bankers originated $5.5 billion, or 68 percent.

In other words, mortgage bankers dominate FHA transactions, virtually without any regulation by the government. Of course, they like their privileged status. In an amusing plea for the government's continued laissez-faire approach to the industry, the executive vice-president of the Mortgage Bankers Association of America, Oliver H. Jones, wrote in the July 1972 issue of the *Mortgage Banker* magazine:

"Before the would-be regulators move into the field of mortgage banking, they should consider the economic significance of a financial institution that has the freedom to be flexible in adjusting to change; the freedom to move into commercial lending, into financing apartments; the freedom to seek mortgage funds from all types of financial institutions, from the securities markets, and from pension and trust funds. . . .

"By adding mortgage banking to the list of regulated financial institutions, the nation would simply create another economic vacuum. Once created, such a vacuum can only be filled by still further federal intervention."

Since strict federal regulations of commercial banks, savings and loans, and other kinds of banks have hardly pushed them against the financial wall, the argument by

Jones is wholly without substance. He even admits that mortgage bankers simply are anxious "to avoid the strait-jacket of limited lending powers."

About fraud, misrepresentation, and double-dealing by mortgage bankers, Jones says, "The burden of proof is not on the mortgage banking industry; it is on the FHA."

But the burden of proof has been taken up by federal grand juries in half a dozen cities, and half a dozen congressional investigatory committees and they have all proved the mortgage banking industry rife with corruption.

More interesting in Jones's article is his assertion that mortgage banking is already regulated.

"All investors, including FNMA and GNMA and FHA and VA perform or have the authority to perform the supervisory functions," he said. "Investors audit their mortgage banking correspondents and require regular financial, delinquency and other reports from their correspondents. If they do not like what they find, they can terminate their correspondent relationship. FHA also audits mortgage bankers and requires a variety of reports. If FHA does not like what it finds, it can literally put the mortgage banker out of business by terminating or suspending his FHA-approved status."

The actual fact of the matter is that banks and other investors who buy FHA mortgages from mortgage bankers are extremely careful about the ones they accept. Because mortgage bankers rely on these institutions for the money they use to make mortgage loans, it would be a rash individual who would try to pull a fast one on his capital source. Money, after all, is the raw material of the business.

But mortgage bankers sell most of their mortgages to Fannie Mae, and the good old lady is much less choosy. FNMA does protest when delinquencies and foreclosures rise too high, sometimes for two or three years running. But nobody is overly concerned about delinquencies, because the mortgages are insured, and once the government pays them off they are no longer on the record books. When district FHA directors have moved to discipline mortgage bankers, they have found that the firms have powerful friends inside the central offices in Washington. In 1972, when FHA offices began demanding that mortgage bankers confirm credit and job reports, the mortgage bankers fought against the requirement, because as they discovered fraud it spoiled their relationships with speculators who brought them so much money.

FNMA, by the way, accepts FHA mortgages as good on face value. After the mortgage banker writes his application, nobody—not FHA, FNMA, or anybody else—goes beyond the figures on the form. Sometimes, FNMA suspends a mortgage banker in disciplinary action. But its audits are not sent to FHA, even though FHA pays off the bad mortgages; the commercial reports are used for FNMA purposes alone. FNMA does audit mortgage bankers—once every three years. It does not audit the credit underwriting.

The lack of control is widely known in banking circles, and strongly deplored by responsible financial institutions. Isidore J. Lasurdo, executive vice-president of the Green Point Savings Bank in Brooklyn, asked Hart's subcommittee for ". . . all mortgage companies to be licensed and regulated so they can operate in a more responsive and responsible manner. Supervisory authorities should regularly examine not only their records . . . but their overall objectives and operations."

John Payne, Jr., president of Empire National Bank and the man who was so badly burned in his acquisition of UISC said, ". . . It is not enough for individual mortgage companies to tighten procedures and quality controls—the mortgage banking industry needs legislated and regulated standards such as the banks of the country have through their banking regulatory authorities. Such regulation in combination with quality standards applied without favor by mortgage guaranty or mortgage insurance agencies—will enable us all to compete on an even basis. And, as most of us in 'the mortgage banking business do business in many states, I believe that uniformity of these regulations and standards among all the states is vital."

By the end of 1972, New York state's three largest mortgage bankers—Eastern, UISC, and Inter-Island—had either been indicted, suspended or were under investigation for fraud in FHA transactions. The federal grand jury indictments handed down on March 19, 1972, against Eastern Service Corporation and its president also included nine other corporations and thirty-nine more individuals. Among them were Herbert K. Cronin, the $27,000-a-year chief underwriter of the district FHA office in Hempstead,

Long Island, the then No. 3 man in that office, and six other FHA employees. Most interesting of all, Dun & Bradstreet and one of its executives were indicted on charges of creating fraudulent credit information for Eastern, in order to get FHA mortgages.

The indictments came three days after Secretary Romney said in Detroit he was "angered and determined to eliminate incompetence, conflict of interest, favoritism, graft, bribes, fraud, shoddy workmanship, and forms of 'legal' profiteering that take advantage of technicalities to defraud the homebuyer and the tax-paying public."

The same day, in a meeting in the offices of the *Detroit Free Press,* Romney accused me of "muckraking" and "yellow journalism" for my articles about the FHA scandal in Detroit.

When the first New York indictments were handed down, the assistant United States Attorney, Anthony Accetta, who presented the case to the grand jury said, "I wish we didn't have to have these indictments. I wish the FHA system hadn't been so thoroughly corrupted. I wish the government had not suffered such a social and financial loss.

"I don't see how anyone who is black or Puerto Rican could have faith in the white system after being shaken down like this and then losing his house two months later.

"The low-income Italians I grew up with were the same kind of people as the Puerto Ricans and blacks being victimized here—basically hard-working individuals trying to get ahead in a new country."

The loss in New York was estimated at about 5,000 houses, collectively worth at least $100 million. Approximately $10 million of this money went to the mortgage bankers in the form of points.

The speculators who have drawn so much attention in the FHA scandals could not have existed without the mortgage bankers. The mortgage banking industry created them, not the other way around. The mortgage bankers paid for all of the speculators' activities and financed the blockbusting. Their outrageous points and "juice" interest rates forced speculators to double the sales prices of the houses they sold to poor people through the FHA. The mortgage bankers accepted fraudulent credit and job reports, or made them up themselves, in order to defraud the FHA into approving the mortgage insurance applications. FNMA and other investors accepted the mortgages on face value because, after all, they were insured against any loss.

Without the collusion and active participation by the mortgage bankers, the FHA scandal could not have come about. They are the pieces of the puzzle that makes everything fall into place.

8

We Got Troubles

JOYCE RENFORTH knows what it's like to be a victim of the FHA disaster. At the time of the following interview Mrs. Renforth was an ADC mother and the foreclosed buyer of a used Section 235 house. She lived in Warren, Michigan, a Detroit suburb.

"In November of 1969 I had to leave the house I was living in, and a man called me from X Real Estate and said that they had a house that I could probably buy. I was relieved to have somebody call me. They took me inside the house, and I saw it and I didn't want it and I told them so.

"I said that, 'It's just too small for my family.' I had a boy and three girls living with me. There was no visible defects that it wasn't livable or anything, it was just that I didn't want it. I talked to the real estate firm on the phone two or three days later, and they told me, 'That's the only one that you can buy, it's the only one that you can have right now.'

"It seemed that something trashy like that was the only thing somebody on ADC [Aid to Dependent Children] is supposed to be able to handle. It cost $16,000. I told them that I couldn't take the house because it was too small for my family. He said that I couldn't get a bigger house for six months.

"The real estate man said all I had to do is keep the payments up, fix it up a little bit and he would get me another house within six months' time. And since he said that it was the only one available, I went and took the papers to a neighborhood legal service and had them check it out.

"The day that I moved in was March 4, 1970, and it was raining like crazy and there was an awful lot of mud around the place. It was like a mud bath and there was a leak in the utility room over the water heater. That was the only sign that there was anything wrong, except for a small hole in the wall across from the front door. There was no way of locking that door because the doors and the front and the back of the house weren't level.

"And that hole. When I saw it, oh my gosh, I mean it was just a little hole. But gee, what became of that hole. It just got bigger. There was water leakage through there, and that was in March.

"I had been in there a week and the ceiling fell out of the utility room over the water heater and there was a red tag on that water heater. It had been on there for two years saying that the water heater was not installed correctly. And actually, before I moved out, the ceiling was so messed up in that utility room that all the outlet pipes fell off the house. This water heater sat in a fountain of water, and it became a fountain of water in the living room.

"And you could see that hole in the wall get bigger and bigger. You could see that water was just dripping down in there. All that was inside of the wall was soaky mush. It got big fast. By May, a whole bunch of insects started flying out of that hole. I had an exterminator come in and look at it and he said that it was just full of termites. He said that condition had been there a long, long time.

"When I moved out, all that was left in this hole were some shingles, aluminum siding. That was the only contact between the outside and the living room, just a piece of aluminum siding. The rest was just gone. It had disintegrated. Pieces kept falling away. There were piles of it continually falling on the bottom of the floor.

"Then I found out that the roof was bad, it was really bad. It cost $300 just to get the roof replaced, and the termite control cost $300 to $400, and I was told that everything under the walls would have to be taken out to find out how extensive the damage was. Then there was the trouble in the utility room, and the water in the front room.

"There was a big area in the ceiling that fell out, and it

fell out in two or three different periods. I was in bed the one time. It was a week after I was in the house. It had been raining steady and all of a sudden we heard this crash.

"The plumbing was really bad. It was leaking in the bathroom toilet, and the whole water faucet had to be replaced because it was leaking and there was no way of stopping it.

"There was also trouble with the furnace. It was a blow furnace. Now you see, I've got asthma and I'm allergic to dust and I was continually sick, continually sick. I had these sinus headaches and I was taking Dristans constantly and other medication, and all this dirt was blowing around from the furnace.

"We were in there three months and I was in the kitchen, cooking, and suddenly the kids yell, 'Mother, the furnace is burning.' Here were these flames shooting up. Dirt and grease in the furnace were burning.

"I knew that if you threw water on it you would break the block. I ran into the kitchen and got some baking soda, and I threw it on the fire and got that fire out. The house was full of smoke. We had to open all the windows and doors, and if we'd been in bed, we'd been dead, and I told people this.

"I told them that I had been sick with asthma, constant headaches, and I didn't know what was causing it. But since I've been out of the house I haven't had any more sinus headaches. They were caused from that dirt going in that furnace and then blowing through the house.

"I've got asthma, and I have these attacks, and I was having them constantly from the furnace, but I couldn't get out. I couldn't get out of that place, a year and a half later I was still trying to get out.

"I had bought this house under the government 235 subsidized program. I was paying $74.45, and I think the total mortgage costs were $156 something, so the government was paying about $90 a month.

"When things started going wrong, I started writing letters, and I wrote to Romney in Washington. Actually, I started calling people before I started writing letters. I called the FHA in Detroit and they said, 'We don't have to inspect old houses, we have nothing to do with it.' I got four or five of those answers on the phone.

"I figured that I would have to do something, the house was just absolutely impossible, so I started writing those letters to Romney, and later on to Consumers Protection. And I wrote to the FHA Chicago division, the regional office, and I ended up writing fifteen letters to stupid people in the year and a half I stayed.

"And after five months, I contacted my first lawyer, a lawyer from legal service. That seemed like a dead end, because he'd never call me. Finally, he said that there was nothing that he could do.

"So I went back to the real estate company and told them, 'What am I going to do? This house is no good. You said that I could get out of it within six months. The place is falling apart around me.' And they said, 'Yes, we're going to do something about that.'

"But the man who came out actually propositioned me right there. He said, 'You've got to get out of here, no doubt about it. We can get you in a nice house. What would you do if I get you out?'

"And then he started to repeat it, and I said, 'What do you mean?' Then he made it more clear what it was he was referring to, and I said, 'Mister, I'm not interested in anything like that,' and I put it down flat that I wasn't interested. He sort of hem-hawed and said, 'We'll get hold of you next week.'

"He assured me then that the house had been inspected in December by the FHA, in December of 1969, just before I bought it.

"My understanding was that the government was behind these houses when the government gave FHA mortgages on them. I thought they had to be only good homes before they would even put a price on it.

"Well, the real estate company wouldn't do anything for me, and I went to two other lawyers, wrote to a state senator, George Romney, the Better Business Bureau and Bill [William] Whitbeck at HUD.

"After a year or so Whitbeck sent this man down to inspect my house. Believe me or not, the man comes through and he sees these things wrong and the roof coming down in the utility room and everything else and I said: -

"'Can you do anything about it? Can you repair the place?'

"He said the place is hardly worth repairing and walked

out. I never heard another word from the FHA. That was the end of it, and that's the facts. They walked out and left me.

"I also complained to the city. The city came out after the termite inspector in July of 1970 and he told me then that the house was not livable and that it should be condemned. He was from the department of health. And the city of Warren Health Department condemned the house because of improper construction and other improper things about the house.

"One inspector said the problems in the house included: large hole in the wall where the house was infested with termites for at least two years prior to the complainant's purchase of the house; bad roof, leakage has caused deterioration within the walls of the structure and considerable damage to the plaster; thermostat furnace is out of control; all pipes and faucets in bathroom must be replaced; the gas water heater had a red tag on it for two years because of improper installation.

"He said the house won't stand for five years with its present rate of deterioration.

"This is what the board of health wrote:

"'As a result of an inspection by Dean Zimmerman of the Warren Building Department in response to the letter of July 21, 1970, we found that termite damage to the walls in the living room and rafters in the utility room is due to water leaks and damages to the wall and the ceiling. Finishes in these rooms must be removed to check the extent of damage. The roof was not installed properly, shows signs of leaking. Porches and steps are in need of repairs. Upper floor windows are under minimum requirements. Upper floor has no provision for heat.'

"They said I had to go and see the prosecuting attorney in Mount Clemens, so I went there and I saw him. I explained all these things and I remember that I never heard anything more and so I contacted him again and nothing more went, and it seemed that they just dropped my complaint.

"In the fall of 1970 I tried to stop making payments and to put some money aside as down payment on another house to live in. I made up those payments. But in August of 1971 I decided that I had enough, and I stopped making payments for good. I had to get out. I was going to hold back on the payments to find another place to live in. If I couldn't use the money on some other place eventually, I still had hopes of buying. I ended up saving $200. Of course, Social Services knew about it. They knew that the money was in escrow. I went before Social Services and explained, 'I'm trying to get out of this house. What can I do?'

"At the end of November I found another house to rent for $125 a month. I said, 'I'll move in.' ADC gave me a trailer hitch and a dolly and I had to find somebody to move me. I ended up taking things out in my station wagon.

"I moved the fourteenth of December. On the thirteenth of December all my family got the flu. I was trying to settle a house, take the things out of one house into another by car. I was working till midnight at a store, 6 to 11 P.M. on weekends, and my whole family was sick and I was sick. I was working and moving and trying to prepare for Christmas. I was still pretty weak from the flu. You should of seen me just dragging myself, hauling boxes and stuff. Well, on the first Tuesday of the new year I came there to get more goods and found the front door wide open and screening all around the outside of the house.

"The mortgage company had done it. They took all my good dishes, ceramics, my school papers and bike parts and bike. The house was cleaned out, spic-and-span, everything gone. I made a list of about $700 worth of goods that was taken of mine. They apparently got a crew and told them to clean it out, and that's what they did. They took all my stuff. I was panicky. Yet the house was still legally mine for another couple of weeks. I called the police, but it didn't do any good.

"Oh, the other thing was, the house was condemned before I moved out. The board of health came in for a second inspection and they said, 'This house is not livable.'

"Now they're going to tear this house down, and I have to get out, but I can't find anyplace. It seems that I'm going through the same runaround. I get so depressed sometimes that I feel that I'm going out of my mind. I tried to buy another house, and the real estate man talked to Mr. Whitbeck, or somebody at FHA. The FHA said sorry, but this woman has no credit and she won't have any credit because she let a house foreclose. I have no way to get back. I let a house foreclose.

"But I couldn't live in the place. It was falling down around me. I was scared. And now Romney has changed policy, he has made it so ADCs can't buy anyway because we don't have enough income.

"Romney has closed the door because he said that ADC does not qualify to buy a house. But there's nothing available for $120 a month that's worth living in. It just seems like a hopeless cause. I'm stuck here. I can't get out.

"And this has happened now when I've worked myself off of Social Services. I started attending Wayne State [University] six years ago, and I have taken care of my kids and put myself through school, and I'll start student teaching this fall. Now I want to be self-sustaining. I want a job that will pay decently enough so the kids can live adequately. I wanted to have a house that the kids could live in and not be dragged out of.

"I don't understand why the government could allow such bad houses to be sold. That's what I've been asking for the last two years. I've been a victim of it. I plead to everybody and I have gone to everybody, and no one will do anything. The house was no good, and it was sold for $16,000 or $17,000. Who's got the money? Can you tell me? Who?

"I think it is monstrous. I think it's disastrous. I fought to make things better. I fought while I was in college. I wrote these letters. I contacted these people, and sometimes I was in a frenzy. All I wanted while I was in that house was to get out, and I couldn't get out. Legally, there is no way out for you.

"It was just like a doggone jungle."

(An inspection by the author of Mrs. Renforth's house found a hole in the roof, concrete crumbling, front steps breaking away, the concrete-block floor cracked, eaves rotted, the garage tottering over, paint peeling and an American flag pasted in the front window.)

On December 10, 1971, HUD's Office of Audit released a study for official use only under the formal title: *Audit Review of Section 235 Single-Family Housing.* In polite and careful language the auditors confirmed what others had suspected and charged: that FHA appraisers were criminally negligent if not outright corrupt; that 26 percent of all new subsidized houses and 43 percent of the used houses were substandard or uninhabitable; that HUD-FHA didn't know what they were doing; and that the general attitude of FHA employees was let the public be damned.

To make the report, HUD investigators went over the inside and outside of 1,281 houses in February and March of 1971, in fifty-two FHA areas. This sampling was of the 150,000 new houses and 50,000 used houses insured through the fall of 1970 under the subsidized interest program. The houses were selected on a random statistical basis and made up a big enough sample to safely predict that the troubles uncovered were typical of all 200,000 houses. The auditors didn't look at any of the houses insured under Section 221-d-2. But because the FHA was, if anything, more careful about its procedures under the subsidized program, congressional investigators concluded that even worse conditions existed in houses sold under the un-subsidized program for the poor.

About half of the houses inspected by the two-member teams were made in inner city areas. An additional 2,000 complaints made to HUD were reviewed, and 284 houses—201 new and 83 used—were looked at. The investigators also followed up on deficiencies by going into case files and sometimes speaking with real estate brokers and mortgagees.

The inspectors found deficiencies in 173 of 672 of the new houses inspected, for a total of 25.7 percent. One hundred of the houses had what the auditors politely called poor workmanship or materials—evidence, in other words, of crimes such as noncompliance with minimum property requirements, "poor or lax inspection procedures," incomplete finish work, and "other examples of lack of enforcement of the builder's warranty."

Typical violations were:

- Inoperative electric ceiling heat
- No kitchen light switch
- All wall corners cracked from ceiling to floor
- Terrazzo floor not bonded to foundation slab
- Loose stairway handrail attached to Sheetrock instead of studding
- A two-inch difference between the high and low spots of the foundation slab
- Plywood roof sheathing that stops short of the apex ridge
- Interior grade plywood for exterior work
- No back steps

Problems like these are enough to drive buyers mad, but the auditors didn't find them beyond the pale. What they got more steamed up about were the "significant deficiencies" they discovered in 11 percent of the new houses, problems which affect the "safety, health and livability" of about 16,000 new houses being paid for by the American taxpayer.

These troubles included:

- Leaking drain pipe causing standing water under the house
- Inoperative electric furnace
- Malfunctioning and overheating gas furnace that made the interior so hot that doorknobs couldn't be touched
- Malfunctioning circuit breakers
- Sagging Sheetrock ceilings
- Cupped hardwood floors
- Six inches of standing water in the crawl space
- Cracked foundation slabs
- Leaking roofs
- Wings settling away from the rest of the house
- Falling porches
- No drainage

The used houses were much worse. The inner city houses had something wrong with them 53 percent of the time. In suburban and rural areas, 34.5 percent of them weren't right. Six percent of the total were so bad that they should not have been insured or sold under any conditions. Many of the houses were just plain slums. Their deficiencies were:

- Rusting electric water heater set directly on bare ground in a hole under the house
- No furnace
- Wall plugs hanging loose
- Short circuits and condemned wiring
- Cracked walls throughout the house
- Falling ceiling tiles
- Rotted floor joists
- Floors with a six-inch pitch
- A house built on a natural spring
- Holes through the walls
- Basements flooded with sewage

- Rotted windowsills and frames
- Rotted walls
- Falling chimneys
- Rotted gutters and downspouts
- Falling exterior bricks
- Buckling porches
- Rotted steps
- Garages toppling over

".. . We believe many unsophisticated buyers of older inner city housing have not been fairly treated," the auditors said dryly. "The values stated on appraisals have been high and the condition of a number of properties at final endorsement have been poor to bad."

The auditors found a great deal more than bad houses. They discovered a corrupt and morally bankrupt FHA. Breaking down FHA procedures into seven areas, they concluded:

Appraisals. Many appraisals were defective because property values were questionably supported and inadequate repair requirements were written up by the federal employees. "We identified related problems of attitude, morale and communication or understanding of departmental objectives or policies."

Supervision. The supervision, review and other administrative control over the activities of appraisers was "generally insufficient."

Crimes. HUD didn't follow up with criminal or administrative actions against obvious violations by real estate firms, builders or mortgage companies.

Complaints. "The handling of mortgagors' complaints about existing housing was generally inadequate." The same for owners of new houses.

Closing costs. HUD let mortgage companies and real estate firms commit fraud in closing costs, often winking at double fees and worse.

Mortgage companies. HUD didn't pay any attention to what was going on.

The auditors reported to Romney and other top HUD and government officials that they found "significant deficiencies" in the performance of appraisals. The apparent violations in houses were ignored and overlooked by appraisers even when they were easily observable. The appraisers, in at least 3,000 projected cases, didn't note problems in houses that were so bad it cost more to repair them than they were worth.

"The physical condition of a number of the houses we inspected was so bad that we could not understand how an appraiser could have ever been inside the house without requiring correction of the obvious defects," the auditors said. What they meant was the appraisers either didn't do their work or were being paid off. The auditors also discovered that the comparable houses which are intended to establish the value of an FHA house frequently weren't comparable or didn't even exist.

A question the auditors struggled with and were defeated by was why the appraisals were so bad. Part of the reason, they theorized, was that the appraisers were overworked. The FHA required them to appraise four houses a day and that may have been too many on which to do a decent job.

But another, more subtle reason was what the auditors called "problems of attitude" and what others may characterize as racism.

The report noted that:

"Some of the appraisers interpreted the abolition of 'redline' area prohibitions [which excluded certain declining inner city areas from eligibility] as 'take anything in the way of property.' Some appraisers interpreted the caution that ruled out requirements for essentially 'cosmetic' repairs as 'make no requirement for repairs/improvements.' Some appraisers appeared to 'pass the buck' by relying, unduly, on repair contractor certifications and the buyer's sophistication and knowledge (*caveat emptor*). *Some appraisers accepted deficient houses with an attitude that 'this is good enough, because it's better than what these people had before.'*" [Italics added.]

Many of the appraisals were inflated and allowed speculators to make "excessive profits." Real estate sales commissions ran as high as 13 percent of the sales price. Points, which the auditors call "mortgage placement fees" went up to 16 percent of the mortgage amount. Speculators bought the houses after the FHA appraisal for a fraction of the appraised value.

"In a few cases, the assigned value appeared to be inflated to the degree that a basic question exists concerning either the competence or the diligence of the staff or fee appraisers involved," the auditors suggested. ". . . We believe the values established by HUD in a number of appraisals have been high and the condition of a number of houses at the time of appraisal was poor to bad."

The HUD auditors were anxious not to offend their bosses by putting too fine a point on things, and sometimes their caution becomes humorous. For example, what the auditors called "imprecise" wording by appraisers for required repairs consisted of replacing one broken refrigerator with another broken one to satisfy an order to "replace refrigerator"; or the installation of ornamental flower-bed fencing instead of a real fence to satisfy a requirement to "install fence at rear of lot."

Substantial fraud was found at the time of sales in the padding and manipulation of closing costs. In one case, a 221-d-2 house valued at $7,500 plus $350 closing costs, or $7,850, was bought for $7,850 plus $756.28 in closing costs. Like swindles were found in "a substantial percentage of similar cases. . . ."

Most of what went wrong with appraisals wouldn't have happened if FHA administrators had followed the rules and checked on their work. But they didn't. In Dallas, for example, no field reviews were made from August 21, 1970, to March 7, 1971, although hundreds of them were called for by HUD regulations. The auditors were also startled to find that HUD doesn't ask for a record of who does what appraisal. And there isn't any way to find out unless a case number is known and checked in the case file which is stored in Washington.

Any apparent irregularity in an FHA transaction is supposed to be referred to HUD's Office of Investigation (OI), but the auditors learned that few, if any, such referrals were made. At the same time, when irregularities were referred to the Justice Department but not prosecuted, HUD didn't take any administrative action against the offender.

As a matter of practice, the Justice Department prosecutes only a few cases of most violations of federal law and bases its decision on which ones to go after on several practical (and political) considerations. The typical determinants are the likelihood of conviction and the deterrent value that a conviction might bring. The U.S. Attorney's office just doesn't have the manpower to go after every criminal who is taking advantage of the public trust. In the case of FHA crimes, the Justice Department up until recently placed a very low priority on what it considered white-collar mischief.

But the auditors found that when the Justice Department didn't decide to take action, HUD didn't take administrative action, either.

Administrative action, however, is a very effective control, because the FHA can simply refuse to do business with somebody it suspects of a wrongdoing. In 200 cases, the auditors disclosed that HUD didn't even refer the complaints to its own Office of Investigation. When auditors' reviews in Washington, Richmond, Virginia, Pittsburgh and Philadelphia disclosed that eighty-five subjects involved in forty-eight insured transactions needed to be investigated, area offices still had not even referred them to the OI after 100 days. Yet the regional director of the OI stated that a high percentage of such cases involved prima facie violations that come under the jurisdiction of the FBI. The question is why area directors don't try to make speculators and mortgage companies answer to crimes they know exist.

"Presently, most of the field offices either: (a) take little or no administrative action against individuals or firms involved in detected irregularities; or (b) persuade the offenders to correct the conditions, without referral to the Office of Investigation; or (c) have the offenders placed on the Undesirable Risk Determination (URD) list, precluding that offender from subsequent participation in HUD's programs," the auditors told Romney.

If the FHA doesn't prosecute or even raise its voice to housing criminals, it also doesn't pay any attention to the justified complaints by homebuyers who have been abused and swindled.

The office of audit said serious complaints were not resolved promptly, "if at all," although such action "is an urgent necessity."

When the FHA did respond to complaints, it frequently did not have the buyer's case file because it was stored in Washington. In those cases, it went to the mortgage company that serviced the account to find out if required repairs had been made. Such certification, which is supposed to be made by the mortgage company prior to closing the procedure, is much like asking the fox if the chickens are in safely to roost.

In some Section 235 houses, the government is required to pay for violations or defects that are deemed to have existed at the time of appraisal. But it appears that if the homeowner is victimized by apparently deliberate acts of concealment, the homeowner can't get help. In other words, the homeowner can have the government repair defects to his house only when he has not been swindled.

The law "appears to exclude defects that were actively and intentionally concealed because such defects might not reasonably be disclosed even through a conscientious appraisal/inspection," the auditors wrote. "We observed a number of houses in which we believed that defects had been actively and intentionally concealed."

Finally, the auditors found that the FHA insured mortgages even when HUD's own appraisers called the houses unfit for human habitation. The FHA insured mortgages even in cases where the entire monthly income of the buyer barely covered the mortgage payment.

The line between criminal negligence and criminal collusion appears to be extremely fine.

At the same time the HUD auditors were digging through the muck in the single-family programs, they were also looking, although much more superficially, through the 236 multi-family program. The results of this twin investigation were presented to Secretary Romney on January 29, 1972. It was cautiously researched and very carefully phrased because HUD really didn't want to tell anybody that the program designed on the surface level to subsidize persons of modest means was more completely planned to subsidize the rich.

Actually, the stated goal of Section 236 does not say anything about the government aiding the poor. HUD itself says that the purpose is to "encourage private enterprise to engage in the development of good rental and cooperative housing for lower-income families."

The assistance program, HUD says, is an aid to help private enterprise build low-cost housing. Once again, HUD and the FHA intend to support the activities of money-lenders and money-makers. The interest supplements, which reduce payments on the apartment's mortgage to what it would cost for principal and interest at a 1 percent interest rate, mostly help the lenders and the builders. As we will see, the government assistance is not passed on to the low-income renter the way one would expect because HUD policies encourage windfall profits and outrageously padded costs.

Persons who live in Section 236 projects are required to pay a rental figured on the basis of principal and interest payments at 1 percent interest mortgage, or 25 percent of their monthly income, whichever is greater.

The mortgages are for forty years, which means that the government interest subsidies for each project come to approximately twice the mortgage cost of each project. That is, a $1 million apartment building will cost the government $2 million, in direct subsidies.

To get builders to build and investors to invest in the Section 236 apartments, the law provides for some impressive incentives. First is the builder's fee, which guarantees general overhead and costs, and the builder's profit, which is defined as whatever builders are making at the time. (Except nobody ever figures that out, and the builders define their own normal profits, which are quite good.) General overhead, which doesn't have to be accounted for, is 2 percent of the total construction costs. If a builder chooses not to make his own profit calculations, HUD allows 10 percent builder-sponsor profit and risk allowance, plus the 2 percent overhead figure.

The Department of Housing and Urban Development does not place any controls on land profits in Section 236 deals. In fact, the department allows HUD appraisals in excess of land purchase costs to be represented as cash investment in the project. If you bought a five-acre farmland site for $5,000 and got the land rezoned for multiple-family dwellings now worth $100,000, HUD would allow you $95,000 credit as an investment into a 236 project.

In addition, the law provides investors accelerated depreciation for income tax purposes and a tax-free reinvestment of gains when the profits go back into other projects. When existing properties are rehabilitated under 236 guidelines, up to $15,000 per dwelling unit may be written off against personal income in a five-year period.

Comments HUD: "For specific information regarding favorable tax treatment, consult a tax advisor or the Internal Revenue Service."

The whole thing is explained by HUD in this way:

"Assume a project with total cost, excluding land and builder-sponsor profit-and-risk allowance, of $1 million. HUD administratively allows a builder-sponsor profit-and-risk allowance (BSPRA) of 10 percent or $100,000. Assuming a land cost of another $100,000, we have a total project cost of $1,200,000. [Note: The land cost actually is the HUD appraisal, although the land actually may have cost only $5,000.] Under HUD regulations the minimum required sponsor's equity is 10 percent of the total project cost or $120,000. In the resulting mortgage it should be noted, however, that the $100,000 allowed for the builder-sponsor profit-and-risk allowance may be counted toward the required 10 percent sponsor's equity in the project, thus resulting in an actual cash outlay by the sponsor of only $20,000 or 2 percent of the project's construction cost.

"A limited distribution sponsor eligible for BSPRA would be limited to 6 percent rate of return on his equity of $120,000."

That is, a $20,000 cash investment gets you equity of $120,000, plus a return of $7,200 a year, plus the tax breaks.

The Department of Housing and Urban Development says that it wants to make the production or rehabilitation of low-income multi-family housing economically attractive. It is perhaps the only one of its objectives in which it has succeeded without qualification.

The HUD auditors investigated 62 projects in twenty-one area insuring offices representing 9,450 living units and compared them with 124 conventionally financed projects.

What they found was a whole lot of stealing going on. They discovered that because of the stealing, windfall profits and cost padding, the FHA 236 projects had a basic rental price that was much higher than private apartments and offered less for the money. They learned that architects and contractors gouged the government, charging up to four times typical fees. They revealed windfall land profits of 65 to 195 percent. Against the law and the intent of the law, the auditors found the apartments located in industrial sites or isolated sites, away from schools, shops, recreation and medical care—locations that were against the law and the intent of the law. Because of these problems, they found that many of the projects were going broke because people refused to live in them. They found a mess.

The most obvious contradiction of what Congress hoped would be a program of real assistance for the renting poor is in what it actually costs to live in one of the 3,800 projects finished or under way in the fall of 1971. In 93 cases out of every 100, private one-bedroom apartments cost less than comparable ones backed by HUD. The same holds true for 84 percent of the two-bedroom and 59 percent of the three-bedroom apartments. The actual dollar differences range from two dollars a month more for a one-bedroom in Atlanta to sixty-four dollars a month more in Seattle. The spread in two-bedroom living units is from one dollar a month less in Tampa to fifty-four dollars a month more in Hartford, Connecticut.

In practice, this means that the subsidy doesn't reach the tenant. If Mr. and Mrs. John Q. Public and their two children are entitled to a $50-a-month supplement in Hartford where a two-bedroom rents for a hypothetical $200 a month, they are paying $4 more out of their own pockets to live in the "subsidized" government-backed building than they would if they moved out and rented a wholly private apartment just like it.

But the private apartment wouldn't be the exact duplicate. It would be better—larger, better built, and in a more attractive neighborhood.

The reason why the Section 236 projects rent for higher prices than private ones is because private real estate developers make more profit by keeping costs down while building well enough to attract high occupancy. In 236 projects, the profits, all along the way, are hidden in higher costs for inferior amenities and construction.

Consider architectural fees. The customary fees for design and supervision on private apartments vary between $75 and $125 per dwelling unit, with $125 being about the highest figure anybody will pay. But in three projects insured by the HUD field office in Dallas, architects' fees averaged $499 per dwelling unit, or $374 more apiece than they charged for private work.

In San Antonio, the conventional architectural fee per unit was also $125, but the government paid or allowed $415. The spread in Hartford was between $145 and $439.

Nationally, HUD architectural fees ran $434, or $209 per unit more than what private money bought. Since for every mortgage dollar HUD will pay back $2 in interest, the national architectural payout per FHA-backed living unit in the 236 program is in excess of $1,000 of which $418 is a pay-off to fraud. When HUD announces another 100,000 apartment units in a 236 project, it has just cost the American taxpayer $41.8 million for phony architectural fees.

The title "housing consultant" has a nice, professional ring to it, and many of the 236 projects sponsored by so-called nonprofit organizations were associated with one. In the public mind, the housing consultant is an expert who is brought in by a socially conscious, nonprofit organization such as a church in order to get low-cost apartments constructed. But HUD personnel told the auditors that it is generally understood that a consultant primarily serves as a project "packager." The consultant decides he wants the fee, which ranges from $15,000 to $27,500 or more, finds a nonprofit sponsor and prepares the application to HUD. He doesn't save the nonprofit sponsor time—in fact, it takes slightly longer to get a 236 application processed with the help of a consultant than without one—and he doesn't save any money. He does make a nice profit, however, for himself.

It sometimes seems that HUD, which constantly complains to Congress about insufficient money to hire enough personnel to administer its programs, has allowed its money to freely flow into private hands. Builders profited on the work they did and made even more money through a device called the incentive allowance.

In theory, the incentive allowance sounds good. It says that if a builder works well enough to come in under cost, he gets paid something for it, as a reward. The Department of Housing and Urban Development always gives these builders an incentive allowance of half of the money saved, although it could give as much less as it wanted to.

What gets goofy here is that HUD regularly overestimates the cost of one of these projects by about 5 percent, with the overestimations appearing in project financing costs and construction costs. The padding is not done accidentally, but deliberately, apparently because HUD bureaucrats would rather pay out money to builders in "incentives" than change mortgage totals after a project is completed.

In Topeka, Kansas, a well-known builder who had a history of completing similar buildings in less than twelve months was allowed fifteen months to build a 236 project. He finished it in eight, and got an incentive payment of $25,153. He didn't get rewarded because construction costs were any less. The savings came in interest, property taxes, mortgage insurance premiums and general insurance—costs that properly should not have been projected in the first place.

If HUD overestimates how much projects will cost to build, it underestimates how much it will cost to run them, or allows project backers to underestimate annual operating expenses so that the projects will look financially feasible. In one defaulted project in Sacramento, California, annual operating expenses were underestimated by about 50 percent. The Department of Housing and Urban Development should have caught the error, but did not, probably because HUD usually does not know how much things cost and doesn't try to find out.

The auditors found across the nation that estimated expenses for taxes, insurance and utilities "bore little resemblance to the actual expenses," and that these amounts were "consistently underestimated."

Underestimation of operating costs is one of the main reasons why projects default.

The easiest money for backers of these projects comes in inflated land evaluation. Regulations by HUD call for 236 project land to be evaluated on the basis of what comparable land is worth. Unlike HUD, conventional mortgage companies evaluate land for mortgage purposes at what the owner paid for it if he acquired the land in the past year. Housing and Urban Development appraisers appear to make up their own prices, based wholly on air. In three typical cases, the auditors found profits of 71 percent, or $61,947 in one month; 195 percent, or $95,600 in three months; and 83 percent, or $139,375 in twelve months. The investigators could find no basis for the higher evaluations, either in land improvements or by comparing the land with equal land. The comparables cited by the appraisers sometimes didn't exist. The auditors found "compelling need to restrict inflated land valuations and preclude large profits." They did not, however, call for criminal investigation of the HUD employees who made the evaluations, or the investors who profited from them.

Along with allowing land profiteering, HUD permitted the apartments to be built in undesirable locations more than one-third of the time. Some of the projects were built on land so dangerous as to be topographically unfit. One site in Atlantic City, New Jersey, was adjacent to a junk yard. Another in San Antonio was next to a rubble-strewn creek, across from which was an auto wrecking yard. A third, in Michigan, was between an unfenced railroad track on one side and an auto wrecking plant on the other. An Indiana project shared large power transmission towers and lines.

About 25 percent of the sites investigated were one to three miles away from any public transportation, shopping areas and other necessary facilities. People who lived in these apartments, who don't have much money to begin with, had to purchase one or more cars just to exist. Lower rents meant higher transportation costs, and any advantage from the government subsidy was cancelled out.

And some tenants of these projects made so little money, they couldn't eat after their rents were paid. A project in Pontiac, Michigan, found persons making $1,872 a year paying $1,285 of that tiny amount for rent.

Renters in the 236 projects frequently suffer from illegal assessments by project managers who are usually associated with or run by the sponsor. These abuses include illegal deposits or overcharges for draperies and rugs, charges for utilities that are supposed to be included in the rent, and rental and cleaning deposits that are never returned when the tenant moves out. They are hotly disliked in suburbs where 236 projects are located, often in extreme concentrations that strain educational, social and police facilities. These residents are almost invariably white.

One ongoing reality of American suburbs is that they are predominantly Caucasian, and a fact of HUD is that the 236 projects are almost all suburban. Those that have been established in cities have been rehabilitation projects, for blacks. Most of these projects, because of the high cost of rehabilitation, union gouging, vandalism and profiteering, have gone broke.

It would be unfair to say that none of the objectives of the 236 program have been met: Hundreds of thousands of single-family and apartment units have been built that are better than mobile homes and, for the time being at least, better than shacks. But when they are paid off, they will average in cost $60,000 to $80,000 each. Many of them have been so badly built, it is doubtful they will last for the life of the mortgages. Because of their concentration and construction, they are the slums of the future, and that future is dawning now.

9

Country Ridge Baltimore
Life in the Swamp

May 4, 1972
Statement of the Hon. Clarence D. Long, Congressman from Maryland, before the House Legal and Monetary Affairs Subcommittee, Cong. John S. Monegan (D-Conn), chairman:

"I appreciate this opportunity to appear before this committee. Your committee has done a great public service in exposing what appears to be the nationwide breakdown in the administration of federal housing programs. I understand that the majority of your investigative activities and testimony has centered on the fraud and maladministration of FHA programs in the inner city.

"Now, as I am sure the committee is aware, the scandal does not stop at the city limits—nor is it confined to existing housing. The same situation—although less extreme—happens in the suburbs and in new housing.

"What I want to present to the committee this morning is a case study of gross negligence on the part of the Baltimore FHA office in reviewing, approving, and administering a new FHA 235 project of 122 homes in Baltimore County, in Essex, Maryland.

"Last summer I started receiving numbers of complaints from the homeowners of the FHA 235 Country Ridge project in the Essex area of Baltimore County. These complaints covered a wide range of problems; unworkable windows, collapsing living room ceilings due to leaking bathroom fixtures, flooding basements, kitchen stove ovens burning children, substandard fire walls, leaking roofs, et cetera.

"Because of the increasing number of complaints about FHA housing projects I had received from constituents throughout my district, I decided to find out what happened at Country Ridge. Although our case study was a Section 235 project, the problems in Baltimore County encompass the full range of FHA programs.

"I first asked the Corps of Engineers to make an independent investigation of the causes of the flooding basements. The corps' report concluded that 'the basement leakage and dampness resulted from the following deficiencies: (a) a poor or marginal site; (b) poor design; (c) poor workmanship.'

"Now, this is a stinging indictment of one federal agency by another. At this point in the record, Mr. Chairman, I would like to include a copy of the Corps of Engineers report."

The Hon. Clarence D. Long, is a small, scholarly man with a deliberate manner who regards American government with a sorrowful mien. There's an air of dignity about him, and people who don't know him usually have a hard time sensing when he's angry. But on May 4, 1972, in the big chamber in the Sam Rayburn Building in Washington, where Cong. John Monegan's Legal and Monetary Affairs Subcommittee was continuing its investigation of the FHA scandal, there was no question about his emotion. Mr. Long was mad. He was, in fact, a great deal angrier than the other witnesses who came that day to testify about the great housing disaster called the FHA, because he seemed to feel that his constituents, his office, Congress, and he personally were all being led down the primrose path by the Baltimore office of HUD.

What he had to offer on May 4 was a chilling little story about the Country Ridge subdivision in Essex, Maryland, which he described as a case study of gross negligence on the part of the Baltimore HUD office. Country Ridge isn't much as FHA scandals go. The subdivision consists of 122 six-room houses worth $16,500 each. It's a subsidized 235 project, and the federal payoff on the mortgages will eventually cost taxpayers approximately $4 million. (By my reckoning, Cong. Long said $2 million.) But one of the problems with Country Ridge is that it was built in a swamp. Another problem is that Country Ridge really isn't itself, because for some incredible and still unexplained reason the Baltimore FHA reviewed and approved the plans for the wrong development. The Country Ridge that the FHA approved and committed federal money to was actually the plan for the Maple Crest development that had been built by the same contractor three years earlier. And the plans and specifications for Maple Ridge did not even conform with the FHA's own minimum property standards.

One might say that Country Ridge was built with mirrors. Of course, Mr. Long didn't know this when he started his investigation. All he knew was that the voters who lived there were flooding his office with complaints about floods of their own—in the basements of their new houses.

Long asked the U.S. Corps of Engineers to take a look into the complaints, and he had one of his staff members named P. Stockton do the same. Corps Col. Louis W. Prentiss, Jr., reported back to him that the basements were flooded, all right, because good ol' Country Ridge was built in a swamp next to a small tributary of the Black River. The permanent ground water level was at, and sometimes above, the level of the basements of the houses.

Worse yet, none of the normal and required precautions for building houses in river water were followed. The protective, watertight covering that is supposed to go under the basement floor wasn't there; the basement gravel foundation wasn't there; the proper drainage system hadn't been put in.

Long started to brood about it all, and decided to investigate some more on his own. He called in an FHA inspection team from Washington and other FHA inspectors from the Baltimore office to look at all 122 homes. The investigators found more than 1,000 defects in the houses; one house alone had 28 problems. Ninety-six percent of the houses had problems that demanded corrective action by the builder. At the same time, Long discovered that the original FHA inspectors who signed inspection forms did not take note of a single defect while the houses were going up.

According to Long, the FHA allegedly inspected each

Country Ridge home three times during construction. He said "allegedly" because the builder's disregard of government requirements simply couldn't have happened if the inspectors had done their job properly. The homeowners had concluded that there was some kind of hanky-panky going on between the FHA employees and the builder, Victor Posner Enterprises.

The owners also thought something was wrong because they could get no action on their complaints from the builder, the project manager owned by the builder, or the Baltimore FHA.

Nor could Long himself get any satisfaction from the FHA. The Baltimore office told Long that it could not tell the builder how to make necessary repairs. Nor did the Baltimore officials have anything to say about misleading advertising for the project that promised a playground for the children of Country Ridge. Perhaps this was due to highway department plans for a freeway to be built directly through the lot that was to have been the playground. Nor, Long said, did the FHA inspectors have any complaints about the stoves that had burned owners and their children numerous times. Long wrote a letter to Sec. George Romney demanding to know what HUD was going to do about all of this. He suggested it was worth Romney's personal time because the annual subsidies totaled more than $100,000.

Among Long's unanswered questions was why the FHA approved the site in the first place, because the Baltimore office knew since 1969 about the marshy condition of the land. On August 11 of that year, an FHA site engineer sent a memo to Allen T. Clapp, then director of the Baltimore office, which pointed out:

"There appear to be two problems at the site: one, the low land adjacent to the marsh will undoubtedly flood during tidal conditions on Deep Creek; and the other, questionable soil conditions for foundations in several areas and whether or not easements should be permitted throughout the entire tract in view of its proximity to marshy land."

The FHA responded by ignoring the engineer's suggestion to disallow building there, and specified construction plans to hold out water. Furthermore, the FHA either didn't make the inspections it had certified were done, or lied about compliance with them. The only beneficiary was the builder.

An investigator in situations like this can draw only three conclusions about the FHA inspectors who did the work. Either they were incompetent to the point of criminal negligence, or the inspections weren't made, or the inspectors were paid off to ignore the violations. Otherwise, why didn't they see that the required four-inch concrete basement floors were sometimes one-half inch thick? Why couldn't they tell that cinder blocks were used for the basement walls instead of concrete blocks as the government required? Why couldn't they figure out that the black tar material for the outside of the basement walls was sprayed on instead of being thickly troweled on as the specifications said?

Long's staff found these failures "extremely strange."

It's worth quoting from Long's conclusion to his study because it describes so well what others have found out about the FHA:

"The best way to describe the FHA's role in this affair is one of negligence and indifference in their actions and attitude toward protecting the consumer—the homeowners of Country Ridge.

"There seems to be a basic attitudinal problem on the part of the FHA office. They appear to be far more interested in receiving the annual 'George Romney Production Award' for meeting or exceeding production goals—sent down from the administration in Washington—than they are in assuring that the homeowners get a well-constructed house. Last year, after the '235 scandal' hit, the FHA defended itself by rationalizing that it viewed itself solely as a mortgage insurer whose interest is in the adequacy of the security for the loan rather than decent, safe and sanitary housing for people.

"Secretary Romney, after many directives, supposedly changed this role, and the FHA was to be consumer-oriented. Despite these directives, little apparent change of attitude has taken place—at least in Baltimore.

"It must be emphasized that the prospective homeowner cannot rely on the mortgage company who finances these homes at prevailing interest rates plus points with FHA insurance on the mortgage. His only protection then is the FHA.

"There are many indications in the Country Ridge affair that seriously question whether the FHA deals at arm's length with developers. There is such emphasis on increasing production put on these FHA area offices by Washington that an unhealthy 'mutuality of interest' develops between the FHA, the developers and the mortgage companies, which blurs the line that should sharply separate their roles and self-interests.

"Under these conditions, the FHA personnel get sloppy and lethargic. They not only fail to protect the interests of the homeowner, but don't even protect the interests of their own agency, let alone the interests of the taxpayers. It must be remembered that the federal government is insuring over $2 million in mortgages on this project alone, and is paying an estimated $100,000 in annual subsidies.

"Once these projects are approved by the FHA, as in the case of Country Ridge, the financial risk is borne not by the builder or the mortgage company, but by the homeowner, the federal government and, of course, the taxpayer. This is becoming all too painfully clear in Detroit, where homes are being turned back to the FHA at the rate of 400 per month [650 in November of 1972] compared to 96 per month last year. The reason, according to the General Accounting Office, is poor and slipshod FHA inspections and appraisals.

"Under these conditions, one would assume that the FHA would be vigorous in protecting the interests of the homeowner and the agency itself. However, this staff report seriously questions the FHA's vigor in protecting the homeowner, the agency and the taxpayers."

About six months after Long wrote to complain to Romney, HUD finally showed him the results of its own investigation into Country Ridge. The verdict was guilty as charged. One of the things HUD found already has been mentioned: The Baltimore FHA reviewed and approved the plans for the wrong development. The HUD investigators revealed that the houses were not built to specifications, that specifications were faulty, inspections inadequate, quality control checks not followed as required, and:

- Ninety-five percent of the windows in the houses were defective
- Seventy percent of the basements had water problems
- Half of the dry walls were improperly finished
- Fifty percent of the houses had cracking kitchen floor tiles because the sub-flooring was improperly laid

- One hardwood floor in five needed repair
- Seven of ten lawns were improperly graded

In this, a classic case of HUD learning what it had botched when it was too late to remedy the problem, the belated self-criticism came six months after the one-year warranties had expired on all but eleven of the houses in the subdivision.

As an ironic "Catch 22" twist for the poor people who bought houses in Country Ridge, the builder may have no legal responsibility to fix the houses because the FHA approved the wrong program with the wrong name.

Finally, the week before Congressman Long testified, the builder and the Baltimore FHA officials held a secret meeting from which the homeowners were barred, the press was refused attendance, and Long was not even invited.

Long pleaded for criminal and administrative action to be taken against the builder and the FHA officials who committed crimes in the Country Ridge subdivision, and for a shake-up to be conducted within the entire FHA.

"The shake-up of the FHA means not just changing its face, but a real turnaround, putting in a new leadership that is consumer-oriented rather than builder-oriented," he said. "It is the most important thing to be done. We need people that we can have some confidence in. These home-owners have no confidence in the leadership of either the regional or the Washington office."

During the past few years there has been a great deal of talk about the "crisis of confidence" that citizens have about their government. The causes are usually attributed to alienation or governmental indifference to real needs. What the Country Ridge experience shows is that the problem is much more serious than that. For 122 young, white homeowners the crisis in confidence has come about because they were defrauded by their participation in an expensive, federally backed program, apparently with the compliance and perhaps the active participation of the very same governmental officials who were supposed to look out for their interests.

There is no way for an apologist to explain to these people that the government is not responsible for building their houses in a swamp. The fact is that the FHA knew about the marshy land and let the builder, who was backed with federal funds, go ahead anyway. There is no excuse for the certification of every one of the houses by FHA officials when, in fact, more than 1,000 defects existed. There can be no explaining away as simple error the FHA's approval of another, inadequate project instead of the equally inadequate but illegally built Country Ridge.

Over the next thirty years, the Country Ridge home-owners will have to pay $2,030,000 for the houses while we, the taxpayers, will be helping them out with an additional $4 million in interest subsidies. The final payoff will total about $6 million for 122 houses sitting—or floating, as the case may be—in the tributary of a river. Given the ground condition, it is doubtful these houses will last as long as thirty years. If they do, the federal government will have to invest additional millions of dollars in them to correct faults that should have been taken care of in the first place.

The example of Country Ridge questions the morality of our government and also questions the sanity of our society. An individual who tries to build his house in a river runs a good chance of being required to have his head examined. A society that pays a builder and mortgage company for building 122 houses in a river is due for mass analysis. The endeavor is so stupid and corrupt that it would not be believed in fiction. But you might as well laugh about it: It's true. And you'll be paying for Country Ridge until 2001.

10

Detroit, Michigan

The Ruined, the Abandoned, and the Dispossessed

If you were paid $5,000 for every word you read in this book you would have some $400 million, about what the FHA has paid for repossessed houses in Detroit alone as a result of the FHA scandal. The chapter title above, for instance, would be worth $45,000, or three houses.

The previous paragraph is worth $250,000—seventeen houses.

As regular as clockwork, through the closing months of 1972 and as far into 1973 as the government can project, dozens of FHA employees in the Detroit district office are processing twenty new foreclosures a day, representing a loss of about $14,000 an hour around the clock.

If you seem to hear a roaring sound, don't worry about it. It's the bulldozers and wrecking cranes going about their busy work of destroying more than 3,000 houses, many of them in sound condition, smashing the walls and pushing way the debris of about ten houses every day.

The crackling sound you hear comes from the fire in the abandoned houses, about 1,000 fires a year in 1970, 1971 and 1972. About half the fires are set by children playing with matches. One in five is set by professional arsonists to collect fire insurance. One fire in ten is lit by tramps and thieves. The rest may simply be an act of God.

The grunting and thumping sound comes from the twenty or thirty families a day who are abandoning their FHA houses to the arsonist, the vandal and the thief. The hammering comes from workmen nailing sheets of plywood over the windows and doors in a fruitless attempt to keep disaster out of the empty house. The whistling sound comes from the wind as it blows through 25,000 empty houses, about 10 percent of the city's housing stock.

Finally, there is the babble of 120,000 refugees who lived in these houses and lost them, and then somehow lost themselves. Where do 120,000 people go? Nobody knows, but they seem to have disappeared. Have they doubled up, or fled to the suburbs or the South? Perhaps they have been devoured by private greed and governmental indifference. Perhaps they have been erased by benign neglect. But they are gone.

A disaster so extensive numbs the imagination because it seems that nothing short of a natural calamity or war could bring so much destruction and so much suffering. But the trouble in Detroit is the government of the United States and the unholy deal it struck with private business to deliver what is called mortgage production.

In this Orwellian bureaucracy, the figures and statistics become more real and more important than the actual houses and the people who bought them. The mortgage companies and real estate speculators were allowed to do as they wanted in their search for profit, if they simply filled out the right forms and went through the proper internal procedures to fulfill FHA requirements. The government didn't protect the citizens of Detroit, and it didn't even protect itself. From 1968, when the crisis began, well into 1971, the Detroit FHA office didn't even have internal legal counsel to make sure the laws were followed, although it underwrote hundreds of millions of dollars in mortgages and worked with the sharpest and some of the least principled businessmen in the country.

The person who is in charge of the Detroit office of HUD, the largest HUD office in the United States, is a giant of a man about the size of a professional football tackle. His name is William Whitbeck. Whitbeck didn't take over the Detroit office until mid-1970, and he is not responsible for the scandal. In fact, all of his efforts have been toward stopping it in some way. He hasn't been very successful, for several reasons. First of all, he had no way of knowing how serious things had become until 1972 when foreclosures rose from 50 a month to 500 to 650. Secondly, as a result of extensive discussions with Whitbeck, I'm convinced that he simply couldn't believe the mess things were in. As he became increasingly aware, he began to shut down the FHA machinery. But that didn't solve anything—it only made conditions worse, because traditionally 90 percent of all mortgages in Detroit were insured by the FHA. There isn't any other way to sell houses in Detroit. Other kinds of mortgages are available in different cities, but not in Detroit. Finally, Whitbeck couldn't stop the disaster in Detroit because he continued to believe that most people were honest and would willingly obey the law, and because he was a lawyer who sincerely believed that people were innocent until they were proven guilty.

When I first went to see Whitbeck early in 1972 I was dumbfounded to hear him say he discounted my accusation that FHA appraisers were corrupt, because nobody had ever been caught in the act of taking a payoff. Nine months later, after he had suspended three of his top officials while their activities were being investigated by the FBI, after he had suspended from further FHA transactions dozens of businessmen and real estate firms, and after he had been roasted time after time by congressional committees, Whitbeck's faith in the virtue of his people and the real estate and banking industries had been shaken considerably. (Forty-six indictments naming ninety-three defendants had been handed down by a federal grand jury sitting in Detroit as of May 15, 1973.)

"Where there's smoke, there's fire," he admitted.

Whitbeck also knew that his career in government had been broken and he had a problem that he couldn't solve. Detroit had been ruined by the FHA.

Perhaps both of us came to that conclusion at the same time. One warm night in late summer of 1972, after long hours of discussing the FHA and Detroit, we got into my car and went to see what we were talking about. For five hours, until the sun rose and we were exhausted with sorrow, we drove up and down the shattered streets, counting deserted houses. The total finally rose into the thousands and we lost count while we traded information about which group of speculators dominated this ruined area and which firm had destroyed that one. That was the night I realized that the city and the FHA both were beyond hope.

One of the houses we may have passed that night was a tiny frame house on Burlingame, built in 1919 for $1,000. In 1960 it was worth $1,500. In 1970 a speculator sold it FHA to a welfare mother with four children for $12,500. There are more than twenty-one things wrong with it, including a basement full of rats.

We may also have driven past the two houses of Cecilia Demankowski, a welfare mother since her daughter was born twenty-two years ago when Mrs. Demankowski was 13. She gets $109 every two weeks from the Aid to Dependent Children (ADC) program. She was sold two houses with FHA mortgages within a nine-day period, one for $11,150 and the other for $9,700. She lived in one house for twenty-four hours and never entered the other one. She made no down payment on either house and never made any mortgage payments. She couldn't, of course, because half of her welfare allowance went to pay rent on the apartment she lived in.

Mrs. Demankowski is what is known in Detroit as a "ghost" buyer. She didn't want to buy the houses and financially she couldn't. But her name and signature were used by speculators to complete two sales so they could cash in.

There may have been thousands of ghost sales in Detroit but nobody will ever know how many because it's nearly impossible to track down the people who once lived in the abandoned houses. It's even more difficult to find them if they didn't exist in the first place—because a ghost buyer is just a signature on a mortgage and a phony job and credit report. The phantom real estate business may be the easiest way to make money in the whole history of crime.

It works like this. The speculator has purchased a house for $3,000 and has had it appraised by the FHA for $12,000. He signs the purchase offer himself and assembles credit and job information, either by forging the documents or by getting them for a real person with the same name as the ghost. The information is forwarded to the mortgage company, which gets FHA underwriting and approves the mortgage. The mortgage company does not investigate the job and credit information: none of the mortgage companies did in Detroit because the FHA never required them to. The FHA never investigated the information either, because it assumed the mortgage companies checked them out as they do for conventional mortgages. But the mortgage firms felt checking was unnecessary because even if the house foreclosed they got paid by the FHA.

So the mortgage for $12,000 is granted, and the speculator is paid $12,000 for the house. His profit is $9,000. The house is deserted, no payments are ever paid, and the mortgage is foreclosed. The abandoned house now belongs to the FHA.

One variation of this technique is one in which the speculator rents out the house after a ghost sale and collects rent from it until the government comes to board it up. But in no case does the government get any of its money back.

A classic case of this kind involves fraud and conflict of interest in a house on Caroline, in Taylor, Michigan, part of the Detroit HUD jurisdiction.

It began with the meeting at church of a devout, quiet woman named Betty Munson and a Bible-records salesman named Jerry Cohen. Miss Munson had injured her leg, and Cohen and his wife went out of their way to befriend her. She grew to like and trust both of them.

In July of 1970, Cohen arranged to buy the small frame house on Caroline by putting $300 down on a purchase agreement. The price was $8,250. The same month, Cohen applied to the Veterans Administration for an appraisal on his prospective property.

The VA assigned a man named James Siemasz to appraise the property, Siemasz, a large, boyishly handsome man who looked like an advertisement for the Rotary Club. was also chairman of the Taylor Planning Commission. He owned, with his father, the successful Van Born Real Estate Company. Both of them worked on a part-time basis for the VA as fee appraisers, getting $37.50 for every appraisal they made. Over the years, James Siemasz had done about 1,800 appraisals for FHA and the VA, worth some $67,500 in fees.

Siemasz appraised the frame house on Caroline, where he met Cohen for the first time, on August 18, 1970. Cohen paid him at least the standard fee of $37.50 for the appraisal. and Siemasz decided that the house was worth $13,400.

The appraisal may have seemed a little high, even to Siemasz, in light of the fact that his father, William J., an FHA appraiser and city assessor for Taylor, had assessed the house for taxation at a state equalized value of $2,425.

Meanwhile, Cohen found out that VA regulations prevented him from selling the house for more than the $8,250 he had offered to buy the house. He wanted to sell it for $13,400, and turned to Siemasz and through him, the FHA, for an answer.

Three weeks after the appraisal was made, Cohen asked the younger Siemasz to be his real estate agent for the house—even though he didn't own it at the time. Siemasz agreed.

On September 9, Cohen appeared in Siemasz's office with Miss Munson and said she wanted to buy the house. Miss Munson said later that she never wanted to buy the house, but that Cohen did. And he had explained to her that because he was self-employed he couldn't get FHA-backed financing on the house. (That is untrue.) He wanted her to sign the papers for him, and she agreed to do it as a favor to a friend.

Miss Munson said that Cohen asked her to supply credit and job information for the FHA so he could finance the house. He promised her he would assume the payments and live in the house once the financing cleared.

So on September 9, Miss Munson signed a purchase agreement to buy the house. James Siemasz signed as both witness and real estate broker.

"Mr. Siemasz was the one who knew about the whole deal," she said. "He said they do that all the time on FHA mortgages. He said he knew they [the Cohens] were going to move in after the mortgage cleared."

The $100 down payment, according to Miss Munson, was paid by Cohen. She didn't notice that the sales agreement listed Cohen's wife, Doris, as the seller of the property.

Shortly thereafter, Siemasz went to the Motor City Mortgage Company to apply for FHA financing of the sale. The FHA sent its own appraiser out to the house, and the man inspected the house carefully.

Hulett Ezell, then a tenant of the house, remembered the FHA appraiser's visit. "The old guy rapped on the walls and said, 'Oh, this house isn't very sturdy',," she said, "He said he didn't think it would get an FHA approval."

He wouldn't give it one. The FHA rejected the application on September 24, saying, "Subject property not in marketable condition to typical purchaser. If reopened, submit itemized list of repairs."

Motor City Mortgage told Siemasz that the application had been rejected. A broker for the firm, Chester Urbanek, said he forwarded to Siemasz a list of repairs cited by the FHA.

"There was a whole page of conditions," Urbanek said. "The house was rejected because of visual appearance and livability."

Siemasz told Cohen about the rejection. Later, Siemasz said, he was asked by Cohen if it wasn't possible to get FHA approval based on the VA appraisal that Siemasz had done.

"I told him if the FHA had rejected it when it first came across their desk, they would probably reject it again," Siemasz said. "He asked me to try it, I said I'd try it."

Siemasz then made arrangements for his appraisal to be forwarded to the FHA. In cases where VA appraisals are transferred to the FHA, approval is virtually automatic. The FHA approved the new application with an appraised value of the house for $13,400.

With his profit now assured, Cohen bought the house for $8,250 on December 5.

Nine days later he resold it FHA to Betty Munson, for $13,400. The FHA officially insured the morgage on January 21, 1971.

Cohen took his $5,000 profit and left for California.

Siemasz said he got a $480 commission.

Betty Munson got a house she never wanted and never lived in, although she did struggle to make the $131-a-month payments on it. The abandoned house was condemned by the city and boarded up. When Whitbeck learned of the case in 1972, he allowed Miss Munson to foreclose it, and the government paid off the mortgage company. Later on, the Cohens sent a card to Betty Munson from California, saying, "The Lord is good. A stronghold in the day of trouble; and He knows them that trust in Him."

Neither Siemasz nor Cohen have been charged with any crimes. It is unknown if the FBI is investigating the case.

In another case investigated by HUD, a man known as Jerome Ford was named on an application for an FHA home he never tried to buy.

"I never talked to any real estate company. I just stayed at my present address," he said. "I have never gone looking at a house or apartment. Why do I want something new when I already have a house?"

Edward Schwarz, executive vice-president of Citizens Mortgage Corporation, said Ford's name, mortgage application, alleged signature and credit report, which correctly stated he worked for the House of Seat Covers, was sent to Citizens by Beneficial Real Estate Company. There have been suits against Beneficial's owner, William J. Hahn, and he has since been suspended by the government from FHA transactions.

The mortgage application, dated February 11, 1972, was signed by Hahn, and the Wayne County Tract Index showed Beneficial as the owner of the property from November 16, 1971.

Whitbeck's investigation of the case disclosed that various records, including those in his offices, showed ownership of the property to be in at least three different hands.

"This is mind-boggling," remarked Whitbeck.

The disclosure came after HUD had rejected the "Ford" mortgage application because of fraud in an accompanying employment verification letter. As a result, the Detroit office asked HUD to suspend Citizens from all further dealings with the FHA.

Schwarz, who admitted the job letter was phony, said he was shocked to discover that the entire application appeared to be fraudulent.

"I thought they had stopped that kind of thing now that the heat's on," he said. "We're subject to the integrity of others."

The Department of Housing and Urban Development eventually suspended Citizens from FHA transactions for thirty days. The action was noteworthy because Citizens is one of the largest mortgage companies in the Midwest, and because it is also a subsidiary of the billion-dollar U.S. Industries.

The suspension letter to the firm from George O. Hipps, Jr., director of the FHA's Single Family and Land Development Division, said: "Our discussions clearly indicated your awareness of the negligence on the part of your company in submitting applications [for mortgage insurance] to our Detroit area office. It is also apparent that you were violating our processing procedures regarding the handling of verifications of employment and deposit.

"Your violation of our procedural requirements has left me with no alternative but to suspend the approval of [your] corporation for a period of thirty days from the date of this letter."

U.S. Industries executives would make no comment. But Schwarz said that the "whole world" of mortgage companies and banks in Detroit have "deviated from standard procedures" in FHA transactions because "we let builders and realtors order credit and employment reports.

"I feel they [HUD] have known of these practices for some time," Schwarz said. "This didn't start yesterday. They're now pointing out that industry is in the soup with them and we're the guys who are in the fishnet.

Citizens Mortgage wasn't the first mortgage company to get into trouble in Detroit, and it won't be the last. More than a year earlier, in February of 1971, another kind of mortgage company misbehavior was revealed by the housing expert of the *Detroit News*, Don Ball.

The disclosure involved false statements submitted to the FHA by a mortgage company about the completion of required repairs. As a matter of policy, the FHA appraiser indicates what repairs must be done on a property to qualify for FHA underwriting. It is up to the mortgage company, however, to make sure that the repairs are done.

The house in question was purchased by Mr. and Mrs. Rogers W. Anderson of East Canfield, for $11,150 on July 17, 1970. Anderson is a disabled veteran. The house was sold to them by Quaker Management Co. Quaker's owner, David Cohen, had purchased the house earlier in the year for $2,200. Two days before Cohen bought the house, the city of Detroit had ordered it to be demolished because it was in such bad shape. Cohen knew about various problems with the house, and he signed an agreement with the Andersons to fix things such as the heating system, the plumbing, and substantial structural flaws. Three inspections of the house were also required by the Detroit Department of Buildings and Safety Engineering. The inspections and the repairs were required by law before the mortgage company got FHA insurance on the property.

In fact, the Auer Mortgage Company sent FHA a signed

certificate stating that the inspections and repairs had been completed. But only one inspection had been made, and most of the repairs were not made.

When the fraud was uncovered, the mortgage company's defense was that it had no control over the activities of its employees. "We employ three competent inspectors to check such homes and report to us on the completion of required repairs and inspections," said a vice-president of the mortgage firm. "One of our inspectors is a former FHA staff appraiser and reviewer, and another is a former contract broker for the FHA. The third also has had contacts with the FHA in the past. We pay these people ten dollars per inspection and trust their judgment. We can't be held responsible if they submitted false reports."

But to the weary investigator, it sometimes seems that the only kinds of reports submitted by FHA employees and former employees who are doing FHA business are false ones.

One of the most colorful real estate investors in Detroit is Samuel T. Antonelli, a young, gun-toting former fee appraiser who hoped to make a fortune as an FHA speculator. He was indicted in March of 1972 on nine counts of arson and was convicted later in the year of the arson of the house he owned.

According to the Wayne County Prosecutor, William Cahalan, Antonelli was charged with arranging the arson of three properties he owned in Detroit to collect the insurance on them. Antonelli was fired by the FHA from his fee appraising work because he was suspected of conflict of interest.

Antonelli worked his way through law school with the FHA fees and told me that he realized then that the big money came from buying houses cheap, getting a high FHA appraisal on them, and selling them to poor people.

Antonelli carried around a gun in a shoulder holster and liked to let his suit coat hang open to show it. He said he never got as rich as he wanted to, despite selling dozens of FHA-insured houses, because the big profits were made by the mortgage companies who charged 24 percent interest a year.

On January 31, 1972, he was suspended from all HUD transactions, and on February 19, a U.S. grand jury looking into FHA crimes in Detroit returned three fraud indictments against his firm and against one of his salesmen.

But the arson indictments offended him the most, and he complained to me that he was afraid they would affect his plans to become a juvenile court judge. He was also offended that indictments were returned against him when he thought the larger speculators in town were more deserving of criminal prosecution. That was one thing Sammy and I always agreed on.

The big speculators in Detroit haven't escaped scot-free, however. Early in 1972, the government rocked the multi-million-dollar empire of Detroit's largest real estate speculator, Gerald A. Waechter, and suspended him, his father, his wife, his brother-in-law and his real estate firms.

At the time, Waechter owned an estimated $500,000 worth of houses he planned to sell to poor people under the Section 221-d-2 and 235 programs. The suspensions were made for violations which, according to the government, allegedly included:

- Concealing the identities of homebuyers who had previously defaulted on another mortgage
- Listing the names of fake buyers in cases where real estate companies collected rent payments and made no mortgage payments
- Taking money deposits higher than the proper amount
- Lying about the source of the down payment

At the same time, the government also suspended and black-listed Patrick J. Meehan and his Meehan Properties, believed to be the second largest group of speculators in town. Meehan operated and advertised under the friendly title of "The Irishman." From 1969 to 1971, The Irishman bought an estimated 1,200 old houses in Detroit and sold at least 1,000 of them at inflated prices through the FHA programs. He still owned 200 of them when HUD suspended him on charges of falsifying documents to get FHA insurance. Later in the year, the state revoked Meehan's real estate broker's license on other charges.

But dozens of other firms and speculators continue to do business with the FHA, and a number of them are guilty of crimes ranging from fraud to conspiracy. The government says it doesn't have enough men to investigate all the charges, and that's probably true.

The most interesting speculator in Detroit is Jacques

Mayer Grunbaum, alias Jack Green alias Jack Meyer, who was arrested by the federal government on Novermber 26, 1972, on a charge involving an FHA fraud.

Green's operations in Detroit had a dimension that others didn't, because he is a naturalized citizen of Canada who lived and did business in Detroit for many years as an unregistered alien. Shortly before he was arrested, business associates and enemies reported to the Justice Department and IRS that Green was selling out his property and preparing to move to Israel. For some reason, perhaps because he is said to be personally charming, Green appeared to have more personal enemies than other Detroit speculators. These enemies called me about Green at least once daily for six months to inform me about his business transactions and even his private activities. All the information I ever received about Green was turned over to federal authorities, and it became a fascinating suspense story to see if government investigators would have a case against Green before he left Detroit.

Green's greatest skill lay in mustering HUD approval for sales of his homes under the 235 subsidized mortgage program, which most other speculators found impossible to obtain. He first got into trouble for advertising in Detroit's black weekly newspaper for welfare mothers to buy FHA homes. They were told that various churches would make the down payments for them on houses sold by Green, although it was actually Green who (illegally) made the down payments. The newpaper and Green's firm were swamped with applicants, and a former employee of his told me that they sold houses as fast as they could write.

Of course, most of those houses have since been foreclosed and abandoned.

The FHA suspended Green for violating the down payment regulations, but Green continued to sell houses with FHA mortgages by persuading certain mortgage companies to process the applications through HUD.

He also got wonderfully high appraisals from FHA employees on his properties. In one case, Green purchased a dilapidated eight-unit apartment building on Joy Road in northwest Detroit for $12,000, and divided it into two four-unit flats. The division was necessary because the low-income single-family program only applied to properties with no more than five units. An FHA appraiser placed a $15,500 value on each of the two parts and required no repairs. Green's profit was about $19,000.

In another case, he bought a three-unit property for $5,800 and sold the units separately with FHA mortgages for $8,500 each. His profit was nearly $20,000. In each of these cases, the owners have since defaulted and the government has had to pay off the mortgages.

The federal magistrate before whom Green appeared held him to a $50,000 bond which Green later skipped out on. The real identity of Green is uncertain. For although U.S. records show him born in Pforzheim, Germany, he claims French nationality, is a naturalized Canadian who lives in the United States without having registered as a resident alien, and tells his friends that he is from Alsace-Lorraine.

Compounding Whitbeck's troubles in cleaning things up in Detroit is the fact that the bad guys aren't emotionally confused or mentally retarded street thugs, but are instead well-educated, wealthy and ambitious persons who know as much as or more about the federal housing programs than the government bureaucracy does. And Whitbeck's office can't keep track of what's going on either, because its personnel are truly inferior, or because they don't want to.

A big part of the FHA's efforts in Detroit lately have been toward disposing of its inventory. Romney boasts that the FHA doesn't abandon any houses—it destroys them or fixes and resells them, although it can be questioned whether or not leveling a house with a bulldozer constitutes abandonment. In any case, Whitbeck's deputy director, John Kane, the most obstructive, nonresponding, and bad-tempered government official I have ever met, came up with a disposal plan in the fall of 1971.

Under Kane's program, HUD would sell repossessed houses at minimum prices to qualified non-profit corporations in the housing field. The corporations would rehabilitate and sell the houses at the lowest prices possible to low- and middle-income familes. These would be sold with FHA mortgages that provided for only $200 down and subsidized interest payments. One extraordinary result of this program was that the FHA would pay off a mortgage for $15,000, resell the property for a "nonprofit" corporation for $100, which in turn would do minimum repairs and sell it once more with a subsidized FHA mortgage for

$15,000 to an owner who would abandon it, costing the FHA $15,000 more.

In the most notorious of these instances, an organization called Slocum Mission, Incorporated, which allegedly existed to provide financial assistance to the Slocum Mission and Orphanage in Monrovia, Liberia, in West Africa, purchased eleven of the repossessed houses for $29,795. They cost the FHA $182,000. Slocum resold them for $208,000.

Neither the Slocum Mission in Liberia nor the couple who set up the nonprofit group can be located, although they are sought by investigators and by the construction companies who worked on the houses and who still have not been paid for the more than $25,000 worth of work they did.

Kane allowed the nonprofit groups to choose the houses they wanted to rehabilitate under the weird program, and the Slocum Mission group selected some of the finest houses in HUD's inventory, in northwest Detroit's best neighborhoods. One house on Mendota, which Slocum sold for $19,150, was given to them free. Another on Monica later sold for $17,500, was given to Slocum for $1,350. Another which HUD sold to Slocum for $217.48, was in turn sold by Slocum for $16,900.

Although the houses were to be marketed by Slocum for minimum prices, the FHA appraisers set values on them about 25 percent higher than what equal houses on the same blocks sold for. Although the HUD program required Slocum to submit a list of rehabilitation specifications for each house and a cost estimate, the firm didn't. The eleven houses, under HUD's guidelines, should have sold for a total of $112,000—but actually sold for $208,000.

Kane set up the program and presumably monitored it, so an investigator must assume he knew what was going on. If he didn't, an investigator must question his competence. But Kane was transferred from Detroit to head the Milwaukee HUD office as a "reward" for this extraordinary program, which will cost the American taxpayer an additional $500,000 in interest subsidies on the eleven houses, and which apparently allowed the Slocum masterminds to profit by $182,000. He was transferred back to Detroit and given the director's job in the spring of 1973 when Whitbeck finally called it quits and took a job with the state of Michigan.

Despite widespread abuses in Detroit, the local office took no action against its employees, except for the dismissal of all fee appraisers, until November, 1972. At that time, three men were suspended while the FBI looked into their activities. Housing and Urban Development has never said who the three were, but my sources inside the office told me that all three were high-ranking officials in the property management division.

At the same time the three were suspended, Whitbeck barred more than a dozen contractors who were paid by the FHA to repair its repossessed houses, and he fired three property managers, real estate firms which the FHA had hired to watch over as much as 25 percent of its burgeoning inventory. The property managers and contractors had been responsible for an estimated $3 million in contracted repairs, and Whitbeck's drastic action indicated that something—fraud perhaps—was dramatically wrong.

Among other problems, there were signs that contracts for rehabilitation work were inflated by as high as 300 percent, that the work done was of poor quality, and that sometimes work paid for by the government was never completed—or even started.

Up until the suspensions occurred, the Detroit FHA office allowed the property managers to solicit bids for repairs and then forward them to HUD to award the contract to the low bidder. This procedure allowed property managers to work sweetheart deals with contractors in a round robin in which three contractors submitted inflated bids, one of which was slightly lower than the others. The "low" bid would get the repair contract. The property manager got a kickback.

If, for example, a house needed $2,000 in repairs to bring it up to code for FHA resale, two of the bids submitted would run about $7,000 and the third would come in at $5,000. Sometimes repair contracts were let on houses that were subsequently torn down. Whether or not any work was ever done on them is open to question.

I had suspected something was seriously wrong in the property management division since early in 1972, when I walked into its offices and started questioning clerks and leafing through bid files. The department manager caught me at my snooping and hysterically chewed me out, flatly forbidding me to look at anything unless he was lurking at my elbow.

There are three major reasons for the disaster in Detroit, all interrelated: fraud, collusion, and corruption; incompetent and criminally negligent administration; and capital manipulation.

The first of these evils has been sufficiently documented to make the point, but the corruption couldn't have grown to such an extent if the FHA office in Detroit had been correctly managed.

To begin with, the HUD area office in Detroit was inadequately staffed in its appraisal, inspection and property disposal sections. Nationally, HUD tried to handle a 66 percent increase in FHA applications with only nine percent more help. As Nixon was reinaugurated, HUD, because of administration orders, was reducing its central office staff and cutting back 5 percent of all employees. The situation was much more acute in Detroit, which handled more FHA applications than any other district office in the country.

To compound its difficulties FHA, which had been an independent agency, was formerly merged into HUD in September, 1971. The result was chaos. The already disorganized agency was further disrupted by a series of organizational changes that brought in unskilled and ignorant bureaucrats to handle the complexities of federally backed housing programs.

Two changes in philosophy accompanied the confusion. The first of them was a change in the FHA's traditional posture toward insuring mortgages; instead of insisting that the properties have "economic viability," the department began operating under the idea of "acceptable risk." Acceptable risk was never defined, and in practice it meant that everything goes.

The second change, one introduced by the Nixon Administration, was of decentralization. The theory behind it that district offices are closer to their own needs and problems and can pay better attention to them than Washington can. But in practice it turned out that the central administration had no way of knowing how bad conditions were until it was too late.

Milton Semer, now a Washington attorney who was chief counsel for the FHA under President Johnson, has firsthand knowledge of what this meant. Semer said his most important job was to read and investigate compliance reports from district offices. Compliance reports are internal HUD investigations of problems and complaints. They gave Semer and the central office an early warning system and allowed him to dispatch experts to district offices whenever it seemed that something serious was going wrong. The forwarding of compliance reports to Washington was one of the procedures that was halted under the decentralization program. An important safeguard had been administrated out.

The Detroit HUD office failed to make field reviews of the minimum of 10 percent of all appraisals in speculator-dominated areas, although the reviews were required by FHA's own regulations. When field reviews were performed, which was in less than one case out of a hundred, they were superficial and inadequate.

Despite the fact that HUD knew thousands of houses in the inner city were substandard and fifty or sixty years old, it went ahead and insured them anyway, for reasons that nobody has ever been able to figure out, and contrary to warnings that it was headed for trouble by doing this.

To make matters worse, FHA got no support from other government agencies. By the end of 1972, despite widespread knowledge of crimes and abuses, suspensions and indictments, the Michigan Department of Licensing and Regulations had not suspended or revoked the license of any real estate salesman or broker in connection with the FHA scandal. Of course, the licenses of many speculators couldn't be revoked because they were unlicensed to begin with. Licensing is not required for people to buy and sell houses on their own account.

Neither the Wayne County prosecutor nor the Justice Department moved to investigate violations of the law until 1972, when it was too late to save the program. The Justice Department, in fact, described FHA corruption as "white-collar crime," with a very low priority. Mysteriously, the county prosecutor never moved against speculators at all.

The third major reason for the Detroit scandal was the manipulation of capital. Basically, none of the problems in the city ever could have developed without the active participation and profitable involvement of mortgage capital sources—the mortgage companies and, behind them, the banks, insurance companies and pension funds that provide most of this money.

In most cases, the speculators didn't have enough capital

of their own to carry out the widespread buying and selling that the scandal was built on. Although initial purchase prices of houses from private owners were low, the speculators still had to borrow the money from mortgage bankers. Then, to buy more houses, more money had to be borrowed.

These loans soon generated strong inflationary pressures, because the average short-term interest rates were 2 percent a month, and sometimes higher. A speculator with all of his own money tied up in property and a $100,000 outstanding loan was forced to cough up $2,000 a month in interest alone; the alternative was to lose the investment. The heat of high interest payments was the main reason speculators developed the practice of "flipping" properties to each other for immediate profits often from $150 to $1,500 on a house. Every time a property was "flipped," the price finally paid by the purchaser went up.

The mortgage bankers had speculators in another kind of bind at the time of sale because of the standard FHA mortgage discount practice of "points." Although government regulations limit the amount of interest to be paid by an FHA homebuyer, points are the mortgage banker's way around the rule with the government's acquiescence. One point equals about one-eighth of 1 percent interest between the FHA limit and the going rate for interest. At the time of sale, when the FHA seller completes the deal with a buyer, a point is worth 1 percent of the sales price.

Between 1969 and 1972, the FHA interest limit was 7 percent, plus one-half of 1 percent to pay for the FHA insurance. At the same time, regular mortgage money was getting 9 percent interest or higher. So the 2 percent difference worked out to sixteen points, to be paid by the seller to the mortgage company. A speculator who sold a house FHA for $10,000 in this example would have to pay sixteen points, or $1,600 to the mortgage company. On the other end of the transaction, the buyer owed the mortgage company $10,000 at 7 percent interest. Assuming the owner paid off the mortgage over thirty years, the $1,600 received by the mortgage company at the time of sale would have justified its receiving only 7 percent interest instead of 9 percent—by the arguments of the mortgage companies.

But in actual fact, the low-income FHA mortgages in Detroit and other cities didn't last thirty years—they often didn't last a year. When a buyer was foreclosed in the first year, the FHA paid the holder of the mortgage 100 percent of the money owed, plus 7 percent interest on that loan.

Now we see that the mortgage company's yield to maturity, the amount that it actually got for making the loan, was 23 percent, or $2,300 on the $10,000 loan. It got sixteen points, $1,600 at time of sale, plus 7 percent of $10,000, or $2,300.

It was to the financial advantage of the mortgage lenders to make the loans and then allow, if not actively encourage, buyers to default. Although some of this windfall went to the secondary mortgagee whose role will be discussed, the mortgage bankers prospered as FHA was gutted and the cities ruined.

Because FHA insurance protects the mortgage lender in the case of foreclosure, the mortgage companies abdicated their traditional role and responsibility for screening potential homebuyers and ensuring that the property was structurally sound and valued fairly.

When an individual buys a house with a conventional mortgage, the moneylender very carefully investigates his income, savings, job and credit, and thoroughly examines the house to make sure that it is sound and priced at a fair market value. Otherwise, the mortgage company could lose money if the owner loses his property. This procedure was stopped for the low-income FHA mortgages because it didn't make any difference to the banker what the house was worth, or if the owner stopped payments. In fact, it was to his benefit if the house did foreclose.

This critically important point was not realized by HUD until 1972. But even then, neither HUD nor FNMA took any steps to bar imprudent mortgage lenders from doing business until congressional investigators caught some of them red-handed.

Needless to say, the low-income FHA business was so profitable that some mortgage companies established speculators in business. As Bob Lindsay said, "They had PR men running up and down Mack Avenue," looking for people to lend money to.

There is a third way in which mortgage lenders waxed rich from the FHA disaster. It came from the first part of the equation, when the speculator bought the house from its original owner. Most likely the house had been mortgaged, and at a much lower interest rate than was paid after 1968. The mortgage company money which the speculator used to pay the first owner came back to the original lender, thus freeing the banker's capital for new, profitable uses. One of these uses was to lend money to speculators at 24 percent interest a year and to finance the FHA transactions. An alternative use was to make mortgage loans in the suburbs where the former owner went to buy a new house at a much higher price and much higher interest. In other words, the mortgage companies—and the banks behind them, and the insurance companies and pension funds behind them—were behind the first sale to the speculator, and behind the sale of the first owner's house in the suburbs, and behind the FHA sale and foreclosure.

It becomes apparent that the lamentations of speculators who have been indicted that *they* are not the big crooks, but that the mortgage bankers are based on fact. The mortgage bankers made more money than any other party in the shuffle without having taken any risk, because they were backed 100 percent by FHA. The FHA actually insured the mortgage interests' profitable destruction of the inner cities.

When I came to Detroit early in 1971, I intended to stay only a short time, perhaps only months. I stayed well into 1973, because the destruction of a city of 1,500,000 mesmerized me. I couldn't take my eyes off the strange sight of the federal government ruining houses, blocks and neighborhoods.

Now in Detroit's inner city, one-third of the people who want to work are unemployed, and at least one-half of the houses are destroyed. I imagine that a child growing up in these neighborhoods has the impression of being a survivor of a particularly cruel and senseless war. The people are not only poor, but they have no place to live.

If I were a child living on Detroit's Lower East Side, my impression would be that the government comes in the night to turn people out of their houses and to board the houses up, so that nobody but criminals and addicts can use them. From listening to my parents, I would believe that the government works with real estate men to put you into "trick bags," promise you something, and then throw you out in the cold and bulldoze it down so you can't get it.

If I were an angry child I would think of the rich Mr.

Banker roasting in his fine fourteen-room mansion in Grosse Pointe or Birmingham after an arsonist torched it the way the arsonist torched houses where I grew up. I might be tempted to act out my fantasies and torch the city myself, the way my older brothers did in 1967 when forty-three died in uncontrolled riots. Or I might be tempted to cover all my hostilities under the comforting, cool blanket of heroin.

In any case, I would hate property, because property is what my family didn't get, and what the white man destroys in my neighborhood. I wouldn't know that Secretary Romney and other high officials attribute the growing blight to my acts of vandalism and my theft of marketable goods from the ruins, and I wouldn't understand if I heard them talk about it. It wouldn't make sense to me because I would know that for every house the ignorant black people tore down, the government itself tore down ten.

But what will finally astound me is the day the same government that ruined my neighborhood writes off and tears down all the houses that are left and backs the real estate men and mortgage bankers in their new city project on the cleared land. I would be delighted if I could live there, of course, but there will be no chance of that. The clean, sturdy, roomy units will be for the middle and upper classes who have always appreciated the convenience of living close in. The houses and apartments won't be for me. I'm too poor. Too ignorant, they say, too careless with property, too angry to behave properly in school.

I have been told by housing and financial experts in Detroit that the write-offs and new construction are already in the works.

"What the FHA scandal actually is," they tell me, "is the most expensive urban renewal project ever attempted. It seems like an ass-backwards way of going about it, but it works. There's no doubt about that."

The idea that the disaster in Detroit may have been deliberate is one that haunts me. I know some men who build new cities, and they are among the most intelligent men I have ever met.

The Detroit mortgage bankers say they knew the disaster was coming as soon as the 1968 Housing Act was passed, because of HUD's administrative laxness. If they saw that, they could also have seen it all as a vast urban renewal plan, beastly expensive, but so complicated and overwhelming that nobody could protest until it was too late.

But I can't believe it's possible, can I? My alternative is to believe that nobody could have stopped the scandal in Detroit—that nobody in power knew about it—until it was too late to do anything about it.

But I can't believe that, either.

11

William Whitbeck

Bill Whitbeck was the director of the Detroit area office of HUD-FHA, the largest such office in the United States and an office where foreclosures and loss have reached astronomical levels. Approximately one house in every ten in Detroit either belongs to HUD, or soon will. The loss in Detroit has been estimated at $100 to $500 million, and the half-billion-dollar figure is closer to being accurate. Here is his story, as told to me in a series of interviews in spring, 1972.

I contended for a period of time that the housing and FHA problem in Detroit was merely a larger version of the same problem that HUD had elsewhere, that it was the St. Louis problem, the Philadelphia problem, the New York problem, but just more houses. I don't think this anymore. I think Detroit is the worst situation the FHA faces, and that housing is the worst problem Detroit faces.

Most of the people who live in the city are closely tied to the automobile industry. Consequently, as the automobile industry fluctuates, so do their incomes. This directly relates to what they are able to spend for housing. But there's an anomaly here which I can't understand: why the automobile industry is booming, yet unemployment remains high, particularly in the areas where we have our worst problems—the inner city and the middle city. I have never seen an economic analysis of this condition, but it's one factor in Detroit that I don't think is present to such a degree anywhere else in the country.

A second factor unique to Detroit as a large city is the city's housing characteristics. There are just more single family homes in Detroit than there are proportionally in any other city in the United States. There are 300,000 of them, Chicago, Philadelphia, St. Louis, and New York all developed as apartment cities. Detroit developed as a single-family city and it remains that way.

We're getting these single family houses back. Almost all of the 650 houses a month coming back are 221-d-2s, 321-d-3s, which are special risk d-2s, and a very, very few 235s. But that doesn't mean that the 235 program is less subject to default.

A person can default for a lot of reasons. He can default because he has lost a job or income; he can default because of sickness, marital problems, or because the house was a bad house when it was insured. But he's much less likely to default if he's paying $90 a month rather than $140 a month. It doesn't mean that the 235 program is structurally any better than the 221-d-2, it just means that it's economically better for the buyer.

There have been numerous instances of outright fraud regarding false credit reports and false employment letters, again a situation entirely unique to Detroit as I understand it. The automobile companies took the position that they would not provide the employment data to anyone but their employees, so this whole system of employment letters blew up, contrary to our regulations that employment verification should not pass through the hands of anyone but the employer, the lender, and the FHA. It was not to go through the hands of a third party, most particularly the buyer. But the system grew up whereby these things were routinely given to the third party. I heard of instances and saw a couple myself where the broker had letterheads of Chrysler, GM and Ford in his office, and he would just type an employment letter himself.

Blame for the fraud can be spread pretty broadly. First

of all there was the speculator, the guy who bought and sold houses for the little people. He was unregulated, not even required to have a broker's license since he was buying and selling on his own account. There was a middleman, a mortgage broker; he packaged loans either directly for the lending institutions or directly for the seller, the speculator. Also involved were the lending institutions and the mortgage companies. The fault was shared equally by the end-lenders, the big life insurance companies who buy loans, Fannie Mae [FNMA] and HUD.

It is difficult to say how much corruption there is inside HUD. There's a remarkable difference between the constant allegations of employee misconduct, fraud and bribery, and being able to prove them. When an allegation is made, I try to nail it down to specifics to get someone to name names, to name ties, to name instances that could be turned over to the FBI and to the U.S. Attorney. I have been absolutely unsuccessful in respect to actually pinning down within my own agency any such specifics. No one in this office has been indicted. [A few weeks later, four of Whitbeck's employees, including the chief of the property appraisal department, were indicted on bribery charges by a U.S. grand jury sitting in Detroit to hear evidence on the FHA scandal.]

We plotted default patterns for the whole single-family operation, to see if there was any pattern between given appraisers, lenders, speculators. We were able to ascertain statistically that the pattern just wasn't there. You couldn't say that X appraiser consistently handled the appraisals for Y mortgage company or Z speculator. That pattern was not there.

But that doesn't mean that—and this is contrary to all my legal training—that where there's that much smoke there's not a little fire. It doesn't mean that the employee has a criminal nature, however. Perhaps it was negligence. Just plain sheer negligence existed and perhaps still continues to exist. Now that is almost as tough to deal with as criminal behavior is. I'm presently going through the painful process of attempting to remove some of the causes of negligence. The procedures are intricate, to say the least. They are heavily weighted with rules, regulations and an overlay of court decisions which stand in favor of the employee. Only time will tell if we're going to be successful in terms of winning those cases in front of the Civil Service Commission.

In places like Philadelphia, allegations of criminal activity went right up to the director. It seems to me that if I were in the full-time investigating business for the federal government and I were seeking out corruption, I would look at any situation where the government interfaces directly with private industry. I think you don't find too many instances in federal government where that occurs routinely. But where you do find it, the defense industry for instance, you find these huge cost overruns because they interface directly.

OK, HUD does the same thing: we interface directly with the real estate industry. I don't think that the real estate industry is more or less corrupt than the legal profession or the newspaper profession; it's about the same. But there is a lot of money involved. I think that the real estate industry has been a kind of modified capitalism at its best. A situation where a lot of money could be made fast, decisions had to be made, money changed hands quickly, profits were there. The entrepreneur who was successful, daring and perhaps even a little unscrupulous tended to do pretty well. When you get a federal agency in a situation where it's interfacing directly with that kind of industry, I think fraud and corruption are inevitable. That is a very bleak estimate of human nature, but it's true.

Back in the 1930s, I think that some genius made a fundamentally wrong decision about the FHA when he first decided it would be self-supporting. As a matter of fact, it was going to be an agency that was going to make money, it was going to be a successful insurance company. Then they made a later decision that administrative costs, particularly salaries, would be low. So they set up a thoroughly decentralized structure of FHA insurance around the country. They kept those grade levels for employees very low.

So what do you do when you pay people at the GS 9 and 11 [Civil Service] levels to make very big decisions, decisions which involve millions of dollars? They had made a very brutal decision that they would not hire extraordinary or even moderately qualified people. So what do you do? You write yourself a cookbook that does two things. It tells anybody of average or below average intelligence exactly how to do it. This is step one, this is step two, and this is step four million and three.

And the second thing that you do is break down the decision process so that each person does different things, like on an assembly line. One guy turns the screw, one mortgage credit examiner reviews a certain part of a case and that's all he reviews. It's all done according to the cookbook. It's nine feet long, and it's called the FHA manual. It may have been fine in the thirties and forties, but when you get into a multi-billion-dollar insurance program that interfaces with private industry, with low salaried employees of moderate competence, you've got a situation that is almost guaranteed to go haywire. I mean it's almost bound to happen because the cookbook doesn't work and the cookbook won't work in the inner city of Detroit.

It won't work with an unscrupulous speculator because it's premised on good faith and it's premised on carrying out the instructions. It just isn't going to work. My predecessor sat in Detroit running the largest insurance program in the city and in the state without the benefit of full-time legal counsel, making multi-million-dollar real estate decisions every day. It passes comprehension how that could have happened. He did not have a lawyer and he was dealing with the very best law firms in Detroit, the highest powered individuals in the real estate industry. They were coming in that door one after another, and he didn't even have a lawyer. It's like having a high school team playing against a professional team. You trot out on the field with your manual under your arm and brother Smith runs right over you.

I would criticize my own agency fundamentally on the point of evaluation. It strikes me that like most governmental agencies, HUD has no early warning system. Bells should have been ringing all over this country in 1969. Those bells were not ringing. No one was saying, for God's sake, what's happening, those defaults are starting to inch up. Those bells didn't ring, there were no bells. There was no way that George Romney or Robert Weaver could know what was going wrong. I think that the department came to the realization that they had a massive problem on their hands about the time that the newspapers came to that realization and the United States Congress came to that realization. Almost simultaneously. Had we had a systematic evaluation of the system, we would have had that warning a year in advance, but we didn't have it.

When I came to this office in August of 1970 I had no idea at all that we were going to be faced with enormous defaults and foreclosures. None whatsoever. I think that I came in with my eyes open in respect to the magnitude of what the office was doing. I was careful to read the production reports and I knew that it was a big operation. Frankly, my first four or five months was spent just trying to create a new office. I was setting up an area office in enormous turmoil, recruiting personnel, setting up systems and procedures, transferring the files from the regional office, taking over the state of Michigan in terms of the HUD program. I'll criticize myself on two points. First, it shouldn't have taken me or my staff four or five months to find out what was going wrong, even given that enormous turmoil. We were operating out of file cabinets and file boxes in the midst of the enormous transfer of power and responsibility, but it shouldn't have taken me so long to begin to center on the single-family programs. It wasn't until January of 1971 that I fully comprehended it.

The second thing that I fault myself with is that it took me too damn long to realize that at the back end of the operation we were taking property back. Every month that report would come in with those repossessions, and it took me too damn long to realize that we were being swamped. You cannot run an operation dealing with 2,000 and 3,000 and 4,000 recalls, with seven realty specialists. I think that I missed that one by about six months, in terms of my reaction time.

The fundamental decision to tighten the screws that we made in January of '71 was the right decision. Unfortunately, we only made half a decision. We tightened the screws, tightened the appraisal procedures, dispensed with the private individuals who were obviously abusing the programs and tried to bring the activities of the mortgage companies into compliance with our regulations. It resulted in rather less production and a smaller volume of cases and that was all to the good. There was just no way in the world the office could have done a good job in processing 60,000 applications and insuring 35,000 mortgages. That was just impossible. It could not be done. I think that we have brought ourselves into the position where

we are now doing reasonably well. For instance, we require city inspection of the houses and are trying to make
the mortgage companies assume at least their legal responsibilities, if not their moral responsibility. I would never
change that. But we've taken enormous heat from the
industry, from the public and from the press. They are
asking, what the hell are we doing? You're not insuring
homes for people anymore, you're nit-picking, you're tying
everybody up with red tape. Well, so be it if that's what it
takes.

But because we tightened up, people were getting hurt.
They weren't able to sell homes because we were loading
on these repair requirements. They weren't able to buy
homes because we were stiffening up our whole system
whereby a person qualifies for FHA insurance. We caught
it from both directions. Some of the criticism is justified
and some of it isn't. I wouldn't change my decision, however, I think it's the right one and I'm going to stick with it.

There are problems everyplace. We had fundamental
personnel problems in the property management section.
Again, it's the question of straight interface with the private system. When you're talking about repairing property
and selling it, of using private repair contractors and private area management brokers, you get into a situation
which was foreign to anyone in the department.

Properties that were taken back in the inner and middle
cities were being vandalized. The availability of good,
qualified repair contractors was limited. The area management brokers who managed the whole system certainly
were not sophisticated in terms of construction techniques.
The checks and balances, the spot checks at the agency
which should have been performed could not be performed
given the volume and the absolute scarcity of the staff. So
in essence you had a machine running without any of the
checks that would have ensured that a home was properly
repaired or that the repair costs were reasonable. We were
simply swamped, overwhelmed by the volume.

The area management broker under the old system would
solicit repair bids on a regular basis from qualified repair
contractors and then select a low bidder. Several of our
investigations have shown conclusively that bids were not
being rotated, that there was complimentary bidding. As a
matter of fact, some of the firms who were bidding against

each other were operating on the same blocks, same addresses, same secretaries.

We have some remedies. Our remedies are a lot more flexible than those of the Justice Department. The Justice Department has only one remedy and it is criminal prosecution. Of course, the burden of proof that they must sustain is very heavy, there's no question about that. Whereas, in terms of administration, our first line of defense is to get rid of the bad guys, which we've done, with suspensions. They've been suspended from doing business with HUD anywhere. Recently, we suspended a number of repair contractors and area management brokers on that basis. Our burden of proof is much less than is necessary for criminal prosecution. We simply have to show that it is not in our best interest to continue to do business with these people. But it took a special investigating team three or four months of concentrated effort to amass enough evidence even to take that action. Given the complexity of the situation, you just have to go case by case. Our second line of defense which we are exploring is a possibility of a civil suit to recover damages.

We anticipate at least another year of high repossessions, in the neighborhood of 500 or 600 properties a month. We presently have 11,500 homes in our inventory. Assuming that we will add 500 a month for the next twelve months, I think that it's quite possible that the Detroit area office will have 16,000 or 17,000 repossessed homes. There were many other houses that we tore down or resold. We will have torn down 3,000 houses by the end of the calendar year.

We are tearing down some housing that could be made sound. We have more or less divided our approach into three classifications. Priority area one is the outlying area of the city and parts of the middle city. In that area, if we repair a house, we can sell it at a reasonable price and with some considerable assurance that the buyer will be getting a decent product. Except for extraordinary circumstances, he will not default it.

Priority area two, the middle city, is more questionable. In that area we will be taking a higher risk when we sell a house. We will take back probably 10 percent of those we insure. In priority area three, the inner city and parts of the middle city, I'm convinced that when we repair the house and sell it, we're going to experience intolerable defaults. We will simply be recycling these homes unless something else is done. That something else has really got to be done jointly by the federal government, the city, and the state.

What you're really talking about is, what the hell do you do about an inner city? Do you clear it or do you refurbish it? Do you build a gilded ghetto? Without action with respect to education, law enforcement, the economy, if we sell a house here we're recycling it. Consequently, if that something isn't done, we may well be forced to tear down homes that could be repaired. We simply know that to repair them and sell them again, we'll get them back again. It is better from the federal government's point of view and better from the city's point of view not to repeat that experience. Consequently, the house gets torn down.

I think that the 1968 Housing Act allowed private capital to transfer the risk to the FHA in a lot of cities, but I'm not entirely convinced that this cause-and-effect sort of thing was so in Detroit. First of all, it seems to me that private, uninsured mortgage loans were never too extensive at any time in the city's history. Detroit is somewhat similar to Chicago in the sense that the conventional mortgage industry was not making conventional loans. Certainly, they weren't inside the old red-lined area. The predominant method of real estate transfer prior to the middle 1960s was done on contract. A lot of people are looking back nostalgically at the land contract system as not having been as bad as everybody thought it was at the time. I still don't agree with that.

I would say the question of private capital transferring the risk to the federal government probably happened in New York. Apparently conventional loans there were steered to speculators who bought the property and resold it FHA-insured and paid back the conventional lending source. So the banks got out of the very risky conventional loan and into the fully insured FHA loan.

Detroit is a little different. What happened in Detroit is that the white flight from the city was facilitated by the FHA to the nth degree. Not only did the readily available FHA insured mortgages facilitate somebody selling and leaving the city, but of course we insured the other end of the transaction, when he bought a new house out in the suburbs. We just greased the skids the whole way. It's no wonder that Detroit lost 190,000 people from 1960 through 1970. The system was there like a greased runway.

I don't know what has happened to all of the people who lived in all of the houses we are getting back. It's sad to say our attempts to trace persons who have defaulted and abandoned have not been successful. We have been able to reach some people who are in default and still living in the homes. The question we ask them is, "Why are you not making your payments?" Most of them name one of four or five reasons: loss of income, sickness, marital trouble or a poor house in the beginning. But we don't know why people made the decision to abandon. I have some theories on it, but I can't prove them in terms of surveys.

My theory is one I sort of share with the mortgage bankers. Properties in Detroit are not appreciating. They're staying steady or dropping in value. The term of ownership is shortening. Now it's down to two, three or four years, because the guy has children and he's in a neighborhood where the schools are bad, there are crime problems, and he may have employment problems. He wants to get out, he wants to leave. I don't think that he is looking to go to an area where he'll have a better chance in raising his family or avoiding his problems, he just wants to go to another area, he wants to get out of this area because it's bad. So he says, "I want to sell."

He sits down with a piece of paper and an envelope and goes to a real estate broker. It's not very complicated arithmetic. He figures out that he has built $400 or $500 worth of equity in two or three years, and it's going to cost him $2,000 to sell the home. Well, that's a net cash loss of $1,500 and he doesn't have it. He wants to get out, so he abandons. He rents a truck and comes up in the night, packs his furniture and he goes. Whether he goes to another area in Detroit or to New York or to the suburbs you can't say. But he leaves. It seems to me that he is probably circulating within the city. You're not getting a lot of actual flight back to the South or wherever, but I couldn't prove that because we can't trace him. It's almost impossible to. We took a sample of well over a thousand cases and we were able to reach exactly forty.

I think that the fate of the inner city in Detroit is a very low population density and a large number of vacant lots after houses are torn down. That is bound to happen as we accelerate our demolition program and tear down more houses. I'm not convinced that that is at all desirable. A lot of vacant lots in a blighted neighborhood is comparable to having abandoned houses.

I thought for a period of time, until we actually did the painful task of mapping every property that we owned, that all the defaults could end up as a land mecca, that HUD would acquire enough property that we could assemble a parcel which would be cleared and redeveloped. But that isn't going to happen. We have no area where we own a whole block, no area in the city. We may own 60 or 70 percent of the property on the block, but we're still dealing with some private owners. We have no way of getting our hands on the property and so HUD is a land banker.

HUD is now talking about an alternative to the subsidized interest programs. Fundamentally, it's a radical approach. Maybe you could view it as socialism, but the whole concept is to make available to the eventual consumer money or some substitute for it. You give the housing grant to people who qualify for it economically and simply say, "Alright, this is your housing allowance, do with it what you wish. If you wish to rent, fine. Buy, fine. It just must be a standard home." It would mean direct payments to the recipient without any of the present interface, without any of this tampering with the private system of mortgages, brokers, speculators and mortgage bankers and the whole array of characters. The whole approach is almost overwhelmingly attractive. It has enormous administrative simplicity, and it is very simple to introduce. It may be initially very costly, but in the long run it would mean much less cost to the government than the system of long-drawn-out, thirty- or forty-year interest subsidies.

In one of my favorite nighttime thoughts, I wonder how many members of the United States Congress who voted on the Housing Act in 1968 realized that the 235 and 236 programs were absolutely cumulative in terms of cost. Every time a mortgage was insured, a subsidy kicked in, and the cost is going to continue for thirty years in the case of the Section 235 and forty years in the case of the Section 236. Politics is a game of mirrors. When do you stand the cost? Do you want to stand it all at once, or do you want to spend it over forty years? It is very unlikely that very many congressmen or senators fully realized the accumulative effect of these costs, that they were voting for a program that would cost billions and billions of dollars.

My own personal view is that the whole system of massive government intervention in urban areas has been counterproductive. We fundamentally changed the nature of the real estate business in the United States, perhaps irrevocably, by the passage of that legislation which was built on previous legislation. Without a single test of whether or not economically or socially it made any sense, without ever having tested the concept of low-income persons owning their own homes, we just walked into the situation absolutely blind. The result in some instances has been catastrophically bad. In most instances it has been fairly good, where the social factors are tolerable. But where you're dealing with complex social issues, the results have been bad. I don't care who the judge is, when you get 25, 30 or 40 percent defaults on Section 221-d-2 mortgages in certain areas, that's bad, that's intolerable.

Ford tests a new automobile going to market. They test for design, they test the engineering. We didn't do that. HUD didn't do it, the federal government didn't do it. Congress responded to what was viewed as a crisis and responded in crisis terms with a monumentally new approach that will eventually cost hundreds of billions of dollars.

It strikes me that before we do that again, before we go out on some other tangent, we damn well better test it. Hence, I think Congress is wise in requiring a test of the housing laws. The department is wise in carrying out that test on a long-term basis, five years, to actually see what happens, what effect it is going to have and how it is going to work, before we go to the housing allowances as a new system of producing housing.

I have a very corny reason why I have stayed with HUD despite all the problems and the personal heat: pride, stubbornness, our lives, our sacred honor. You get into something, and I don't know, you can't just back out. I can't think of the word for it. Committment is not the word. I suppose ego is a good word, the most descriptive one that I can think of. Hell, my parents were not wealthy. I worked my way through school and never faced a situation that I didn't think I could at least manage if not conquer. I don't think that anybody is going to conquer this situation.

Speaking very candidly, this job has been a career-breaker. This situation probably means that I will have to start all over again. When I leave the government, I will have to begin again.

12

Chicago

The People Speak

"I spent a month looking into some of the new Chicago suburban subdivisions that included regular and FHA housing for a series that I did for the *Chicago Sun-Times*. I couldn't believe the things I saw built, by some of the largest new home builders in the country. One subdivision was built on a flood plain. Of course, every time the river rose what always happens to a flood plain happened: it flooded everybody's house. There isn't even a law against it. Another subdivision was built between a sewage lagoon and a garbage dump. When buyers asked what that thing was over there, the real estate salesmen said, 'That's a forest preserve.'

"The man who owned the dump heard about it, and erected a large sign that said, 'This is a dump.' The builder put another sign up in front of it. So the dump owner posed as a buyer and went to the subdivision. 'It was the most amazing thing in the world to be told my dump was a forest preserve,' he said.

"The houses were literally falling apart. The walls were coming away from the foundation. One house's foundation dropped three inches the first spring, because it had been built on frozen ground. You could put your hand between the bottom of the wall and the floor.

"I did a four- or five-part series about it. I got more telephone calls and letters as a result of that series than anything I have ever done as a reporter. It seems that everybody's getting screwed. I could spend the rest of my career writing about housing—it would never come to an end.

"I think that what's been going on in the FHA is the biggest scandal I've ever seen. It may be the biggest scandal in our history."

Thomas J. Dolan, reporter,
Chicago Sun-Times,
October 10, 1972

On November 29, 1972, Tom Dolan reported that a federal investigative team was looking into the affairs of some 30 potential defendants in the FHA scandal in the Chicago area, about half of them being FHA officials and half construction officials.

The investigative team, formed about five months before in Washington, included architects, auditors, and FBI agents. They were assigned to collect detailed evidence "on possible bribery, shoddy workmanship, and housing fraud" in six suburbs: three to the south and three to the west of Chicago.

Dolan said the investigators had learned that homes were built over natural springs and some had walls that were sinking. Violations included faulty plumbing and electrical and heating construction.

The defects, as usual, should have been discovered by routine FHA inspections and FHA internal reviews.

On July 27, a federal grand jury working under the direction of Assistant U.S. Attorney Anton R. Valukas indicted four FHA officials, seven contractors and two real estate brokers on charges ranging from bribery to making false statements on FHA contracts and inspections.

The most notable of these indictments included two officials of Kaufman & Broad Homes, Inc., one of the nation's largest home builders. The officials were Royal Faubion, former president and general manager of Kaufman & Broad's Illinois division, and Maurice Sanderman, the firm's Illinois controller.

The investigations centered in Country Club Hills, Mokena and Park Forest, the south suburbs, and Carpentersville, Valley View and South Elgin, the suburbs to the west.

Dolan reported that in Rainbow Valley subdivision, built by Kaufman & Broad, federal agents had documented dozens of defects, including bedrooms without insulation, buckling and uneven floors, improper wiring materials, leaking roofs and cracked foundations. Most of the houses were Section 236 subsidized units.

In South Elgin, federal inspectors found houses built over natural springs. One of the homes had a constant stream of ground water pouring through the basement.

The most unusual thing about investigating the FHA scandal has been its reasonableness. Simple inductive reasoning led me first to conclude that the problems were vast ones, but it was deductive reasoning that led me to information about how the "scam" operated.

But after I started to look into cities other than Detroit, I learned that all my fancy figuring was unnecessary and there were people around who could explain it all to me based on their own hard experiences. By coincidence, I found the two most knowledgeable FHA participants in Chicago, one on either side of the official divide of the formal bureaucracy. They are Gail Cincotta ("Physically, I'm a housewife") and John Waner, head of the FHA Chicago District office.

Both of them believe a conspiracy exists between real estate and mortgage interests to defraud the government and the people. Both of them have ethnic backgrounds, and both of them are intelligent, compassionate people. Outside of these things they are entirely different, each seeming to think the other is part of the opposition. But as their insights demonstrate, they are both victims in some way.

Gail Cincotta may be the most unusual housing expert in the United States. She is a large, fast-moving woman with a kind of huge Wayne Cochran bleached blonde bouffant hairdo that is noticeable all by itself. But don't let that delude you about her achievements. With no advanced education, she not only taught herself the intricacies of housing, finance, and the FHA, but has taught thousands of others as well.

Gail Cincotta created the National Peoples Action on

Housing, known as the National Housing Coalition; she did this virtually alone, with no money and only a sense of the truth to guide her.

The coalition has affiliate organizations in almost every large city in the country. Its first national gathering in Chicago early in 1972 brought 2,500 delegates, senators, and representatives, all major media—and Gail—for a marathon productive bitch session about the FHA.

I think the most interesting thing about it was the working arrangements reached by ethnic whites, poor blacks, and Spanish-Americans to fight the FHA to keep from ruining their neighborhoods. Their efforts may prove to be worthless as the low-income programs are killed, but their mutual understanding of each other's problems has been very rare in recent times.

Gail Cincotta and her family are among a handful of whites still living in her neighborhood in the Austin district of Chicago—a determined few who stayed while the once all-white area was "changed" by speculators and mortgage companies and the FHA.

John Waner is a handsome bull of a man who, as head of FHA's Chicago office, seems to hold a job below his station. He doesn't need it. A wealthy and prominent contractor who once ran for mayor of Chicago against Richard J. Daley, and lost, Waner only does the job because he thinks it's important. He is honest and he runs the only truly open FHA office in the country. Gail Cincotta and John Waner don't very much like each other.

But that isn't important. What is important is that they describe the FHA situation in Chicago far better than I can, so I'll let them. Note, however, that many of the abuses they describe came under the Section 203 program in low-income areas, proving that greedy men can manipulate almost anything.

Gail Cincotta Speaks

My name is Gail Cincotta. I'm 41 years old. I'm a housewife. I'm nonsalaried. I'm past-president of the Organization for a Better Austin here in Chicago and leader of the West Side Coalition in Chicago. I'm also chairman of the National People's Action on Housing.

I've lived on the West Side of Chicago all my life. I live

in Austin, a community that's undergoing racial change. I work on the real estate problems. I'm tackling them by understanding what the realtors do.

This past March [1972], we pulled together a conference in Chicago because of our frustrations with the FHA here. We had gone to Washington, and that only led to more frustrations. By reading the papers, we found out that the FHA was a national scandal and it was being covered up in every city. That's why we decided to have a conference.

We called together every community organization that we could find. The conference was held at the end of March. We had 1,600 registered delegates at the conference for two days. We handled about 2,500 people, who came from all over the country. They were part of grass roots groups that had been fighting urban ills. There were 365 different groups represented. We organized. We're kind of new, but we are pulling ourselves together.

When I first got into housing, I wanted to know who made the decision in areas like Austin that there would be a black or brown movement into it. Originally, it appeared to me that it was made by realtors, blockbusters and panic peddlers. You know, there's no open housing anywhere that I know of. There's a closed market.

For example, you'll find a four-block area set off and suddenly hit by a bunch of realtors. There were about 35 realtors in Austin when it was practically all white, a reasonable number. But a couple of years ago, in the midst of the change, we identified the signs of 300 different real estate companies here, and each company hires from two to sixty real estate men.

We thought that was the answer. But when we started digging into the problem we found the whole community was under FHA. The only mortgages that were being made were FHA. We discovered that the banks and the savings and loans were pulling out of the area and the FHA was coming in to fill up a vacuum. The realtors were coming in and using FHA to move people from old ghettos to the new ghetto. The whole problem became more complicated.

What we saw was a whole economic thing, almost like a conspiracy of people deciding that this area was going to go, or they were going to make it go, and some people were making a hell of a lot of money off the racial change.

The first step is when the banks and the savings and loans refuse to give mortgages or loans for rehabilitation and repairs on the houses. The second step is when the speculators come in to panic-peddle. They used to be less sophisticated and just say the blacks were coming. They don't do that anymore. Now they say, "This is an FHA area."

This means that the term "FHA" becomes synonymous for "blacks only." Conventional mortgage money is synonymous for "whites only." One of the ways we learned that is when we got hold of a book called SREA, Survey Real Estate Appraisers, and laid out the information in it. The book told who bought a house, who sold it, what they paid for it and what kind of financing they had.

In our area, the book showed financing was 90 percent FHA. Based on its figures, you could draw a line on North Avenue, 1600 north, and find that above that line into Oak Park [a west-side suburb] all the houses were sold with conventional loans. In Austin, all the mortgages were FHA. You see, you can draw on a map where FHA is and where conventional money is.

The speculators' markups are fantastic. On Hubbard Street, two blocks from here, a speculator bought one place for $7,500 from a white family. He sold it to a black family for $14,500, and it was riddled with code violations. We assume that he told the white family: "I'll take it off your hands, fix it up and sell it." But he didn't do a thing to repair it.

The same speculator bought another house for $5,000 and sold it for $14,500 FHA. Two other houses he bought as a package deal for $15,000. He resold them FHA for $16,500 and $17,500, all filled with violations. In another case, a speculator bought a house for $2,000 and sold it FHA for $19,500. We've had cases where whites were getting $10,000 for their houses and the blacks were paying $25,000 for them.

Whites feel that they're being pushed out and blacks and browns feel that they're being deserted. They inherit the older homes with problems, and the whole community undergoes change.

Under FHA, the banks were charging up to fifteen or sixteen points, which is 16 percent. That means that anybody who can sell his house with a conventional mortgage will never use FHA. But you can only get conventional mortgages in white areas. An FHA mortgage is used in mixed blocks and fringe areas where people can't get conventional money. They can't get it because the banks and the savings and loans have pulled out.

The directors of the regional FHA office say they're color-blind and can't help who gets FHA mortgages. They say they abhor the point system, but nobody's done much about it. And the mortgage bankers charge five to fifteen points.

The FHA here was using both regular and fee appraisers, and a lot of fee appraisers that they hired were realtors. I guess they're doing service for their buddies, because a couple of them are under indictment now. One of the classics was a staff appraiser who was also an active realtor in the same area, Austin, where he worked for the government.

So far, about five realtors have been indicted or have been found guilty. They are really cool guys. They knew all the angles and they were advertising illegally. "Free FHA appraisals," they advertised on their windows, which we found out later was against the law. Huge signs, "FHA right away." You can be an old neighbor fast, you know.

They walked their mortgages through FHA. That's when you know somebody at FHA and you can walk it through from one desk to another. In a couple of days you can get your mortgage walked right through with all the OKs. The FBI has been looking at some of these deals because of all the complaints about the houses. You'd have to be blind not to see all the code violations in the houses. You just know there had to be a payoff. The FHA never saw the houses, they just gave a blank endorsement.

But the classic answer of the FHA is that the people who bought the houses are better off now than they were before. That's kind of the whole attitude of the FHA. You can have a woman standing in her living room with the whole ceiling out and the plumbing leaking, and John Waner will say, "Well, she's better off now than she was before, and we helped her."

I've been down to talk to Waner many times. Usually it's very hard to get an appointment, although it's easier now that we picketed his house. One time we went down to Waner's office and he said we locked him in. We were locked out, we never got in. Afterwards FHA put grates over the elevators and built extra doors in the corridors so you can't get into the office. They're very anti-people, from Romney on down, in the HUD administration.

Romney usually refuses to deal with people. When we had our second conference in Baltimore, he refused to come. He sent a flunky, and the people booed him off the stage.

Later, we heard he was going to be speaking in Park Forest, Illinois, [a south-side suburb] so different groups from Chicago went and picketed the building so he had to come through us. We confronted him on the sidewalk and got to talk to him.

Well, somebody swore, I guess, and he was very upset. He was more upset about one swear word than all the things wrong with the houses. He just doesn't want to deal with people. With community people they're really uptight, they feel we're a mob. After one meeting, an FHA official said the people were Communists and Bolsheviks—just troublemakers. None of the HUD officials want to recognize the problem at all.

I heard Romney testify in Washington and he put all the blame on the people, saying that they have to be educated. Our premise has been, if you give people a wider choice of locations to live in and good houses, at least you're giving them a fair chance. But when you move people from one bad situation into another, you can't blame the troubles on them.

Romney says the scandal is the Democrats' fault because they held office four years ago. There was an article in one of the New York papers which talked about Romney living in his $126,000 house. Now, that is only one of Romney's houses; all the others are in the slums. Anybody else would have resigned in disgrace or tears, or been kicked out, but Romney still goes on.

Under the Section 235 program, we've found really terrible construction; so bad that even John Waner agreed with us. They sell these houses for $24,000. They take a fifty-foot lot and cut it in half and put two houses up on slabs.

As you watch them build, the slabs are cracked. They put up the frame and then they put up four-by-eight-foot board like plywood paneling. Over this they slap a thin brick veneer. The whole wall is only four inches thick. The inside drywall construction is not plastered.

You end up with a very thin, long house. They look like

bowling alleys. The blacks in this area call them shotgun houses—one shot will go through the front door and clean out everyone inside.

We've also got a few Section 235 rehab houses. They are in deplorable condition. You walk into the house and it hasn't been painted for fifteen years. The plumbing is rusted and rotted, the siding looks like it has been eaten off all the way to the roof, and it has big holes in it. The FHA blames the problems on the kids. The kids don't have a chance. In Philadelphia, where they have a tremendous problem, the FHA solution to lead-based paint on the walls was to varnish over it. Incredible stuff.

Many of these neighborhoods that are FHA eventually are taken over by urban renewal. You know, it's funny . . . the last ripoff you get in most cities is the arson. The last money that's made off the changing community is the burning and the abandonment.

I don't know if anybody has mentioned it, but in a community like this, older people had 3½ and 5½ percent mortgages. The banks were unhappy about that. It was bad money. It is worth it to clean out a whole area if you can get 8¾ percent, which mortgages were going for not long ago.

There is a group of people who made money from converting Austin from white to black. The realtor makes at least 6 percent. The mortgage companies get 5 to 15 percent in points, plus interest. If you can convert a whole community, the money flows, everybody is making a buck. And the banks get their money out and put it into new suburban construction where it's safe.

We met with the savings and loan companies about two months ago. They told us the people who were buying the houses were so poor that they couldn't afford conventional loans. They agreed there were no conventional mortgages in this area, but said the people bought FHA because they could get a house with minimal down payment.

But they're the ones who establish the high down payments. You can't get conventional mortgages here at 50 percent down, hardly at 75 percent down. They said the people who live here are kind of old, and it's a changing area. One of the presidents of the savings and loans said, "Oh, my God, you saw the pattern east, didn't you? You just know this is going to be the next area of racial change."

I said, "Here is a self-fulfilling prophecy. You say this is going to happen, and you make it happen."

The real estate companies keep two sets of books, two sets of listings. One for black people and one for white people. White people have to fight to move in here, the agents won't show them any houses. They will only sell to black people. That's because it's more profitable to change a whole community than stabilize it.

I'm one of the few whites still living here. Only about 10 percent of the people here are still white. I stay because I don't like to be pushed around. I lived in Austin all my life. We've been working so hard here. Can we make a difference? Where the hell are we going to move? If somebody else has the power to decide where I'm going to live and when I'm going to move, it really turns me off.

I think there is a conspiracy, almost, of people making decisions about where people like me are going to live. I think that they've called it a natural phenomenon for so long that people began to believe it. But can anybody explain to me that Garfield and Woodlawn [community areas] are natural phenomenons, that Austin is a natural phenomenon?

There has been no choice of housing for minority groups. The banks, the savings and loans, FHA and insurance companies have made the decisions. When you talk to them they make decisions: they say, "That's a high risk area, that's a bad area." They all say the same kind of thing.

Now, the FHA line has moved to North Avenue. People know it because they can't get mortgages and they know it because they meet with these guys, the big shots, who come up with zones, maps and decisions. I can't imagine that they all made the same decision at the same time by themselves. Do you think the realtors did? How come there weren't 300 realtors here ten years ago? How come there aren't 300 realtors in Oak Park or Belmont-Cragen? And how come there's all the money available for FHA mortgages?

Up to now, the consumer has not been taken into the FHA's consideration. All of their programs have been built with the lenders and money people in mind. I think the trend has got to be for the consumers' protection.

One ideal would be to have all HUD-FHA homes guaranteed for up to three years, whether it is new construction or old. Somehow, there should be full-time counseling service for the low-income buyers. Not the present $100 counseling plan that the seller pays, but protection all the way down the line. If you buy an FHA house and find out it needs a new furnace, there should be someplace you can go. There should be legal service, so that all the papers are looked at before they're signed.

I don't know if we need new laws. There are laws on the books now. But when a speculator has been indicted, convicted and is given four years' probation, it makes you kind of wonder if the laws are being enforced well enough. You can have good attorneys working on cases and do a bang-up job investigating, but the judge is the one who sentences them.

There are a lot of existing laws on civil rights, nondiscrimination laws that federal money can't be used to do X thing, that you can't sell bad houses, that you can't discriminate and take money and lend it somewhere else—there's a lot of laws that aren't even being enforced.

Of course, there are politics and money involved in the conversion of neighborhoods from one race to another. They just want to make money. So much of this is economic. If they can keep people hating each other and fighting each other and moving, everybody makes so damn much money. They think, "We're going to clear the whole central city. We're going to put up some more Sandburg Villages [middle-income apartment complexes] and some more University of Illinois, some more medical centers, and we're going to push all the poor people, black, white, and brown, out of the city and have the wealthy move back in.

The people have complained and complained, but the FHA just tries to beat them down. At this point they're still saying it's really not that bad. Romney says he doesn't know why he's blamed for all this, the real problem in the city is crime in the streets and that housing is not to blame.

But the people feel that they have been taken. A lot of them are very angry. Minority groups have always been taken advantage of. It's such a pattern of always being taken by the "man."

The minority groups have a feeling that a new community is a place to pass through. You go there for a couple of years, knowing somehow that you will not be able to stay, you don't know why, it's just a part of the system to move. You move into a place, then urban renewal follows you out. It's just kind of a white, black and brown urban removal.

What the hell can you do, any of us? Our feeling here is, we don't want to kill FHA, we want to clean it up because we had contract buying before which is pretty damn bad or worse.

What we're afraid of is Romney making noises like the whole inner city is beyond help, so we'll just erase it. But if they completely cut it off, you're going to have a lot of people in a lot of trouble.

The FHA scandal is national and it's so bad, I just don't know what else to say. It's sad that they're not listening to people. I think the hope is in the people finding answers for themselves. Nobody else knows them; they might as well give the people a chance to come up with some ideas.

John Waner Speaks

The problems we have had in Chicago haven't been as bad as in Detroit. Our economy is a little more stable, and I venture to say that because of it our repossessions will be substantially less. One thing that is gratifying, we don't have the abandonment here that we find in Detroit and other areas where people just walk away from the houses.

We do see that our repossessions are on the increase. They will go substantially higher than they have been. To some degree we attribute that to the softer economy, but we have had a tremendous amount of speculator activity in this area. I think that I nipped it in the bud. We were a little later in formulating our office than Detroit was. The Detroit office was set up a year before ours. This office was set up in August of 1971, and that's when I came aboard.

I was from April, 1971, the former assistant regional administrator for housing production and mortgage credit, and FHA director back in 1960. At that time, we didn't have any of the inner city problems that we have today because a lot of the areas in the inner city were considered areas of unacceptable risk. Any similarity of the FHA today compared to ten years ago is rather remote.

At the present time, our existing home inventory based

on 221-d-2 and 235 sales is exceptionally small. In the nineteen-county area that this office serves we have an inventory as of July 1, 1972, of less than 1,000 buildings. We manage to dispose of some 400 pieces of property per month, but our foreclosures and delinquencies are about 600. Perhaps I'm a bit off on these figures. But we're repossessing buildings faster than we can dispose of them.

When I came into the office last year, it was no secret that a good many of the brokers throughout the city were taking advantage of the liberal programs that came as a result of the 1968 Housing Act. When I first came aboard in April, I had access to FHA housing production operations, first-hand knowledge of the Detroit situation and other offices within the six-state area. When I was sworn in as area director here, after first making a study of the office, I immediately put in a whole new set of rules and regulations.

First, I eliminated the use of fee appraisers completely within the inner city and Chicago proper, where most of the speculator activity was taking place.

I have found conflict of interest among these fee appraisers. In one case, there was a fee appraiser on our staff who was operating at the same time a real estate business. They all belong to the same club, so to speak, and I doubt that they could give the buyer a fair shake.

So I eliminated fee appraisers and I put out a directive which tightened up all appraisal procedures in the office. We adopted the moderate valuation approach in this office even before it became the law of the land.

Most of the appraisals as a result of the 1968 Housing Act in the inner city were based on comparables—comparable sales. I have found that it is relatively simple for any group of brokers to get together to establish comparables in any given area.

Take a hypothetical situation. Broker A will go into an area that previously had no FHA activity. He would buy a home on a conventional mortgage, paying in excess of what the home was actually worth. He has then established a conventional sale. Next, he calls the FHA on another house, and the first sale acts as the comparable price for the second one. It was then relatively simple to establish sales in the community on the basis of comparables.

By using the moderate approach, which we do now, the

building is appraised on the basis of actual value replacement cost. It's a drawn-out process of appraisal. To some degree we look at the market in order to determine what buildings are going for, but this has no effect on the ultimate appraisal. The appraisal is made on actual value rather than on comparables established within the community.

This eliminates the speculator, the unscrupulous broker, from going in and knocking down a whole community by buying up a lot of buildings, knowing that the prices would be established on the basis of comparables.

We also stopped the speculator who could realize his profit even before he sold the building because he knew the spread between the price he paid and the comparable. We refused to accept this practice because I am very consumer conscious. I've long been critical of the *caveat emptor* concept. Let the buyer beware has always been the vogue in the real estate business.

Most real estate sales prior to the 1968 Housing Act were conducted on the basis of the buyer being a more sophisticated individual who could understand values. With the interest subsidies, a new type of buyer entered the field who was not knowledgeable. But because of his needs for quality housing, he became a prime target for the unscrupulous speculator.

There's nothing wrong in law for a man to engage in speculator activity, legitimate speculator activity. I believe in the free exchange of real estate. I certainly wouldn't want to stop that. But it's unfair to exploit the unsophisticated, unsuspecting buyer because of his great desire for housing. Invariably he's the black buyer and the Latin American buyer, whose only interest is for how little he can get a home. The fact that he could have bought that home for $15,000 instead of $18,000 does not enter the picture because his interest is fixed and his down payment is fixed. He looks only at the monthly payments.

So you can understand, the salesman would go to him and say, "For $200 I can move you into this house." The buyer didn't care whether the house was selling for $15,000 or $23,000, he was looking at the house. And not being sophisticated enough to be able to determine whether the value was there, he signed on the dotted line.

Immediately, he was in possession of declining equity

because the comparable valuation in no way reflected the true value. In 90 percent of the cases, these homes were not properly inspected.

Now bear in mind that the FHA appraiser, even the staff appraiser, is usually a GS 9. The GS 9 category specifically spells out that the appraiser shall be able to make appraisals on the basis of comparables. He has not been schooled in anything else.

The appraiser didn't take anything else into consideration, although he allegedly—and I use the term loosely—was supposed to have knowledge of minimum property standards. Minimum property standards are far less than actual codes in many instances.

So the appraiser would go into a building and find that it was deteriorated. But because it was being sold on the basis of comparables, he would have to establish a price.

The result is that in many instances the buyer of the home would move in and find defects with the electrical system, defective plumbing, defective floors, plaster falling and so on.

I believe in many instances deficiencies should have been caught and the value of the house reduced, but this was not done. The result was that the prices went up more. I think that there is a certain culpability here on the part of our people and our government. The culpability may have been innocent enough, but the fact is, the appraisers were not thoroughly trained to do their job.

Now you ask, "Why didn't you use higher rated employees who would have a greater knowledge?" Unfortunately, it is not easy to upgrade people, because there is a certain grade level that must be maintained throughout the nation. Even if I wanted to put on a GS 11 as an appraiser I couldn't because I would be above my grade level.

However, in my directive I ordered that the city of Chicago has to send out a building inspector for every single instance, and he has to give us and the buyer a certificate that the building is free of any major code violations.

I did a number of other things. We proceeded with training our GS 9s as best we could, taking them out on jobs, for instance. I went out with them personally and showed them the kind of buildings we definitely don't want to approve. We have insisted that every seller of a home must bring the building up to mint condition. We're checking ourselves to make sure that it is.

Now, we'll go out to an old house, and if we see it doesn't have storms and screens, we won't approve it. We won't approve it because that poor, unsophisticated buyer invariably will be sucked in by some suede-shoe boy for a new set of storms and screens. Instead of having just one mortgage payment, he'll have two or three different things to pay for.

I know a case where a woman bought a building at $21,000. She had income from the first floor, her mortgage payments were only $180 a month, so I thought she could survive. Except for one thing—the suede-shoe boys. They went out to sell her additional equipment. She bought a whole new set of storm windows for the building for $1,900 with another $500 in interest. Her payments increased by another couple of hundred dollars a month. Next, somebody came in and inspected her furnace and said, "You need a new furnace."

It's questionable that she needed a new furnace, and even if she did she could buy one for $550. Incidentally, I used to be in the heating business. You can replace any furnace for $550. Hell, they're doing complete heating jobs on new buildings for $900. This woman paid $1,900. Now she had an additional $4,000 [in] obligations at short-term interest rates.

Now, this poor person had all she could do to clear my mortgage credit section in the first place. And yet, the lending institutions in this town found her to be a pretty good risk in extending her credit for items she didn't need. You can bet your bottom dollar that this woman will go broke.

The mortgage companies, along with the unscrupulous speculators, are not interested in the well-being of the buyer at all. You see, when they buy an FHA mortgage or make an FHA mortgage, they charge a discount now of 7 percent in this area. The discount is supposed to equalize any fluctuations in the money market over thirty or forty years. But if the buyer defaults on the first payment or the second payment, the mortgage company throws him into foreclosure immediately in order to pick up the windfall money.

The more FHA buyers who default, the higher the mortgage bankers' yield—not at all like it is with the conventional mortgage.

If there's a default on the part of one of the conventional borrowers, the lender will send out one of his vice-presidents or someone from credit in order to determine why the default is there. He'll do everything he can in order to get the borrower back into good standing.

But this doesn't happen with the FHA insured mortgage. The mortgagee wants to report to his board of directors that his delinquencies are down to a minimum. Naturally, they are because FHA pays off, or he unloads them to Fannie Mae which in turn pays him off, and he reports to his directors, "We're in good shape." And the profits start mounting.

Instead of helping this less sophisticated buyer and asking him, "Why did you miss your payment?" and, "We'll carry you this month," they do just the opposite. If the buyer missed last month and comes in with this month's payment, they'll tell him, "I'm sorry, I won't take it." It's tragic, it's absolutely tragic that this is being allowed.

The mortgage companies have not been checking out credit information for the low-income buyers, either. We do that now. They could care less. They give it a once-over-lightly and then buck it over to us. Our mortgage credit people check them out.

We try to put people in houses. We recognize that with the discrimination that exists in areas like Chicago there's no mobility for minority groups to find homes in the outlying areas. We recognize that if we're going to find some better housing for these people we must bend over backwards to process their mortgage credit applications.

You know, it is our responsibility to pass on the mortgage credit and we do. In 90 percent of the cases we pass, the people can make their mortgage credit obligations. Except when they become the prey of others. Then the buyer owes too much, and he throws his hands up and says, "What the hell, I can't make it." Because we have a one-year redemption law in Illinois, he can then sit out the balance of the year without paying us, without paying any of his creditors. When we finally get that building back we find that it costs us $7,000 or $8,000 to upgrade it again to sell it to someone else. The second buyer invariably gets a much better building because all the things that brought about this first foreclosure are no longer there. It's a vicious sort of thing, but it's there.

The mortgage companies are getting their money from insurance companies, from some building and loan companies, pension funds—the big operators. It's a full-bloom business because they get their points and interest if the mortgage is paid and in the case of defaults they pick up a premium. If you go broke, the mortgage people get 100 percent on the dollar.

I don't know if we need more laws, but I think that there should be more regulations. I honestly believe the mortgage company should have a greater interest in the ability of the individual to sustain his mortgage, not by punishing him with heavy restrictions but by counseling him and making him more sophisticated about home ownership.

The buyer has to be told, "Look, Jack, don't take on any more obligations when you are in trouble. Come and see me and perhaps we can work it out. Do you really need that boiler that someone is trying to sell you? Do you really need that roof?"

Or rather than being sucked in by some suede-shoe boy, the buyer should come in and see me and say, "Mr. Waner, I bought a home that has a leaky roof."

I should be in a position to say, "What can I do?" If I find out that it's true and that one of my men overlooked it, perhaps I could waive the mortgage principal for a while to allow him to make that obligation for a roof and come back with his payments when conditions have changed.

Many of the buyers tell me they don't see the interior of the building before they buy it, and I believe them. Brokers are like that. They say, "Give me $200 and I'll move you in." The buyer says, "I'll take it."

I've gone through that. Hell, I was a kid from the other side of the tracks. When I went out to buy a car the guy said, "I'll sell you this car, it will cost you $100." I said, "I don't have $100." He says, "You got $10. Where are you working? Sign here." I took the car. I wanted that car, don't you understand? I'd never had one, I wanted one.

Congress had every good intention when they passed this Housing Act of 1968 in order to open up areas that were previously off limits. They meant well, but the FHA wasn't geared up for it. They should have been geared up for it. They should have taken these people who worked in these offices and tutored them heavily in what path to walk, what concept to follow. And they should have taught the buyer about value.

Everything does have value, but value to whom? The more sophisticated individual comes in, looks a building over and says it's worth $15,000. If it was new it would probably be worth $30,000, but it needs new windows, new plastering, new tile, a new back porch. One guy will say, "I take it as it is because I can do this work." The other guy doesn't even know how to drive a nail. He can't be sold a house that needs that kind of work.

Even if a house is in good shape, you can't let people over-extend themselves. Take the woman I mentioned before who bought the two-flat. She can't make her mortgage payments. She'll try, I know she'll try, because I know that she wants to live there. What she will do is move in one or two more families to collect their rent. The two-flat becomes a four-flat. We have increased the density, and if we increase the density, that's the beginning of the ghetto, the slum. The very thing the woman ran away from, she has now created.

Lawrence Katz in Milwaukee had a fine approach and I admire him. But he got greater cooperation from the public aid authorities than we do, although I keep asking for it.

I wrote to the public aid officials here and asked them to cooperate with us because of some of the tragedies that I have seen when ADC recipients buy new [Section] 235 subsidized houses. The county has to do more than help them meet their mortgage payments.

If all ADC does is help with the mortgage payments, an ADC mother with six or eight kids moves into the building and the building turns into a slum the day she moves in for a number of reasons. She doesn't have money to set up some drapery rods. She doesn't have money to buy a garbage can for the back, so the litter accumulates. She doesn't have enough money to plant grass seed, or if she does she doesn't have a lawn mower so the grass is overgrown.

I insisted that the county provide some additional funds for these little things that would right now keep her on the level of the rest of the community. Because now, the minute she moves in, she doesn't have curtains, she doesn't have drapes, she puts newspapers on her windows and it stands out, this is an ADC recipient. Then there's a furor in the community. She's pointed out and her kids are, and I don't think that it's fair.

The 235 program was meant to subsidize in order to give an economic mix within the neighborhood. It's certainly not meant to have the poor stand out as being poorer than the rest of the poor. Unfortunately, we haven't had too affirmative a response from the public authorities here.

I have also insisted that ADC provide us with counseling service for these new buyers. I've gone out on Saturdays and visited the buyers of these [Section] 235 homes and in some instances I was so thrilled. You could walk in and the people were poor but they weren't filthy and they weren't sloppy as people want to think they are. The houses were immaculate and the kids well-mannered and everything was going along. You couldn't tell the difference between that particular buyer and the buyer of a 203.

But by the same token, I walked into others and the culture of poverty was so evident. They got the new home, all right, but the newspapers were on the windows. You understand, there was nothing there. It was even suspect if there was enough food on the table. No one had even gone in and told them how to balance their heat.

In once instance, the painters left a tape on the thermostate when they got through. The woman couldn't adjust the heat and it was 90 in the building. I said, "My God, it's hot in here, please set it down." She said, "I can't." So I tore the tape off and I set it on 70. I asked her if anybody had told her about how to do it and she said "No". She said, "The whole house is 90, but I can't get no heat in the back bedroom." So I went to the basement with my regional administrator, got on a ladder and opened the damper for her. And I said, "Now you got heat."

I said, "My God, have we been doing this?" I felt ashamed of myself that I was a party to it. I went back and I raised holy hell. I called a meeting of all [Section] 235 builders and I said, "I'll be a son-of-a-bitch if I'll allow another building to be built under 235 unless you will assure me that you will start counseling your buyers." Also, I said, "Under no circumstances will you ever get a 235 commitment out of this office until you put enough insulation and storm windows and storm doors on those houses."

The abuses we have had were not among the small builders. Small builders invariably delivered a bigger product. The ones who have chiseled have been the major builders, the ones on the stock exchange. I'd rather not mention any names. But major builders are more inclined to cheat because they lack adequate supervision and have utter disregard for complaints. They give slipshod construction because they beat the hell out of the subcontractors to a point where the contractor has to take his profit out of the quality. I don't mind saying that we have taken a lot of action against these firms. I've called one of the major builders and said, "You've got next Tuesday and Wednesday to come out to one of the projects. I'm sending out twenty inspectors in order to train my men on how not to build a building."

13

The Philadelphia Story
Politics and Profit

The first and perhaps most complete disclosure of the FHA scandal came in Philadelphia. Two reporters from the *Philadelphia Inquirer*, Don Barlett and Jim Steele, followed the trail of bad houses and FHA foreclosures into the inner workings of the agency and the real estate and mortgage interests so thoroughly that 116 indictments had been handed down as of May 31, 1973. Among those accused of crimes were a former Philadelphia FHA district office director and the usual assortment of appraisers and real estate speculators.

Along the way the *Inquirer* reporters revealed an extremely suspicious relationship between FHA mortgage banking interests, speculations, and the inner office of Sen. Hugh Scott, majority leader in the Senate of the United States.

As always, the Philadelphia story began with the discovery that speculators were making millions of dollars by buying old houses in bad repair and selling them with FHA-backed mortgages to the poor. If anything, however, the profits were even more startling than in cities like Chicago or Detroit because they sometimes ranged up to 1,130 percent. Speculators had purchased houses for as little as $500 and resold them in two or three months for $5,500.

Meanwhile, speculators advertised the houses as "FHA approved," which was as illegal there as elsewhere, and did nothing to the ancient properties but slap a fresh coat of paint over the dry rot. When *Inquirer* reporters checked twenty-four such houses, they found in twenty-three of the cases that no building, plumbing, or electrical permits were issued for renovations as required by city code.

In one case the chimney was cemented shut. The victimized buyer, Alma Murphy, said, "The gas man said he couldn't turn the gas on until we cleaned the chimney out. He said the fumes would back up and kill us."

A second house had no pipes, a third required buckets of water to flush the toilet.

The ghetto was expanding, and foreclosures by mid-1971 had reached more than 2,300.

One of the first speculators implicated by the *Inquirer*'s investigation was Theodore Clearfield, who had bought a house with no pipes and standing water in the basement for $1,600 and resold it to a poor family for $7,500 only four months later. The mortgage company in this case was United Brokers, the largest mortgage banking firm in the Philadelphia area.

At the same time, the *Inquirer* revealed that Thomas J. Gallagher, head of the Philadelphia insuring office until June 14, 1971, had been given a "leave" from his duties. Not only was Gallagher unavailable for comment, but HUD refused to tell the investigators which appraisers were involved in suspicious FHA transactions, saying: "It's a matter of privilege and also protects the appraiser from any unfortunate things that might be said about him."

The *Inquirer* eventually had to sue HUD to get the appraisers' names and won the case in 1972.

It soon appeared that speculator Clearfield was more than the average broker trying to make a buck or two from FHA dealings. He was, in fact, well on his way to becoming a financial giant. In 1970, Clearfield had purchased twenty-five houses for $222,000 and sold all but six of them FHA for $603,000 under the Section 221-d-2 program. Most of the buyers were women who knew nothing about owning or maintaining a home. They remembered being told their houses were FHA approved.

The Philadelphia FHA office said it had "informally" told

Clearfield it wouldn't do business with him anymore as a result of a critical study of the Philadelphia office issued by Texas Cong. Wright Patman in July of 1970. The Philadelphia office was more than a little confused, however, because Clearfield had arranged for more than forty FHA insured mortgages since the Patman report. The discrepancy was never explained.

In most cases involving Clearfield and the FHA, the mortgages were made by United Brokers Mortgage Company.

The FHA responded to the *Inquirer*'s investigation on August 27, 1971, by suspending 160 fee appraisers who worked for private real estate firms. In every city where the FHA scandal has erupted, HUD responded first to public outrage by getting rid of the fee appraisers as being the most logical sacrificial lambs.

Romney took the issue one step further and ordered a full investigation of "faults, inequities and profiteering" in Philadelphia under the 221-d-2 program. And he sent a team of investigators from the central Washington office.

Barlett and Steele, the *Inquirer* reporters, remained well ahead of the floundering government, and began to point out some curious connections between the private, apparently unprincipled world of FHA, real estate and government.

In the first instance, William L. Tucker, president of Tucker & Tucker Real Estate, sold an FHA house for $9,200. It came complete with a decayed rear wall that caved in. In the sale, Tucker acted as broker for the owner of the house, Penn National Investments, Incorporated, which had received city notice about the defective wall. Tucker was president of Penn National. He said the fallen wall was "just one of those things that happen."

Tucker also had a distinguished wife, a handsome woman named C. DeLores Tucker, Secretary of the Commonwealth of Pennsylvania and a member of Gov. Milton J. Shapp's cabinet. Mrs. Tucker disavowed any interest in her husband's business. She was a licensed real estate broker who was appointed to the Philadelphia Zoning Board of Adjustment in 1968. In a financial statement made public in July of 1970, Mrs. Tucker made no mention of either Tucker & Tucker Real Estate Company or Penn National Investments. At that time she refused to disclose the assets of her husband.

But she did disclose personal ownership of fifteen shares

of stock in United Brokers Mortgage Company, which she valued at $750. United Brokers gave the mortgage for the house with the fallen wall that Tucker sold. She had bought her stock in 1960 for $250.

The heat was on. On September 25, 1971, the district attorney's office issued twelve criminal complaints against Clearfield, not for FHA violations, but for failing to obtain housing code certifications covering the properties. And it was disclosed that Gallagher, FHA district director since 1964, had quietly resigned. Gallagher had been with the FHA for thirty-three years, since 1938.

In mid-October David Lang, the office's chief appraiser since 1954, went on disability retirement.

The word was out that some people in Philadelphia were in serious trouble.

On October 21, the federal grand jury that had been sitting for six months hearing allegations of FHA crimes, stunned Philadelphia real estate people by returning indictments against a real estate broker—Clearfield—a realty firm, and four building tradesmen.

Clearfield was charged with aiding and abetting the submission of false certifications to the FHA about the condition of eight houses. Named in the same indictment with Clearfield were Clayton Kelley, a roofer; Edward Good, a plumber; Bruce Hammer, an electrician; and Ben Johnson, a second plumber. The charges against them also involved false certification of the condition of FHA houses.

A second indictment against Clearfield accused him of falsely representing that houses had been endorsed, authorized, inspected, or appraised and approved by the FHA.

A third indictment, against the G. J. Hines & Sons realty firm charged it with falsely advertising FHA approval.

The same grand jury indicted nine men and another realty firm about one month later, again on fraud charges.

The *Inquirer,* meanwhile, was fighting an angry battle with HUD and Secretary Romney over the names of appraisers who evaluated Philadelphia properties, and Barlett and Steele were hard at work preparing another bombshell. This one involved Sen. Hugh Scott and United Brokers Mortgage Company.

United Brokers was Philadelphia's most active mortgage company in the inner city FHA mortgage business. Its president, Louis Bank, was a personal friend of Senator Scott, and a campaign supporter for the senator since 1956.

Edward E. Pilch, a large United Brokers stockholder, was Scott's $17,000-a-year field secretary in Philadelphia. He was also a licensed real estate broker and insurance salesman working out of Bank's real estate office.

In December, 1969, United Brokers was appointed exclusive servicing agent for all housing rehabilitation loans made by the Philadelphia Redevelopment Authority, on HUD orders. In October of 1970, Secretary Romney appointed Bank to the twenty-member advisory committee of the Government National Mortgage Association, allegedly after a "good word from Senator Scott."

Scott's law firm, Obermayer, Rebmann, Maxwell & Hippel, had handled United's legal work, and Scott had served as counsel to the company. David O. Maxwell, who had been part of Scott's law firm, was appointed general counsel of HUD and FHA in October, 1970, allegedly with Scott's assistance.

Bank, who had made personal financial contributions to Scott's campaigns, also had his employees make telephone calls and send out mailings for Scott's political races. Bank and United Brokers also did similar work for Maxwell when he ran unsuccessfully for Congress in 1960.

Alan S. Lang, United Brokers assistant vice-president, was the son of David Lang, the FHA chief appraiser who retired in September 1971, in the wake of the FHA scandals.

The relationship between Bank and Scott was so close that at one time Bank's private letterhead showed his name on the left side of the page and Hugh Scott, general counsel, on the right side.

As the crowning touch, on December 13, 1971, the day the *Inquirer* revelations appeared, Pilch was aboard the S.S. *Rotterdam* cruising through the Caribbean with some forty Philadelphia real estate brokers and their wives on a junket being paid for by United Brokers. And at least two FHA fee appraisers and private real estate brokers also were on board with the senator's aide, on United's money.

Bank told Barlett and Steele that he had first met Scott eighteen years before, at a time when Pilch handled all of Bank's insurance business and worked for him as a salesman. Scott, then a congressman, asked Bank if he could put his congressional office in a new building being constructed by Bank, Bank recalled for the *Inquirer* reporters.

"Now, he was very rarely there," Bank said. "He wanted

to stay open several nights a week and he said, 'Lou, could you let me use Eddie Pilch to man my office two nights a week and I'll pay Eddie Pilch?' "

Bank, reasonably enough, had no objections.

On the same friendly basis, Bank said, he worked hard for Scott's subsequent elections, and the two men became close. He said that when Scott was elected U.S. Senator he asked Bank if he could use Pilch full time and Bank agreed.

According to Bank, that explained the relationships of himself, Scott, and Pilch, and their subsequent association in the FHA.

At least some mortgage bankers consider lavish entertainment of speculators unethical, but Bank considered it a normal way of life. Nor did he see anything wrong with a senator's aide going alone to entertain the real estate men.

"Mr. Pilch has gone on the trips all the time as a guest [of United Brokers]. Not really as a guest," he told Barlett and Steele. "He has stock in the company. He helps us entertain the brokers. It's part of his obligation because he owns a fairly decent amount of stock."

The cruise cost United about $50,000.

A competing mortgage banker told the *Inquirer,* "It's well known that Mr. Bank always did use the right political law office and therefore had a strong indirect connection with Senator Scott. He was very well politically oriented."

Among others who took the pleasant cruise was John Brucker, vice-chairman of the Pennsylvania Real Estate Commission, and C. DeLores Tucker, Secretary of the Commonwealth, and wife of the speculator who sold the house with the broken wall. Of course, her husband went along with her. The Pennsylvania Department of State, directed by Mrs. Tucker, is in charge of the office responsible for investigating complaints about real estate men.

Eugene Gulledge, the national FHA commissioner, deplored the junket, saying: "There is no such thing as a free lunch. When there is a real estate transaction involved, the purchaser ultimately pays for everything."

Most United customers were the poor of Philadelphia, who bought FHA houses through the 221-d-2 programs.

In 1970, United Brokers processed more than 2,600 mortgages in Philadelphia with a face value of nearly $26 million, mostly FHA and VA mortgages.

At least through the end of 1972, the government had taken no action against United Brokers, Bank, Pilch, or

Senator Scott for their circumstantially suspect involvement in the Philadelphia FHA scandal. But some others weren't so lucky.

Thomas J. Gallagher, for instance, was indicted on May 11, 1972, on charges of taking at least $18,000 in bribes in 1968. The amount of the bribes was raised a short time later to $73,000, including money which he allegedly took from a building contractor from mid-1968 through June, 1971, when he was "kicked upstairs" from Philadelphia district director at the FHA regional offices.

The bribes, from an unnamed contractor who, according to the government, would act as a witness, were allegedly given to Gallagher to process "with rapidity" FHA approval of four multi-family housing projects.

The projects were said to be for low- and moderate-income families.

Clearfield, who did most of his business with United, was convicted on September 29, 1972, on seven charges of filing false house certifications with the FHA.

Two men indicted with him, plumber Goodman and electrician Hammer, were acquitted of the charges against them. Roofer Kelley pleaded guilty of filing false certifications and agreed to testify against Clearfield. Ellsworth Williams was granted immunity in return for his testimony against Clearfield.

New federal grand jury indictments in Philadelphia included two FHA inspectors. When the indictments were handed down, Romney suspended the men and said: "[We are] determined to eliminate incompetence, conflicts of interest, favoritism, graft, bribes and fraud" in HUD-FHA operations.

Observers of the Philadelphia scandal find the scene to be a fascinating network of friendships, acquaintances and working arrangements between a key state official, speculators, the largest mortgage banker in the city, one of the most powerful senators in the United States, FHA top officials, and appraisers, in an unholy stew of misrepresentation, fraud, spectacular profits, guaranteed investments, favoritism, pleasure cruises, and apparent conflict of interest.

It will have to be up to the federal and state courts to say who is guilty of what. At this point, an outsider would find it almost impossible to say. But the victims, the poor blacks and Latin Americans who bought the FHA houses expect-

ing to have their lot improved, have plenty of ammunition
for their charges of an "establishment ripoff."

It is nearly impossible to explain to a welfare mother
standing in the flooded basement of her Philadelphia 221-
d-2 home that it's all right for Senator Scott's assistant to
own part of the mortgage company that will be paid off on
her mortgage when she defaults because of the bad condition of the house. In no way can you explain to her that her
bad house and her ruined credit after default isn't part of
a plot to "get her," when the director of the FHA office has
been indicted for taking bribes, and when the assistant
vice-president of the mortgage company who handled her
mortgage is the son of the chief appraiser who retired
under allegations of impropriety in his office.

In May of 1972, Carmel McCrudden told the Monegan
House subcommittee that the FHA still was not responsive
to the plight of poor people who bought the overpriced,
undermaintained houses in Philadelphia under the 221-d-
2 program.

"We have had numerous lead-based paint poisonings,"
she said. "I have one family, they were renting an apartment. They had one child poisoned; the child is age 2. They
have a child younger than that, and for their safety, they
thought they would move into a home of their own. They
purchased a home under the FHA 221-d-2. What did they
find? The second house contained lead-based paint, and
they didn't know what to do about it.

"The Philadelphia inspectors told them that it would
cost them $250 per room to remove the lead-based paint
and they also told them that if they didn't remove the paint
they would be prosecuted. The city of Philadelphia told
them that if they didn't remove this lead-based paint after
they went to court, it would cost them $300 a day in fines
until it was removed from the home. So, thereby, they are
in the process of abandonment.

"In the case of another, FHA sent someone out there, and
they had the audacity—the audacity—to come out there
and just coat over the lead-based paint with a varnish and
they said that takes care of their responsibility in this case."

She ended her testimony by predicting that George Romney may drive the poor homebuyers in Philadelphia to
Byberry. "Byberry is a nuthouse," she explained. There
was a great deal of laughter in the hearing chambers. But
there was no laughter in Philadelphia.

14

Jack Blum

Jack Blum was majority counsel for Sen. Philip Hart's Senate Subcommittee on Antitrust and Monopoly of the Committee on the Judiciary. His investigations and cross-examinations were responsible for the bulk of the testimony before the subcommittee on real estate and mortgage banking practices in the FHA disaster. He is not an admirer of the housing industry's FHA activities and was both hated and feared by industry lobbyists. I found him always helpful, however, and very knowledgeable. Here is my interview with Mr. Blum in late 1972:

The situation is that there is a dual housing market. There is the FHA market, which is principally black, and there is the conventional market, which is principally white. There's a money reason behind it, something very important to understand.

I never understood why whites who worked next to blacks on an assembly line wouldn't live next to them. But if you're white and you sell your house to another white with a conventional mortgage, you don't have to pay points. It's only on FHA mortgages that you have to pay points. So if you're white and you have a choice, you'll always sell to a white buyer.

If you're white and the blacks start moving into your neighborhood, you know what is going to come next. You'll be forced to sell out for two or three or five thousand dollars. If you're the typical white, blue-collar worker, that's your life savings, because the equity in your house is the only thing that you've got. So when you see that first black turning up, you're going to be ready to toss bombs and shoot the guy.

The banks are fairly well aware of that. When they approach an area that is turning over, they make sure it becomes FHA only, which means black only. The other areas are conventional only. The use of that FHA-only-black-only is in effect the use of a government program to segregate. The way these FHA programs have been administered, blacks and ethnics have cause for anger.

Now there's another thing that you ought to know. The black people, the average Joe on the street, likes the idea of integration. But there are a whole lot of black hustlers who are in the real estate business and who tend to be prominent in the leadership community, and who have discovered that there is profit in ghettoization. They go around the countryside making speeches about how black people like to live together and how ghettos aren't a bad idea. They support the present system, which is very unfortunate. There are a lot of guys like that around because they get cut in. You have to separate some of the black rhetoric from the reality.

It's not just the subsidy programs which have been stolen blind, it is the same FHA mortgage insurance program conceived in the 1930s that has been stolen blind. That basic program was what was hit so hard in New York. There are only four subsidized mortgages in all of New York, but thousands of foreclosures. The foreclosures were caused by plain old crooked maneuvering.

In our hearings, first we caught up with the few remaining New York superhustlers and then we started into the banks, insurance companies, mortgage companies, Fannie Mae, and Ginnie Mae. We got Fannie Mae essentially to admit it fixed mortgage prices. Then we got to talk with quite a number of bankers who bought on the secondary mortgage market. On the opening day of the last set of hearings we got the president of the Savings and Loan Association to admit who was involved in mortgage conversion; this means taking a bad conventional mortgage in a decaying neighborhood and converting it to an FHA.

We have letters to prove conversion in the record. A banker from upstate New York said, "Yeah, we called the mortgage banker and asked them to do it." That was well-documented and well-laid-out. A real hooker in that mortgage conversion business was the guy who testified that his chief mortgage officer was a man by the name of Don Carroll. Carroll was in charge of working out mortgage conversion. He also was the guy who Romney appointed in November 1971, as the clean broom at the FHA office in Hempstead, New York.

I'm trying to dig out another stinko problem in the 236 program. When they set up the 236 housing programs, they were going to sell the tax depreciation to very wealthy people in high tax brackets. However, the 236 projects have been a disaster from beginning to end. Most of them have been badly conceived, with not enough money in them for management. They were set up as failures from day number one.

The problem is that if the project goes into foreclosure, the tax benefits are lost to the wealthy investors. That's because of the recapture provision on depreciation benefits. Let's suppose, for example, that the building you are depreciating is destroyed by fire and you're paid off by an insurance policy. You have to pay back to the [U.S.] Treasury the depreciation benefit you've already claimed, the theory being that you've had a return of capital another way. Well, what happened was that a lot of very rich people got into these 236 buildings and the mismanagement, bad underwriting, and slipshod construction caught up with them. So the projects now are on the verge of foreclosure. They can't make it, they can't hack it, the rents won't cover the costs.

So what's happened is that these very rich people, Republicans almost to a man, have hustled into HUD and they've maneuvered an assignment of the mortgage to HUD. Then they've worked out deals with HUD to forebear on payments so they don't have to make any payments on them. The principal and interest forgiveness permits the depreciation tax benefits to continue.

Detroit is such a disaster area that the Nixon Administration had to put the lid on it. The Administration didn't want that to blow up in any way until after election day, because it was afraid of losing Michigan.

New York is a mess, too. What they are probably going to do there is drive a bus up to the FHA office to load them all in one morning and take them before a judge. Right up to the top of the insuring office. Everybody. The people will be indicted on fraud, bribery, conspiracy, all that shit.

I happen to know about New York because I've been up to my ears in the New York investigation. So I know the whole cast of characters and I know what they've done and I know how. Unfortunately, what's going to happen in New York has to be kept under wraps because the way I learned the details was really quite accidental. It could screw things up if I said too much prematurely. I give you that as a warning, but they got a guy in New York so cold turkey there's no way he can breathe. He's nailed that hard. I think he's in on something like 175 separate counts.

Everything about the FHA is extremely complicated. I sat down with a group of IRS guys about tax areas of violation. I had to literally start from scratch in an educational process with these Internal Revenue Service types telling them where to look, how to look, who was likely to be a good target for investigation.

But the government has a hard job in proving crimes. It takes a long time to develop a specific case. It has to find the transactions. It's tough enough for you or I to lay out the general pattern and make enough of the case so that anyone understands it. It's something else again when a United States attorney has to prove beyond a reasonable doubt that there was criminal activity involved in a specific transaction. He can't just say, "You're a crook, you're going to jail." He's got to come into court with a case, a specific falsification, and then make it stick. That's tough. That's ball-busting work.

I've mentioned Detroit and New York. The office in Los Angeles was closed and the processing of mortgage applications was halted. I don't know specifically what was fouled up in L.A., except that stories fed back to me say the FHA office was a disaster area. Some of the highest foreclosure rates were coming out of L.A., and it had to be closed for cooling off before the lid blew off altogether.

Los Angeles, Detroit, Boston, New York, and Philadelphia offices all had to close, at least for a while. HUD's reaction has been, this is how we cool it until after election day. Now to get a feel of how bad this is, go out and talk to the Mortgage Bankers Trade Association. They came in here to see me. It was really funny. I'm the last guy you'd expect the mortgage bankers to say to, "Help us, help us."

They said, "Now look, you know what's going on, you probably know more of what's going on than anybody in this crazy city. Our volume is off in one year more than 40-some percent." I think the number they gave me for June was down 42 percent. Fannie Mae's commitments have fallen so drastically that the corporation is a little disaster area. The commitments are down to frankly nothing. What's happening is literally a shutdown of the FHA market.

"Now here's the problem," they point out. "A shutdown is all fine and dandy from one respect; it cuts out all the shabby stuff. But it also means no housing for the folks. And what it's also doing," they say, "is driving everybody out of the FHA market and into the arms of the savings and loan associations, who are reaping the harvests in the form of conventional mortgages at high rates under terms which are not necessarily the best." They say, "We have been knocked down, we can't compete with the savings and loans and all of this is because FHA has turned off the spigot."

There's a school of thought in this town [Washington] that believes the S & L lobby coupled with the private mortgage insurance lobby, the MGIC [Mortgage Guarantee Insurance Company] people, are in part encouraging the shutdown of FHA, because that shunts everything to conventional mortgages. But the people that get screwed are the blacks. [There is] no housing for the blacks because blacks can't get insurance from MGIC. Blacks can't get into a S & L conventional, so that portion of the market is closed down. Also, as FHA shrinks the situation becomes one in which the poor are subsidizing the poor. The insurance premium payment from the poor supports the poor, which is not supposed to be the case. The risk should be spread. They don't comprehend that.

Let me tell you what's behind Romney's quitting. The day he got back from the floods in Pennsylvania there was a phone message waiting for him in his office. The call was from a U.S. attorney in New York with the news of what was going to happen to his crew in New York. I'm sure at that point Romney finally flipped out, because he couldn't even appoint his own men. What happens is that they always run some tired old political hack through. George can't select them, it's some party machine that dredges up some shit who is going to be stuffed into the job because the Republican machine came up with him.

So Romney's caught two ways. He does not have the personnel to administer properly, and he has no control over the people put in the job. As a result, he is presiding over a complete and utter disaster.

The second thing that happened to Romney was the Republicans' killing of the goose that laid the golden egg by firing and reorganizing in an effort to save money. They fired a lot of top-grade administrator types and replaced them from beneath with people at a much lower grade who didn't know squat. They wanted to keep the average grade down in order to save on salaries. So everybody who knew how to run the FHA is gone. The people who might have hung in there and kept it honest are finished. As a result, they've got nobody who can run it.

The story that I get from the lobbyists, the mortgage people and Fannie Mae, all the people who know anything, is that FHA now is an incredible disaster. If you wanted to reopen FHA tomorrow, you couldn't because there is no manpower; it would take six months to train a crew to do a proper job.

In the meantime they cover it up and putter around experimentally giving money out, putting money on the street with the housing allowance. They're doing this in Denver and they've got something like it going in Pittsburgh, and it's awful, absolutely awful.

We won't know for two years what the results of the housing allowance experiment will be, and it will probably take another set of hearings like mine to get to the bottom of it. But let me ask you a question. Take the same folks that got cleaned out in Detroit and instead of calling for an appraisal and an FHA inspection and a check of their income levels, give them a blank check and say "Go find yourselves some housing." Do you think it would work better?

Direct payment is one of those passwords like decentralization. It's bullshit. There is no way you can put money on the street directly with no controls. It will be stolen twice as quickly as money on the street with minimum controls. In New York that style of administration is called putting money on the street. You take a package of money and put it out there. What happens to the money you don't really know, but somebody's got it. You just hope it keeps the lid on until the next election day.

And they talk about it that way. The state housing authority in New York says that's street money, it's gonna cool 'em out there in Harlem for another summer. The programs get funded, the brighter hustlers all come in, the money gets stolen and the hustlers are prevented from leading everybody to burn down the business district. It's kind of like a Robin Hood bounty to keep Sherwood Forest the hell out of Nottingham. Maybe it'll eliminate bribery because there won't be any supervisors to pay off. Direct theft instead of indirect theft.

Let's look at the mortgage companies, what kind of creatures they are and the nature of their business. The mortgage company is a very thinly capitalized operation. All you need to get into the business is $100,000 in assets on a balance sheet. You can assemble the assets from any place you want to, get approval from FHA and get in the mortgage business.

Almost anybody can hustle up enough scratch to get into the business. Mortgage companies do their business with borrowed money. They borrow money from commercial banks to originate the mortgages. They borrow on what is called warehousing lines of credit. They make the mortgage loan, then they sell the mortgage off and use the proceeds of the sale to repay the commercial bank.

They make one point on the FHA loan origination and they possibly make a profit on the resale of the mortgage. They might originate a mortgage at eight points, sell to Fannie Mae at six, and put two in their pockets. Now that's half of the mortgage company's business.

The other half of the business is the money it makes servicing mortgages it sells off to Fannie Mae. The typical mortgage company will collect the monthly payments, collect the tax money and keep it in escrow, and collect the insurance money and keep that in escrow. They get to keep all the escrow monies interest free.

Let's say they collect tax money from you on your house

and they pay the tax bill twice a year. Your money is deposited in an escrow account which then gets credited to their compensating balance. So let's say they are borrowing money from Chase Manhattan. They'll have five escrow accounts at Chase representing all the tax payments and all the insurance payments for all the people whose mortgages they service. And Chase will credit the balances as compensating balances against the loans. Chase considers the compensating balance as an associated account. For servicing, the mortgage company collects a fee of anywhere from one-fourth or three-eighths to one-half percent per year. It depends on what the negotiated arrangement was.

Mortgages are sold either with or without servicing. Some mortgages are sold to institutional investors with servicing and some without. Some of the mutual savings banks in New York bought mortgages from New York mortgage companies with servicing, which meant they were actually going to make the collections themselves. When they buy with servicing, they pay somewhat more than they do if they buy without servicing.

The mortgage company will have associated with it an insurance brokerage operation which will funnel the customers in to buy homeowner's insurance and fire insurance. Typically, the mortgage company will be in bed with a title company. The title company will keep an account on deposit with a commercial bank that is credited to the mortgage company's compensating balance.

These procedures are routine all over the country.

The mortgage company depends on the commercial bank for borrowing and depends on the thrift institution as an outlet for what it has to sell, namely the mortgages.

The only people who can loan money for warehousing lines of credit are the commercial banks. Sometimes the insurance company can, but typically it's done by the commercial bank. There are usually borrowing restrictions on which kind of financial institution may make a loan to whom, and the typical warehousing loan is commercial bank business.

The term *warehousing* grows out of the fact that the mortgage company keeps the mortgages in the warehouse until it has a large enough package to sell. What it's doing is accumulating enough to ship out because a large investor isn't interested in buying $20,000 worth at a time.

He wants to buy $1 million at a time. There are roughly fifty mortgages to a million bucks, so this guy will wait and assemble fifty mortgages. When he's got the package put together he sells them all. That's the way they work.

He sells them for a negotiated price, negotiated between the mortgage company and the buyer. Here's where Fannie Mae comes in. Fannie Mae has what they call their free market auction. Of course, it ain't free market, but they do run an auction operation. If you're the president of a mortgage company, you can go to Fannie Mae and she will say, we're accepting bids for commitments. You can go to Fannie Mae and say, "I would like you to commit to purchase a million bucks in mortgages, thirty-day delivery and an interest rate of X—whatever you think a fair interest rate is." Fannie Mae then decides which offers to accept.

If Fannie Mae accepts your bid, you put up a commitment fee, a small fee which guarantees that in any event you will be able to sell Fannie Mae a million bucks' worth of mortgages at the agreed-on price within thirty days.

You then go out and beat the bushes like crazy to find somebody who will pay you more. There is no penalty for not delivering to Fannie; you can always deliver to somebody else. So what happens is the Fannie Mae price becomes the rock bottom. If somebody will pay more for a mortgage, the mortgage goes to them.

Now the reason that Fannie Mae is said to be the tool of price-fixing in the mortgage business is on the other end of the line, when the mortgage company is deciding how many points to charge the speculator. The way they figure it is they will take the Fannie price and add two points, or whatever. Fannie will buy for ninety-six what the mortgage company bought from the speculator at ninety-four. The mortgage company pockets the two points profit. At retail the mortgage company is making a spread of roughly two points over whatever Fannie Mae will buy for.

Somebody said a mortgage company is as good as having a little printing press because you're in the business with no capital, you've got a guaranteed buyer of last resort, Fannie Mae, and you're charging your customers more than the buyer of last resort will pay for the stuff you're going to sell them. So you always have a profit, and people have described the mortgage business as a sort of legalized printing of money.

Now theoretically there are all kinds of risks. Theoretically the mortgage originator shouldn't be making a spread on the difference between the price of Fannie Mae and his origination. In theory he should be originating roughly at the market, the same at the secondary as at the primary, and he should be making his money on the 1 percent origination fee.

My guess is there are interlocking relationships between banks and mortgage companies. Among other things, there are mortgage companies which are owned lock, stock, and barrel by banks. For example, Advance Mortgage Company in Detroit is owned by Chemical Bank, New York. These banks become the prime source of the warehouse lending. Chase Manhattan owns two mortgage companies, one in Chicago and one in Puerto Rico. In fact, almost every major commercial bank has gotten into the mortgage company business.

Now the reason they get into the business is because it gives them a way out from under government regulations. Now if you are a bank, would you write a mortgage in the regulated portion of your business when you could buy a mortgage company and write it under conditions of no supervision?

There are some other interesting questions. The banks are supposed to have some borrowing limitations. The reserve system has limitations on how much lending the bank may do against the amount of money it has on deposit and its assets. It's called the borrowing base of the bank. But a mortgage company is a known depository institution and it works with borrowed money exclusively, highly leveraged. And so by going into a mortgage company a large bank can avoid the limitations of a borrowing base. A company like United Institutional Servicing in New York was at any given period of time a hundred million or more in debt, and a hundred million is more than the borrowing base for a pretty good-sized commercial bank.

See what I mean? They are able to leverage the bank considerably by buying the mortgage company. They borrow the money from themselves, they borrow it from other commercial banks, they borrow it wherever they can get it.

Now the savings and loans are waiting for the FHA to go under. First of all, they traditionally are not originators of FHA mortgages. Let's go back and look at the history. A savings and loan wants to originate a conventional mortgage in its own market for a permanent investment, if it can. The mortgage company has to sell on a secondary mortgage market; its life depends on that.

Now, if you are a mortgage company in Seattle and you want to sell to a bank in New York with limited assets, you've got to produce a piece of paper which has a certain degree of credibility. The New York bank is not going to buy a pig in a poke. If it's a small bank, they can't send a man out to Seattle to check the property. The only kind of mortgage that they'll buy is one which is federally insured. Then it's safe, it's a good investment.

The S & L's [saving and loan companies] operate on a very different principle. They don't do as much of this origination and selling to permanent investors. There isn't that ease of transferability to capital. As a consequence, what they're interested in is developing as much conventional lending business as possible in their own territory.

They did set up a secondary market among themselves called Freddie Mac [FDMC]. Freddie Mac is the S & L counterpart of Fannie Mae. It's a joint corporation owned by all the S & L's and it buys mortgages from them.

To enhance the S & L side of the business, Preston Martin, the head of the Federal Home Loan Bank board has promulgated new rules which, in effect, enhance the non-supervision of federal savings and loan associations. The new rules permit S & L's to make mortgages with only 5 percent down and with a thirty-year life on the proviso that the mortgages are insured by private mortgage insurance. They then authorize any S & L to sell that kind of mortgage to Freddie Mac.

Mortgage companies are not permitted to sell similar mortgages to Freddie Mac. So as a result, the mortgage companies are frozen out of the conventional market. The Federal Home Loan Bank board said it has no responsibility for supervising the private mortgage insurers, and what happens is all the savings and loans are rushing to skim the cream of the FHA business.

They take the top, they take the best part of the 203 potential businesses and let it go conventional with those 5-per-cent-down, private insurance mortgages. They can clean up. But worse than that it means that a large part of capital which would normally go to housing is blocked from the market because it has no route of entrance.

So what we have is a situation where mortgage capital available in savings banks can't get in unless FHA is operating. What we also have is an imperfection in the capital market because a certain amount of money is blocked out of housing. There is very little competition, which tends to increase interest rates for the slob who needs the 5-percent-down mortgage.

The blacks will be cut out, the minority groups will be cut out, the inner city will be cut out. And the guy who is at the top end of the FHA business now, the best FHA customer, will be in a noncompetitive market.

What we're discussing is the kind of stuff that gets discussed by the lobbyists who really understand what's coming off. When we're talking like this, we're at the level of understanding of the hustlers in Washington who hustle the housing programs. You have to remember that most of Congress is just blissfully unaware of any of this. The average member, like some typical liberal who thinks you ought to do something to help the cities, gets told, "Here's a program let's do it because it will help the city."

He doesn't understand the infighting, he doesn't understand the complexity of a flow of money from capital surplus areas to capital deficit areas. He doesn't understand the relationship of commercial banks, savings and loans, savings banks, mortgage companies.

Lord O Mighty, most people don't know whether they have their money in a savings bank or a savings and loan and couldn't tell you the difference if their lives depended on it. So the consequence is that when congressmen vote on housing programs, they vote with an eye toward what they are told the program will produce, not with an eye on how it affects the functioning of the marketplace and not with any real sense of whether or not they are going to leave a better or worse market.

What happens, in fact, is the housing boys meet over tea and divvy up the turf and come up with a housing program that gets them all rich. That's what happened the last time they did this, which resulted in the 1968 Housing Act. But the lid blew off and it was stinko. They got too rich, all of them, and now there's shambles, and what's happening is the biggest shark trying to cut all the other sharks out. The savings and loan lobby is described as the strongest of all the bank lobbies, and that includes the commercial bank lobby.

They are the strongest because they are so grass roots. They are everywhere and they typically have more members of Congress on S & L boards and more local kinds of pressure that they can bring to bear than Carter has little liver pills. The S & L's are especially favored by the administration. "My God!" a local lobbyist said to me, "it's unfair, the S & L's are the only group in town with two trade associations."

One school of thought here says they are going to sell FHA to private interests and another says they are not going to sell it, they are going to shut it down. The business then shunts to MGIC and the S & L's. If they somehow make the existing FHA a private corporation it would be in competition with the existing private mortgage insurance companies. Now that's a tough one, especially because the private mortgage insurers will fight it like hell unless they sell it to them.

As a private corporation FHA can engage in all of that bullshit racial discrimination and anything that it wants to, because who's to say what it does and doesn't do. So if this comes about there will be absolutely no mortgage money available in any way, shape, or form for inner city residents. It all would be red-lined, and you would be back where you started from. You might get the kind of shadow market that you had back in the fifties, the conventional mortgage with a second and a third and a fourth. It would immediately pull the bottom out of the inner city housing market, leaving everybody who is there now screwed to the walls.

But it would mean that private redevelopers who are very hot for that land could put together large tracts by taking present FHA foreclosed property and the devalued property and putting it all together to work with.

I'm a believer in the conspiracy theory. I'm one of the city paranoids and I'm one of the conspiracy theorists of the city; you know, everything is a plot. But I do not suspect there is a plot where all of the parties sat down and hammered out a master plan of the great real estate ripoff. What you actually have is a bunch of private interests who are concurrently moving in a direction which has the smell of great reward. Maybe they haven't all agreed on an end result in advance, but enough of them are working in conjunction and exerting enough pressure that the end result will be the same.

The hope I see for keeping FHA is that Fannie Mae, the savings banks and the commercial banks will say, "Christ, we can't allow it to be knocked off. We'll be cut out of it too much." The hope I see is the mortgage companies will go to their bankers and say, "Hey, listen: This warehousing stuff, this beautiful business, you get a point and a half, two points over prime, no risk. If we get put out of business you are going to lose it."

Chase had $540 million in warehousing lines last year. That's a big piece of change. Now they go to Chase and they say, "For Chrissake, if there is no FHA we're not going to be able to sell on the secondary market, which means that we can't originate, which means that warehousing business is going to go to hell, get on the stick and help us." There's going to be a real dogfight, and how it's going to be resolved, I don't know. One of the intriguing things is maybe this is the first time that you've had this kind of split in the banking community, where one group has gotten so greedy that they're trying to rip off the other guy. Mind you, there is no one in this game who gives a shit about the customers, which is the essential point one might tend to forget.

The administration decided that the best way to obscure the horseshit in HUD was to charge that it was all Cong. Wright Patman's fault because he was sitting on top of their "reform" bill. The "reform" bill is an enormous grab bag. It consolidates certain housing programs without changing them.

The bill was supposed to consolidate and simplify, but every lobbyist in town took the HUD bill and tacked on the end of it his particular bill of goods. You know, authorization for Fannie Mae to do certain things it wanted to do. Authorization for the savings banks to do things they wanted to do. Authorization for the title companies to do things they wanted to do. So finally the things were just heaped on like a Christmas tree.

The bill arrived at Patman's place, and they took a look at it and found it had nine titles, 270 pages and a little rip-off for every hustler in the housing business. Patman's people are by and large pretty straight. They didn't much care for it. They were going over it pretty carefully and found it was loaded with all kinds of sleepers. They insisted on loading in—because the scandals were breaking

—a little bit of consumer protection. They wanted interest paid on escrow money, some protection on title insurance, to eliminate kickbacks. They started fiddling with the bill.

The administration said, "Wright, you're stalling us." The lobbyists got all geared up seeing their little goodies going down the tube and started putting the heat on members: Get the bill out, get it out. They figured if Wright got too much consumer protection stuff in it they would have to flip a coin—do we want it or don't we?

So what happened was, Patman stalled and the administration leaked to Evans and Novak an incredible column which suggested that Patman was being a tyrant. Patman said, "OK, fellas, you want to play this way, we'll haul it all out in the open and we'll all air our dirty linen." That's exactly what happened and you had this incredible show, that incredible open executive session going on.

You had about thirty members of the House providing the greatest free show in town. They sat there and argued amendments they didn't understand. Lobbyists ran up and gave them something which they put into the bill because the lobbyist was their buddy. Then they tried to defend it, and three other members carved them up with arguments that didn't have anything to do with the amendment they were pumping for. Patman, because it was all public, finally got public interest stuff loaded on the bill, and the lobbyists sat there convinced the whole thing was going down in flames. The administration plans to use the hearings disaster as the excuse for its fuck-up at HUD.

We'll never know whether or not the 1968 housing program would have worked if properly administered because it wasn't. Of course there are flaws in the act. It was put together by the banking lobby. The banking lobby's interest was to keep interest rates up. It works like this: If the federal government took fresh money and poured it into the market it would be increasing the money supply which would have the effect of lowering interest rates. On the other hand, if the federal government creates an interest subsidy program it gives poor people the money to go pay for a scarce commodity, which drives interest rates up. That's why there's an interest rate subsidy.

But what you should be doing is increasing the flow of dough into the market and running a government operation to drive the rate down rather than using government money to increase the interest rates for the poor yuck out there.

The really horrible thing about this scandal are those empty acres of space staring us in the face in Detroit, those square miles of rubble in Brooklyn, Newark, and every other goddam place. Honest to God, it's a real horror show. The second thing which appalls me is the budget impact that all of that disaster is having on the cities themselves. It has wiped out their tax base and substituted nothing for it. You have cities in imminent danger of bankruptcy. In fact, the coming legal specialty of the next number of years will be municipal bankruptcy law. I just do not want to be the receiver of the city of New York.

Well, you've gotten my thinking. Not everybody will agree with me. I happen to be the city radical. You're not going to find anybody who is a wilder radical than I am.

15

George Romney

On December 1, 1972, I interviewed Sec. George Romney at the HUD headquarters building in Washington, D.C. Actually, it was the second interview I had with him about the FHA scandal. The first one earlier in the year in the *Detroit Free Press* editorial offices was not a pleasant experience for either of us. Romney was in a bad temper about the almost daily exposures of FHA failures in Detroit by the *Detroit News* and the *Free Press*. He ranted and raved some about how things weren't as bad as all that and anyway, he wasn't at fault. During that interview he made caustic reference to me, and my "muckraking" and "yellow journalism."

After that, I tried for months to arrange a second, taped interview with Romney for this book and never got anywhere. Finally, I called Jim Judge, HUD's director of public affairs and the secretary's chief PR man, and told him that the book would air a lot of dirty linen. I said that in the interests of fairness, I would give Romney one chapter to defend himself and his administration against some 75,000 words of criticism. Twenty-four hours later, I had the interview.

This time I saw the secretary's other side—the charming, white-haired man in a blue wool sweater, who talked freely and, as is usual for Romney in good spirits or foul, frankly. The interview lasted much of the day. As promised, the raw transcript of about 12,000 words and the following edited copy were given to Romney for his approval. He never responded, so I assume it has his approval.

December 1, 1972
George Romney, Secretary, U.S. Department of Housing and Urban Development

Problems with large contractors haven't been the experience of the agency. As a matter of fact, we have had difficulties with many small firms, and in some ways the difficulties with them are worse than with some of those larger firms.

Usually it's possible to get the large firms to take corrective action on units that have not been properly constructed or on work that has not been properly done. Smaller organizations often are no longer in existence or they no longer have an interest in continued activity in our programs. Consequently, it can be difficult to get them to take corrective action.

Now it is true that we have had some problems with some of the larger firms, particularly with some of the people who work for them. Some of the reasons for the difficulties are that they're pressing hard for overall results and providing incentives for people in charge in particular locations. The result has been that the people in charge of their scattered operations tend to press hard in order to benefit from the incentives and meet quotas and goals that have been established by the national organization.

There is an additional factor, too, and that is: We are subject to a substantial inflation. This overall economic inflation has hit housing particularly hard. The cost of housing has gone up more rapidly than the cost of most products in the last several years.

Inflation has created a problem for large and small contractors because Congress established fixed cost ceilings. In many instances, companies tried to cut their costs to produce within the ceiling but still make a profit.

We recognized that as soon as we came into office. We recommended in the winter of 1970 that Congress change this pattern of fixed cost ceilings because there are wide variations of costs in different parts of the country. We recommended the use of a prototype cost formula rather than the fixed ceiling formula. But Congress has made very modest adjustments in the cost ceilings during the past four years. The ceilings really haven't been adjusted to reflect the full cost increases. The result has been a real squeeze on people using these programs in some parts of the country, particularly in the large metropolitan areas.

Congress has received our proposals but Congress hasn't acted on them. They did act on the prototype formula as it relates to public housing, but public housing only. They didn't act on it as it applies to other programs.

The men on the congressional committees that are dealing with housing usually have quite a bit of background. But the problems that we are dealing with are not simple ones. We are dealing not only with the physical aspects of building housing but also with the related social and racial aspects. If it hadn't been for some of the abuses that became apparent in some of these programs during the past couple of years, we would have been able to get the legislation we needed. We just about got it—it was passed by the Senate, and the House Banking and Currency Committee reported favorably on it—but the Rules Committee of the House was confronted with a 323-page piece of legislation. It was too late in the session to get it into adequate shape.

We have very strong authority at the present time to control the activities of the mortgage bankers. We can declare them no longer eligible to participate in our programs, and this means that they lose the opportunity to benefit and participate in our programs.

You need to take into consideration what the mortgage practices were before the subsidy programs were moved into the central city. Then you had the land contracts. Under land contracts people were paying much higher costs for homes than have been true under the FHA programs. What actually has happened here as a result of FHA moving into the central city is that the lower interest rates and lower down payment levels of the FHA program have become available to inner city families. The FHA programs have permitted people to buy houses who couldn't have bought them under the land contract because on land contracts people had to make a bigger down payment.

Under our programs the down payments are rather modest. The control of the interest rates and points results in much more favorable financing than was true under the old land contract approach. I think to some extent the FHA low-income programs enabled speculators to sell at higher prices because of cheaper financing, but this is one of the things that we had to put an end to.

We did it by changing regulations as they apply to the speculators. We no longer permit sales for higher than the speculator's actual cost of the property, plus the actual cost of the rehabilitation and 20 percent for overhead and profit. So I think that as far as the speculator is concerned, we have been able to control abuses.

I believe that basically we have sufficient authority to deal with mortgage bankers who engage in unethical or illegal activity. And, of course, we have done so in several instances. It isn't always easy to establish evidence on which to take action. You need to have evidence to do it. But I am not of the opinion that just greater control would necessarily handle the problems. If there is to be more supervision of these activities, my present thinking is that it would be much better to do it at the state level than at the national level.

There was a lack of recognition that the use of these programs in the central cities poses quite a different problem than using them in the suburbs. The people who shape the programs are quite aware of it now. But they didn't really become aware of it until we began to find what was occurring in actual practice.

That's one reason I complained so strongly about Congress adopting in 1968 the substantially different programs and mandating their use without any prior testing. There was no effort to find out in practice how the inner city subsidy programs would work. Now, as you know, many of the problems that developed were with programs other than 235 and 236; 221-d-2 is one [with such problems]. Some of the conventional programs have had almost as much trouble in the central city as the subsidized ones. It hasn't been limited just to the subsidized programs.

In the cities where we have had the greatest difficulty,

the difficulties that we have had to deal with occurred as a result of the organization that existed before we took over the department. You take the case of Detroit. The bulk of the problems we've had there are problems that resulted from housing units which were involved in 1967, '68, '69, and '70, before we made our organizational changes.

There is no indication that the organizational changes we have made have contributed to these problems. As a matter of fact, the organizational changes that we made put us in a position to deal with problems in places like Detroit. Now we have an area office and an area office director who has authority to deal with the problems right there on the ground.

The changes we mae were to organize the department on a functional basis. When we took over, we had more than one assistant secretary responsible for housing production. We placed all housing production programs under one assistant secretary, so you could hold one man responsible for getting results.

A second action we took was to decentralize the decision-making of the department and place the decision-making responsibility at the levels of the area insuring office. A third organizational change was to recognize that the housing programs would be used in relation to other programs in the department. We are responsible for water and sewer grants, open space grants, urban renewal programs, Model Cities, and many other programs that need to be related to what housing program is being used.

The organizational changes that we've brought about have resulted in our considering the relationship of housing to other programs in the decision-making process. Again, that authority is vested at the area office level, because the area office is in a better position to be informed about local conditions and is in touch with local officials.

It was decided in 1968 that the housing program should be used within the inner city and that we should put an end to red-lining. After all, up until that time the department had been using the programs largely in the suburbs, [which were] very viable economic areas. That is quite a different thing than using these programs to house the neediest families.

Congress recognized this to some extent by indicating

that in housing families in the inner city we should not apply the normal requirements of economic soundness, but should relax the appraisal and other procedures. Congress set up a special risk insurance fund, recognizing that there would be greater risk in doing this.

But the magnitude of this change was not adequately recognized on a national basis. Perhaps the most striking evidence of the contrast was between the way in which the programs were administered by the FHA director in Detroit and the way the programs were administered in Milwaukee.

The Detroit director was the hero of the department. Lawrence Katz, in Milwaukee, was in the department doghouse because he had so much less production. But he recognized that when the FHA was directed to use these programs in the inner city, it constituted an almost totally different approach than what had gone before. He recognized that housing welfare families and needy families would require a degree of concern about the social conditions of the families, a degree of concern that didn't exist in prior situations.

There was no adequate preparation of FHA personnel to handle this much more complex and difficult job of providing housing in the inner city.

Now on top of that, when I took over the department in 1969, the concern of Congress was that we had never been able to get volume housing production for all income families. Just before I took office, Congress had passed the 1968 Housing Act, in which they adopted these new, more complicated subsidy programs, 235 and 236. They adopted the special insurance program to loosen up requirements in the central cities. The pressure was on me to get some results, to get some housing.

I had to do this with the tools which were there. There was no way I could say at that point, "Look, these tools are really not suitable for use in the central cities where the social problems are really much greater than the physical problems."

Consequently, I went ahead to get the volume production that the nation had been seeking for many years. If you want to check back, you might be interested in reading the correspondence from Senator Proxmire of Wisconsin, who was criticizing me then because he was uncertain that I was going to meet Congress's goal of 26 million housing units by 1978.

If I hadn't taken these tools available to go ahead and get production results, I would have been open to criticism on the basis that I hadn't tried.

At that point I couldn't prove the programs were wrong because they hadn't really been tried, and I didn't know about the action of my predecessors. No one indicated the tremendous changes that took place in the FHA procedures as a result of the decision to put these programs into the central cities. They had ample opportunity to do so, but this was never brought to my attention.

So we went to work and we did get volume output. You know about the tremendous increase in subsidized housing units that we were able to achieve. But unfortunately we achieved it against the background of relaxed procedures in the central city.

Furthermore, it's perfectly clear now on the basis of hindsight that what happened was that Congress mandated the use of these programs in the central cities at the very time that private lenders and experienced builders and experienced real estate people were pulling out because of the excessive risks involved. They left a vacuum for the speculators and the suede-shoe artists to move in. And, of course, that's what took place. From an economic standpoint, FHA was directed and mandated to move into the central cities at exactly the wrong time.

Under these circumstances, our personnel were not prepared to deal with the much more complicated responsibilities than than they had had previously.

Now, another aspect to the situation is that Congress over the last several years has added a lot of little responsibilities to the departments that are handling these housing programs. We have to see now that the housing programs comply with fair housing requirements, comply with environmental requirements; court decisions were handed down that said we had to comply with relocation requirements. All of these are desirable requirements, but all of them add to the work load of people dealing with more complicated programs and with much larger volumes than they ever had before. We had to do all of this with essentially the same number of people that the department had in 1966.

If you go back to that year, the first year of the department's operation, we were probably operating with 15,200 people. I got approval to hire 1,723 more. But shortly after the fiscal year started the inflationary problem in the country caused the president to take drastic action about the economy. In addition, he directed all departments to cut their employment by 5 percent.

In the case of our department, we were directed to cut from the 1966 level of employment rather than from the 16,923 employees that we wanted, and it worked out to a 10 percent cutback. Here we were with essentially the same number of employees that we had in 1966 handling almost ten times the volume of subsidized housing and about 600,000 to 700,000 additional units to supervise from a management standpoint. Plus, we had to deal with the more complicated requirements.

There was just no question that we were short-handed and that this created difficulty in processing and handling our programs and our problems.

Finally, last August they authorized us to hire additional employees. Consequently, our area and insuring offices are currently experiencing the benefit of the people who have been shifted out of the central regional offices to their offices, and from the opportunity to hire more people.

As soon as it was apparent that our programs were not being administered the way they needed to be administered in the central cities, and in order to get a quality result and stop the abuses, I gave instructions to our people that they were not to process any housing applications except on a basis of quality. There isn't any question that during 1969 and until the fall of 1970 we were pushing hard for production to achieve the housing goals. But when the problems became known we immediately issued instructions to our personnel that they were to process only on a quality basis.

As a matter of fact, I indicated that a year ago to the National Association of Home Builders, that this emphasis on quality processing would probably cut our subsidized volume as much as 200,000 units in the current year. And that's about what has happened. I shut down the 235 existing housing program because that was the first program where the facts showed abuses existed. That required drastic action. So in January of 1971, I shut that program down. Then we sent out audit teams to look at 235 and 236 and we found out what was really happening.

In connection with 236 we found out that field personnel were foregoing certain essentials in connection with processing applications. I talked to every regional manager in the country about it. I had to get procedures out to every area insuring office director to correct some of the abuses that existed. We've really pushed hard ever since and made one change after another, to make certain that they dealt fully and adequately with the situation.

There is no question that it has taken much longer to get compliance with new policies in HUD than it would have taken in private business. It takes a great deal longer and we've had to push, push, push, even on this question of quality. We had to keep pushing for almost a year before we could really convince people down through the organization that we really meant it, that there wasn't any uncertainty about it.

In private business it may have taken a few weeks. You might still have some deficiencies in a private organization, but there's a responsiveness in a private organization that you don't get in a public organization. I think that it's a problem with government, with civil service. You just can't expect government to function as efficiently as private business.

I think that the first time that we were aware that there were really serious problems was in the summer of 1970. The House Banking and Currency Committee and Chairman Patman raised questions about abuses that apparently existed in the 235 existing housing program. He asked us to check into it.

So we immediately asked for a report from Philadelphia and Washington. Because he wanted me to appear before the committee on a certain date, that only allowed me time to make a quick check into the two cities. We asked our Philadelphia and Washington people to check into specific instances in those two cities.

In the case of Philadelphia, we received a report saying in essence that the conditions alleged by the committee's staff didn't exist. I went out to take a look at a few units here in Washington and the units I looked at were structurally sound ones that didn't look particularly bad. On the basis of that partial knowledge of the situation, I indicated reservations about the allegations of the committee.

However, we continued to check on these cities and other cities. When our central office people checked on Philadelphia, they sent in a report that indicated the exact opposite of what the FHA office in Philadelphia had reported. That's when I really realized we really had serious problems and that's when I had to take very serious action. So I was misled at that early stage by the report which I got from Philadelphia.

Now it happens that since then the head of the Philadelphia FHA area office has been indicted and some of his associates have been indicted. So it would appear that they were giving me a whitewash report.

The first action we took was to require the disclosure of the price paid by the speculator and the amount of money put into rehabilitation. That was the first action. Then we convened all of our field personnel to get from them a first-hand feel of what we were confronted with. I required all top personnel to get out and inspect a certain number of these units and ascertain for themselves what was going on. I also asked them to check the other programs because at that point we were also concerned with the [Section] 235 existing program. Subsequently, we found out that the problems were broader than just the 235 existing. I don't know how many actions we've taken since, but we've made sixty or seventy different changes in our procedures, trying to cope with the situation.

Going back almost to the beginning of my appearances before congressional committees, I've been pointing out that the number of housing programs and the various statutory requirements they have enacted have created a body of housing legislation that is almost impossible to administer. I began to point that out at our appearances for the 1970 budget, the first budget that I had anything to do with.

From that point forward I have either been pointing out the administrative difficulties of these programs or the need for Congress to re-evaluate them, because they aren't as sound as they ought to be.

In 1968 there was much congressional concern about housing in the inner cities. The whole thrust of what Congress did with Section 223-d was to direct FHA to look at properties in terms of whether or not they were an acceptable risk rather than if they were economically sound. Congress very specifically stated that they did not expect the special risk fund to be actuarily sound. They indicated that the department could come back and ask Congress for appropriations to cover the losses that would occur as a consequence of being in the insurance business in the inner city. The economic situation didn't make an awful lot of sense, but maybe other purposes were being achieved.

An awful lot of people in Congress today seem to have short memories as to what they were setting up back in 1967 and 1968. The department did ask for the first time for an appropriation to cover losses in the current fiscal '73 budget. However, it was not approved by the Congress. Therefore, it is a factual statement that to date the operation of these programs is not costing the taxpayers anything. I have my own personal official department projections which indicate that although the special risk fund will not be actuarily sound, it will not cost the taxpayers anything because the proportion of mortgages in the fund which have run into great trouble are very small compared to the total number of mortgages. You've got an awful lot of sound mortgages in it, and better than 90 percent of the mortgages have never been in default, much less foreclosure.

Any insurance fund when first set up is quite vulnerable to a heavy run of claims. Give it enough time, however, and it will secure itself if you are doing decent underwriting. We believe our actions in the last couple of years have greatly improved the quality of the underwriting.

We might have to borrow some money from the Treasury to cover losses. As a matter of fact, we have done so to cover some cash payments that we have made to settle claims. But nevertheless, we do have assets in that fund which, if they were liquidated at the end of the last fiscal year, would leave us with $26 million balance. We have projections that would indicate we will be in a worse position than that by the end of the fiscal year 1973. But I think the important element is how much of a threat this is to the taxpayers. By taxpayers I mean appropriated funds. This is an insurance fund. Premiums do come in and expenses are paid.

I think that it has to be recognized that while the problems we are talking about are very critical ones in the central cities and the metropolitan areas, they are not nationwide problems. That's why better than 90 percent, 95 percent of the projects have proven out so far. The 5 percent are concentrated in limited areas and therefore are very dramatic, because of the magnitude of their impact on such limited areas as the central areas of the cities.

The more basic cause here is the pattern of local government that makes it almost impossible to provide housing on a suitable basis in large areas in the central cities. This is because of the confinement of problems to the central cities. In areas like Detroit and the central city of Philadelphia we're having difficulties because there is a pattern of abuse. But on the other hand, on a national basis, it isn't so bad.

In asking what we do with the FHA, I think you're raising the broad question of what we will do with the whole federal involvement in housing at this point in history.

The FHA administers not only the insurance of mortgages but also the subsidy programs and the public housing programs. So FHA is basically administering the federal housing activity of this department. I wouldn't scrap it, but I would make some very basic changes.

I believe that the federal government has become too heavily involved with detailed local projects at the local level. I believe the retail aspect ought to be left to state and local governments, not the federal government.

The federal government's responsibilities should be in the wholesaling end.

The FHA insurance programs which increase home ownership by reducing down payments and lengthening the mortgage term have been a tremendous success. It has been so successful that it has stimulated the establishment of private organizations that now do the same thing. So there isn't the same need that there used to be for FHA. I think that the FHA could very properly be modernized and used for the purpose of reinsuring and providing protection against degrees of risk on projects that might otherwise not be undertaken on a completely private basis. I think that there ought to be a reshaping of the FHA insurance activities.

As far as the FHA subsidy programs are concerned, I personally would be glad to see the subsidization of housing done at the state and local level rather than through the national government. It may be that the national government ought to help fund such state and local effort. After all, national tax policy permits middle- and high-income families to make deductions on their income tax for interest payments on mortgages and property tax payments. This constitutes a form of subsidy for middle- and high-income families that exceeds the amount of subsidy that we're putting in for low- and moderate-income families.

As a matter of fact, currently the subsidization of middle- and higher-income families runs $6 billion a year through these tax deductions.

Now under these circumstances, I certainly don't think that the federal government should fail to give support to the financial or housing needs of the lower- or moderate-income families. But I think it could be done more on a block rent basis. Or, if the federal government is going to help meet housing needs in the lower-income areas, it could properly take the form of family assistance programs that make more adequate allowances for housing.

But changes of this kind might have to come gradually rather than suddenly because too quick a change could affect the supply of housing and cause prices to rise substantially. It has to be geared in gradually.

If the retail aspects of housing are left to state and local units of government, what would the federal role be? I think that the federal government should establish long range and annual targets for housing, and establish the monetary and competitive enterprise policies necessary to meet the goals.

We have been doing that for the last four years. For the first time in the history of the nation we have been assembling together those federal officials who are responsible for monetary and fiscal policy with people from competitive enterprise to see what it would take to achieve certain established annual housing targets.

The federal government ought to assume the responsibility for eliminating the obstacles that exist to meeting housing needs on the most economical and efficient basis. At the present time, we have the housing market badly fragmented by building codes, zoning, and other local requirements. The result is that those who are capable of applying modern methods—not just modern technology but modern management, modern financing, modern distribution— are discouraged from doing so because it is too difficult.

We've been able to get twenty-seven states to adopt state-wide building codes for factory-built housing, but there is still a good distance to go in removing obstacles to meeting housing needs on the most favorable cost basis. The federal government should make it possible for housing materials and methods to flow as freely in interstate commerce as cantaloupes, refrigerators and automobiles.

The federal government should see that greater emphasis is given to programs that will preserve our existing housing stocks, and it should continue to underwrite new community programs and to encourage them as a means of helping to meet housing needs.

The proposal to sell part of the FHA to private interests was advanced by the mortgage bankers about a year ago. They've explored it extensively since and even they have concluded that it is not the thing to do. The mortgage bankers' position now is that they would like to see FHA as it existed in earlier years, spun off from HUD and set up as a separate government agency.

Obviously, when the housing insurance and subsidy programs could be handled without reference to the environment, fair housing, relocation, social conditions and other things, it was possible to process applications faster. The whole process was a good deal simpler than it is now. There is little question that the mortgage bankers and others think so. But I personally don't believe that you could spin off FHA on a private basis and still have the housing needs of this country met.

MGIC [Mortgage Guarantee Insurance Company] and the other private insurance firms are tending to take the low-risk opportunities, the cream, and are pretty much leaving to FHA the more difficult, riskier mortgages.

If you had FHA operating on a private basis you probably wouldn't have the mortgage insurance available that we need for low-income families in the higher-risk areas. I don't think that it's feasible to spin it off on a private basis.

I do think that FHA should adjust its programs to reflect the fact that its very success has created private organizations that are doing a good deal of the job. FHA programs should be reshaped to cover the areas not covered by private effort.

Some of the predictions of the FHA troubles aren't all that accurate. Somehow or other, figures have a way of floating up without a lot of substance behind them. I've heard figures like $4 billion losses and nobody can trace down who is supposed to be talking about $4 billion losses. It's just one of those things that gets a going around and even congressmen themselves pick it up and talk about it.

This 244,000-unit foreclosure figure that builds up a $2 billion loss is a phony figure. What it's based on is the fact that the *Wall Street Journal* once called up about defaults. A default is when any mortgage payment is missed. Just thirty days in arrears. Well, the defaults would be up around 250,000 units. They then used defaults to try to figure out what the loss was going to be. But only a fraction of the defaults become repossessions where we have to reacquire the property and pay it off. So it is a greatly inflated figure. [*Author's note: If the approximately 240,000 figure is a "phony" one, it is one that Romney used several times himself. As we saw earlier, most of the defaults indeed do become foreclosures in urban areas.*]

Now the other thing that ought to be stressed is that despite the difficulties we've had, the foreclosures are concentrated in the central cities. Thus far there is no indication that it is going to cost the American taxpayer anything beyond the provisions made in the insurance programs which are paid for by the people who are buying the homes. Even the special risk insurance funds over the years may well be self-sustaining. In the general insurance fund we have about a billion and eight in reserve to pay off against anticipated losses.

Private enterprise can't by itself meet the housing problems in the nation, not at all. There just isn't any question that the nation's fiscal, monetary, tax, credit, and competitive enterprise policies play a very vital role in determining what volume of housing we're going to get.

At the local level, the property tax patterns play a tremendous part in the ability to meet the housing needs of the people. You can't leave it all up to private enterprise. However, I do think that national, state, and local policies that will unleash private competitive enterprise to the maximum extent are the best way to meet housing needs.

It might be significant to note that Congress has stated several times that it is national policy that the housing needs of the country shall be, to the fullest extent practicable, met by the private enterprise system. So there's national direction of the Congress to encourage the secretary to use private enterprise.

I have been pointing out that families in the inner city

have social problems that are more difficult to resolve than just the physical problems of providing a decent housing unit. As a matter of fact, in many of these inner city areas we can't even underwrite the building of new housing without them being vandalized before they're completed. They are so vandalized that they're not even worth completing. There is no question that you can't solve the problems of families just with housing. Furthermore, there isn't any question but that many of the housing units that have been abandoned were deserted because people were living in high-crime areas and wanted to move to a place where there is greater security.

Another thing we don't realize adequately is how the pattern of confining people with problems to the central city has changed the character of our ghettos. There are all types of poor people. Most poor people are good, decent people who want to live under good social circumstances as well as good physical circumstances.

In earlier years, the ghettos were controlled by the stable poor, the good poor people who have good standards. They knew who the prostitutes and the pimps and the drug pushers and the drug addicts and the other criminals were. But they kept them under control, and they had control of the areas in which they lived. However, the confinement of people with problems to these central cities has permitted the concentration of people with problems in the ghetto areas to the point where in too many instances the ghettos are now dominated and controlled by the undesirable element. The good and stable poor are at their mercy.

This creates an environment in which it is almost impossible to meet housing needs on an adequate basis. Now I think there are answers to these problems. But we are not going to be able to work them out in the central cities within the context of the Balkanized governmental structure which exists at the present time.

You cannot have a central city that is being made the focal point of the problems of the whole real city and deal with the problems in that central city only. After all, the central city is only a segment of the real city. The housing, education, health, transportation, water, sewers, and many other needs of the people in the real city can only effectively be dealt with on a real-city basis.

It is going to be just as impossible to solve the problems of the central cities on the present Balkanized structure of local government as it would have been to save this country on the old Articles of Confederation.

The thirteen independent, separate, sovereign states were jealous of their independence and their sovereignty. They were determined not to have a national government that would in any way interfere with their complete independence. The result was that the nation almost ceased to exist under the old Articles of Confederation.

So the Constitution created a national government that was capable of developing national solutions for national problems.

Now, in the same way, it's necessary in these metropolitan areas where you have hundreds of communities, to develop real-city solutions for real-city problems. If we do that, we will have taken the single biggest step that we can to deal effectively with the problems of the cities.

In any event, I'm not giving up on beating these problems. I think we can meet these problems, but I don't think we can meet them without dealing more directly and honestly with some of the real causes of these problems.

I guess it was Aristotle who said that you really don't know anything unless you understand its causes. I think that in connection with meeting these housing needs in the central city areas there needs to be a recognition of how local government structure has contributed to the magnitude of the problem.

I think that when you take a look at our domestic problems there is no problem more urgent or more sensitive and as little understood as the problem involving the cities, race and housing.

I happen to think that citizenship is more important than any other responsibility other than the responsibility we owe to our creator, our religious faith, and our family. I think that we're at a point in this country at which we need to express our citizenship more fully and at which we need to strengthen the private aspects of American life.

I'm not concerned about our having enough government in this country in the future. We're going to have enough government. It may not be properly distributed or properly organized, but we're going to have plenty of government. The great danger in this country is that we may have far too much government and not enough strength in the private area.

16

Romney City Redû

One More Time

Minus twenty-four hours, it is two years since I flashed on the vision of ruined cities owned by Secretary Romney and the Federal Housing Administration and wondered: Who got the money? The answer, as we have seen, is that it was taken by real estate speculators, mortgage companies, banks and other capital sources that finance and run, for better or worse, the nation's housing. Along the way, we have seen more corruption, conflict of interest, fraud, double-dealing, and nasty trickery than we hope to encounter again. But given the nature of men, money, and government—our government, in this instance, and our society—I am not optimistic that disclosure of the FHA scandal will lead to a more virtuous future. It may only be a prelude of worse things to come. Too many men, from the exposure of vice, learn the devil's tricks and not what should be done.

I hope you will not think the worse of me for confessing that as I learned the tricks of men who became rich by defrauding the government and fleecing the poor I sometimes felt a pang of envy. Wealth, after all, is power, and this equation was so set up that the penalties for getting caught are only a year or two in jail and a $5,000 fine. Balancing that slap on the wrist against a possible return of millions, temptation stirred in me like a feeling of being aroused. The grief and rage of the hundreds of thousands of displaced and ruined people is so overwhelming that it has to be shunted aside or crush me with a sense of despair and ruin.

Now that winter has come again to Detroit I get a dozen calls a week from FHA homeowners, mostly women, whose furnaces do not work, whose roofs and walls are open to the wind, whose basements are awash with the water from broken pipes. They have no money for repairs, they get no help from the FHA, the real estate firm, or the mortgage company, and they ask me what to do. Because I understand something of the situation, they hope that I can get the furnace fixed, somehow rectify their plight, get the house repaired by an intercession with the government. They think, in other words, that the government whose laws rule their lives, is responsible to them for decent housing bought under the shadow of the federal wing. They believe the eagle is a righteous and compassionate bird.

Unfortunately, there is virtually nothing I can do for them. I listen, somewhat impatiently, to their complaint and agree, yes, it's not right that the children are cold and the house is a wreck. I suggest they call the FHA, and they always have done so time and time again, without success. I suggest they call a lawyer who might be interested in taking a flier at a civil suit, knowing that they have no money to hire their own legal aid and that the legal services for the poor are simply overwhelmed. Then I give them the only real advice I have to offer, which is to abandon the house and the mortgage.

Yes, I know their credit will be ruined and they will never again be able to buy another house. Yes, I know the house will be pillaged and ruined, too, and its abandonment will cost the government another $15,000 in addition to the hundreds of millions already spent. Yes, I know it will spread the blight that has eaten away the hearts of all our major cities. But I know it is brutal for children to be cold in the winter and for families to struggle to pay for the worthless houses they were defrauded into purchasing.

Finally, I explain as nicely as possible to the victim at the other end of the telephone line that he is not alone. For some reason, that always cheers him up. I imagine him explaining to friends that lots of other people are in the same boat, so it isn't so bad.

"Yes, you're cold, Jimmy, but lots of other little boys and girls are cold in the cities tonight," I imagine parents explaining. "Yes, we're wiped out and we abandoned the house, just like everybody else," I hear.

I know it's true, but I think it's madness, just the same.

I think of the real estate men and the mortgage men and the government officials in their big houses in pretty, safe suburbs or barricaded highrises, their nice furnishings, climate-controlled environments and healthy bank balances, and I think—I can't help but think—I want to be like them. I do not want to be like the poor people who have been ruined once again in a lifelong series of failures and defeats. My Lord, make me clever and make me cruel and make me rich.

Make me cynical, too. Make me trust not, that I may not be tricked.

Or make the country and its people good.

How to do that, short of a total and violent overhaul of our system, I do not know. Nor, given our cultural history and the character of most of our citizens, do I have much hope of a new order in any case. We are Romans, after all, mean sons-of-bitches who can look at the other guy's death without a flinch.

But short of utopian solutions, there are some things that can be done to the FHA program and the federal government's involvement in housing that might help prevent a similar situation in the future, if not alleviate the situation in the present.

First of all, we should change the nature of FHA mortgage insurance. Instead of having it insure the money source, which we have seen leads to all kinds of devilment, it should insure the mortgage holder against foreclosure and the house against substantial defects.

What it would mean in practice is that an FHA insurance payoff would kick in when the homeowner missed payments for reasons not his own fault—loss of income, sickness, and other kinds of emergencies, including extraordinary costs in maintaining a livable house. Such an insurance program would cost the FHA insurance fund less than having to pay off whole mortgage balances in the event of foreclosure. It would still protect the moneylender, and would make his investment both safe and liquid. It would preserve the city neighborhoods we have left, and make the viable ones more stable. The privately owned home is still the best kind of housing for most Americans, and it's an institution that should be strengthened. Just like it is now, the FHA insurance would be paid for by the homeowner. He should benefit from it, not somebody else.

The other half of this equation is to broaden the FHA program to include insurance against major defects in the property: the furnace, roof, foundation, wiring, and everything else. This insurance would be paid for by three parties: the seller, the mortgage company and the buyer. The seller should not mind, because he would just be backing up his warranty that the house is fit for human occupation. The mortgage company would be glad to do it, because he would be helping to protect his investment. And the buyer would be protecting himself.

Along with this goes a written guarantee by the seller and mortgage company that the property has no major flaws. It ought to be standard with every FHA mortgage and include provisions for summary judgments for the cost of repairs in the event that the house is not all it is cracked up to be. This kind of summary judgment proceeding ought to be good for at least three years and include the federal government itself for payment at the time of repair. In other words, the government pays for the repairs and then tries to collect from the other parties if they are liable. The government couldn't complain about this kind of guarantee because it has properly inspected and appraised the property before giving its approval in the first place.

Points, or mortgage discounts, should be eliminated from FHA transactions. Interest rates, of course, should be regulated in the same way they are now. When private capital refuses to provide money for FHA mortgages then the government should, very possibly through a mechanism such as Jack Blum's national bank.

This probably wouldn't be such a serious problem as capital sources will say it would. FHA mortgage yields will continue to be found very satisfactory to investors who are after a completely safe, and fluid, place to put their money. If the federal government also limits short- and long-term investment interest, as it properly should, it will be no problem at all. The argument that interest limits force capital out of the country in the search for higher yields turns to dust because the government will also strictly limit investments beyond the national boundaries. Multinational industries act in no way in the interests of the Republic. But those multinationals that are ours should not be allowed to act against American interests.

There should be no more interest subsidy programs of any kind. They are too expensive and act as a very serious inflationary force in housing and the national economy. The thinking behind interest subsidies, that our lowest-income people need federal help in home ownership, shouldn't be abandoned. This should be translated into direct federal mortgages with very low yields, down to 1 percent—the same effective interest presently being paid by people under the 235 and 236 programs.

The advantage of this to the government is that it accomplishes the same thing as subsidies do—it lowers the cost of ownership or rental without costing any money. The mortgage loans get repaid, with interest. The money is then available for reinvestment in more housing for citizens in need.

People whose housing is paid for by welfare or other government subsidy should not be expected or allowed to handle the mortgage or rental payments. The money should go directly from the government to the mortgage company or landlord. This procedure should in no way govern where the person lives, of course, nor should it limit his mobility; neither should it be paid for substandard housing. But it's foolish to expect people whose lives are otherwise in disarray to take their housing allowance from the government and give it to the landlord, whoever he is. There is no freedom that I can see in the right to be evicted for nonpayment.

Welfare mothers and others at the lowest end of the economic scale should regain the right to buy houses because, after all, the FHA scandal was, for the most part, none of their doing. They should not be punished because they were the victims, although that is exactly what HUD and the FHA have done. Instead, the right of home ownership should be extended to them once again, but in a carefully controlled program that includes training in maintenance and other aspects of home ownership and strictly supervised follow-up. It must be recognized that some people are incapable of owning and maintaining a house and they shouldn't be allowed to on government money. The training program would also include a testing program to determine who gets houses and who doesn't.

People who have lost houses as a result of the FHA scandal should not be barred from future ownership under FHA programs. The enlightened government does not punish where there hasn't been any fault.

The government should make write-down allowances for people who have purchased urban housing at inflated prices under the FHA programs, so they can sell their houses when they want to without taking a financial loss. Since the alternative is hundreds of thousands more abandoned houses, such a program should be easy to sell. This procedure, coupled with sharply lower appraisals in inner and middle city areas, will make the prices of the properties more in line with their actual worth. It will also take the joy out of speculation.

Speculators don't get sent to the seventh ring of hell, although it's a pleasant concept to play with. Something worse happens to them: They get licensed. The federal government should write a model law that strictly licenses speculators, and then encourage the states to pass it. A speculator is defined as anybody who buys and sells more than three houses a year. Speculators who operate without a license shouldn't face jail sentences; they should face drastic economic retaliation—fines up to $100,000 for conviction on each offense. Confiscatory fines, in other words. There is no better way to deal with economic crimes than to take away what has been stolen and then some.

The same goes for mortgage companies who have been caught with their fingers in the till. In addition, the entire mortgage banking industry should be regulated as strictly as any other kind of bank in the United States, and should be made to operate within rules which govern their investments and profits on those investments, what capital sources they can borrow from, and where they can sell. All mortgage bankers should be strictly audited at least once a year. No mortgage banker should display any federal seal or anything similar to a federal seal at any time.

In addition, the government should sue mortgage bankers who committed acts of fraud in the FHA scandal. The laws to make it possible are already there, and they ought to be taken advantage of.

The FHA should be divorced from HUD and once again operate as a separate federal agency. The average grade level of its employees should be raised, present workers trained to do the work, and better people hired. The cookbook approach should be thrown out the window, and applications should be looked at in their totality, by small, flexible, qualified teams of people who together go through all of the necessary steps: appraisal, inspection, credit and job checks, code compliance, mortgage application, approval or disapproval, closing and follow-up. As an ancillary benefit, it's much harder to pay bribes and keep secret payoffs to a team of five than it is to corrupt a single individual.

Under no condition should the FHA, nor should any part of it, be sold to private business. The fact is that the FHA, properly administered, makes money, provides hundreds of thousands of housing units, and is probably the only basically successful "social" program of the federal government.

The present dual housing market in the United States, created by the real estate and mortgage banking industries, must be ended immediately and forever. The fact is that the nation could quickly be integrated by requiring mortgage lenders to show a geographically integrated portfolio. Affirmative lending, if you will. Such action would not wipe out the ghetto, which is economically based in the final analysis, but it would quickly make it smaller. It would also wipe out the practice of blockbusting, which is also a reflection of mortgage lending policies deliberately created and carefully managed, and would stabilize lower-income white and ethnic neighborhoods. What you would see if the government required affirmative lending policies would be blacks being directed to good housing at prices they could afford in white neighborhoods and suburbs. The racial integration of housing would make the whole question of school busing academic. Ethnics, workers—people —don't want to be moved from their neighborhoods by another race, and they shouldn't be moved because mortgage lenders working in collusion with real estate interests want them to be. Racially changing neighborhoods happen because of criminal conspiracy—I hope this is being said strongly enough—between the mortgage, insurance, and real estate industries. The government, if it wanted to, could stop it immediately. It had better, while there still are cities left.

Certainly Secretary Romney is not altogether off the mark when he says that the cities' housing problems cannot hope to be solved without real action on the social problems. It is no secret that the *lumpen* black population of our cities is going through an ugly crisis that no amount of liberal apologies can cover. It is racked by heroin addiction, violence and murder, illiteracy, crime, and too often disease, and mental illness. The causes are rooted in slavery and racism, and a domestic imperialism, but discussion of the causes is not going to get beyond the fact that several million wretched people lead lives in our cities that are a disgrace to our "civilization." Their lives are also a disgrace to themselves.

Open housing and better federal housing policies will not solve all their problems. But they will allow those who Romney thinks of as the "deserving poor" and those who I think of as the nonpsychotic poor to escape.

What to do with the remainder is probably a taboo subject in our democracy, because no known democratic methods have an answer. But a benevolent totalitarian state would destroy the ghetto by shifting the young from the environment into small decentralized communes where the children would get loving care with affectionate discipline, superior food, sound and attractive housing, the best mental, dental, and medical care available in the society, and education at least equal to the very best suburban or private schools. In the remaining ghetto, heroin addiction and the heroin business would be stamped out with whatever means of violent action were available to the larger society, which in this case is virtually without limit. The physically and mentally ill would be treated with the society's best resources; the mentally retarded and the genetically infirm (I am not talking about sickle cell anemia) would not be allowed to reproduce. The educable would be taught. Productive jobs at considerably higher than sustenance wages should be made available to every qualified man and woman. So should sound housing anywhere in the United States. All manifestations of racial prejudice would be eliminated in a benevolent totalitarian state; the actions, at least, if not the sentiments. Interracial marriage would be actively encouraged by cash grants and important tax breaks. The social goal would be the end of a black and white society within 100 years, and its replacement with a thoroughly mixed brown one.

Unfortunately, there is no benevolent totalitarian state, and there is not likely to be one as long as there are human beings who covet authority and its prerogatives. So the very least we can do as a democracy is to act like one, at least one egalitarian enough to allow people to live where they want to live. And at least provide decent housing.

The existing housing stocks of our cities must be preserved and, as they are an irreplaceable national resource, it is up to the federal government to do it. These structures —private homes, two- and three-flats, and small apartment buildings—are built better by far than any new housing going up except luxury units, and they are frequently sounder than $50,000 and $60,000 homes. The structural timbers are always one-by-twos, and sometimes two-by-sixes and two-by-eights that are simply unavailable nowadays for any price. The brick properties have walls a foot and more thick. They have full basements and proper drainage. Besides, they have much more room and exist in neighborhoods built for a community on a human scale.

The cult of newness is a fad that has already peaked in our society, but millions of people still foolishly assume that the houses in suburban subdivisions are innately superior to the housing stock of the cities. The houses they offer as proof are the $60,000 and $70,000 structures with plastic kitchens and built-in stoves. But most of the new houses available to our citizens are stick houses made of one-by-twos and stapled together, with modular bathrooms and kitchens, unit electrical systems and small, second-rate heating units—1,000 or 1,500 feet of badly insulated space set on a thin concrete slab. The alternatives, for the bottom two-fifths of our population, are factory-built houses and mobile homes.

I find it incredible that the people of the United States choose to destroy sound urban housing and replace it with hundreds of thousands of stick-built houses that will not last the life of the thirty-year mortgage; instant slums, if you choose to call them that, as socially nutritious as sugared breakfast cereals.

City planners, economists, and architects have recklessly praised these structures as disposable houses whose quick construction and rapid destruction keep the old economic wheels a-churning. But we live in a society that cannot even dispose of its "disposable" pop bottles and beer cans, a society that devours irreplaceable natural resources at an accelerating rate while they are disappearing. It reminds me of nothing so much as a cancer that eats away at and finally kills the host.

Because our raw materials are being depleted, we must build now for a future in which there is no wood, no petroleum for plastics, no metals and ceramics, and no fuel for heat. If we had our wits about us we would be building only houses fit to last 200 and 300 years, houses that could be heated with minimal amounts of fuel. Of course we have not. The alternative, as we will begin to find out in our lifetimes, will be millions of cold, badly housed Americans in suburban slums around deserted, partially cleared core cities. This bleak dawn is on the horizon.

I have never been able to understand the announcement by various industries that the renewal of existing housing has been tried and found too expensive. It is simply not true. What is too expensive is the present structure of renovator, contractor, subcontractor, all taking their profits on top of the money made by the others in the economic chain. What is too expensive is short-term rehabilitation money at 2 percent a month. What costs too much are fat, arrogant construction trades unions whose members make fifteen dollars an hour and who too frequently don't deliver productively worth three.

To renovate the existing houses, the federal government should make available to licensed and bonded rehabilitation firms interim construction loans at no more than 5 or 6 percent annual interest. These firms should be able to deliver all the skills and services necessary to do the job —plumbing, wiring, painting and plastering, carpentry, and masonry. None of these workers should be paid more than six to eight dollars an hour, but they should be guaranteed wages fifty-two weeks a year, benefits and vacations. Each of them should be able to perform several jobs. The present long apprenticeship period required by the building trades for new members is an exclusionary tactic to keep black people out and to drive up wages by severely limiting the number of people available to do the work. But it does not take as long to learn how to be a plumber as it does to become a brain surgeon. In fact, it doesn't take very long at all. Given decent training, any construction trade can be learned in a year, at least to reach the level now practiced in the United States.

The people who want this training and the jobs that would be created by the massive rehabilitation of our urban properties live in our cities now. They have brown skins, great manual dexterity and a surprising interest in jobs that pay $10,000 to $15,000 a year. There are also an ungodly number of black men and women who are qualified to create the rehabilitation firms, assuming that nobody else was interested because of limited profits.

Only two things would be necessary to make such a program work. First of all, payment for materials, wages and overhead must come as the work progresses. The thing that kills most small construction firms and that has bankrupted so many minority contractors is the lack of working money, and the high interest costs. The second aspect is regular, competent inspection of the work being done by federal teams. Confiscatory economic sanctions against contractors who bribe the inspectors, and decent administration will make the procedure honest.

Obviously, I do not happen to be among those who believe that government in the United States has to be dishonest, incompetent, or both. I am frankly bemused to hear people say that a department like HUD-FHA, with approximately 16,000 employees, is "too large" to be properly administered. The problem is not the department, but the people who are in charge of it. Political appointees all, they usually have their heads screwed onto the wrong place. But competent administrators would solve HUD's problems almost overnight.

The largest purchases most people make in their lives are their homes and it is most unsettling that the *caveat emptor* philosophy of the undisciplined marketplace still rules. We are now gaining the right to expect that the wheels of our automobiles won't fall off on the highway. We should certainly be able to expect that the houses we buy do everything they are supposed to do. Since the automobile industry didn't get "enlightened" until it was kicked in the ass a time or two, the same favor should be paid to the construction, real estate and mortgage industries. They don't know it now but they will be very proud of themselves once they actually behave like the ethical businessmen they pretend to be at Rotary Club meetings. After all, they are always boasting in their press and before congressional committees about how essential and important they are to the United States. I am the last one in the world to disagree. I do believe, however, that the behavior of people who are so essential ought to be responsible for something beyond making bales of money.

The *Oxford English Dictionary* defines *mortgage* as a "dead pledge." In the seventeenth century, lawyers spoke of it like this:

"It seemeth that the cause why it is called mortgage is, for that it is doubtful whether the Sellor will pay at the day limited such summe or not, & if he doth not pay, then the Land which is put in pledge upon condition for the payment of the money, is taken from him for euer, & so dead to him upon condition, &c. And if he doth pay the money, then the pledge is dead as to the Tenant, &c."

Our society is obligated now to pay the sum due to save our cities. If it does not pay, the cities will be lost forever. They will be dead. It has been many months now since I first had the dream of blocks and blocks of empty houses, and I think that I finally understand what that dream was about: A dream of empty houses is a dream of death.

A dream of empty houses is a dream of death, of America's cities, of the hopes its poor share for a better life, of a good society that protects its citizens from the elements.

But as we have seen, the houses and the neighborhoods have been destroyed. We must rebuild them while there is still time. Now.

Brian D. Boyer
June 30, 1973